THE FABER POCKET GUIDE TO
Musicals

James Inverne

ff

faber and faber

First published in 2009
by Faber and Faber Limited
Bloomsbury House, 74–77 Great Russell Street, London WC1B 3DA

Photoset by Agnesi Text, Hadleigh
Printed in England by CPI BookMarque, Croydon

The right of James Inverne to be identified as author of this work
has been asserted in accordance with Section 77 of the Copyright,
Designs and Patents Act 1988

*This book is sold subject to the condition that it shall not, by way of trade
or otherwise, be lent, resold, hired out or otherwise circulated without the
publisher's prior consent in any form of binding or cover other than that
in which it is published and without a similar condition including this
condition being imposed on the subsequent purchaser*

A CIP record for this book
is available from the British Library

ISBN 978–0–571–23751–7

10 9 8 7 6 5 4 3 2 1

For Kareen, who helped me hugely as ever, and for my son Doron who, being two at the time of writing, if anything slowed me down. Always a pleasure. He, I hope, will one day find this a useful guide to some great shows (once he hits double figures). She, as ever, will have to put up with my choice of musicals.

Contents

Foreword

Having been lucky enough to grow up during the majority of the Golden Era of the American musical, I was fortunate enough to see the original productions of many of the great musicals: *West Side Story*, *My Fair Lady*, *Hello, Dolly!*, *The Sound of Music*, *Funny Girl*, *Cabaret*, *Oliver!* and *Fiddler on the Roof* are just a few of the wonderful shows I thrilled to with their original casts. So by the time I started my own career working in the theatre in 1965, I was already steeped in the unique excitement that only the musical theatre can give. My first jobs in the theatre were working on such classics as *Camelot*, *Hello, Dolly!*, *Oliver!*, and *Hair* – the latter being my last appearance in a musical when I joined the cast in the celebrated nude scene – mercifully for one night only!

Even though I wanted to produce musicals since I was eight years of age, and therefore was unquestionably precocious and ambitious, I never dreamed that I'd live through, never mind take a leading role in, the rise and rise of the British musical. In the process, I was also able to help take the musical beyond the confines of London and Broadway and make it a world-wide popular phenomenon.

As my grey cells start to reach their sell-by date, I look forward to reaching for James Inverne's enjoyable and handy critical compendium of musicals and remind myself not only of the great nights in the theatre I've spent, but also those that I have regretfully/mercifully missed!

SIR CAMERON MACKINTOSH

Opening Number: Introduction and the Entire History of the Musical Theatre (abridged)

I can pinpoint precisely the moment I realised how much I loved musicals. It was 1986, I was eleven and enjoying a fairly routine lunch in a London restaurant with my parents and sister. We'd taken the train up from Bournemouth that morning so Dad could attend some business meeting. Any excuse to come to the capital was to be grasped, but truthfully there wasn't much in this one for my sister and me. Then, as he awaited the bill, my father produced some theatre tickets from his pocket. 'A surprise,' he announced with a typically theatrical flourish. 'We're going to see *Les Misérables*. Right now.' I had already seen the show once and adored its heady mix of operatic bombast, the inevitability of revolutionary events bearing down on the personal tragedy of Jean Valjean and his nemesis Javert. But I'm not sure that my reaction was what my parents had been expecting. There, at the lunch table, cocky almost-teenager that I was, I burst into tears.

It was a mawkish moment, I agree. Had it been a (very bad) musical, I'm sure someone would have burst into song. As it was, my mother looked at me, vaguely perplexed, and asked, 'Are you pleased?' Pleased was not the word; the prospect of engaging again with that magnificent mix of music and drama (direction by Trevor Nunn at his best) was actually overwhelming.

Does everyone react to great musicals like this? A friend of mine, a fellow arts journalist, once opined that, 'Anyone can like musicals. To love them as much as we do, you have to be Jewish or gay.' As the first though not the second (he was nearly both; half of one and all of the other) it set me thinking. There are commonalities to be sure between Jewish culture and the tuners (as trade magazine *Variety* invariably calls them). To generalise – a certain dash of schmaltz, an easy sentimentality and a heart-on-sleeve keying into deep emotions through music (this from a religion that places its music at such a premium that in the Middle Ages German cantors had to be afforded guards to protect them from angry congregants who didn't approve of the tunes). And that's no surprise; for a people small in size we Jews have had a disproportionate impact on the formation of musical theatre. Irving Berlin, Moss Hart, Richard Rodgers, Larry Hart, Leonard Bernstein, Jule Styne, Stephen Sondheim and many, many more of the musical's leading lights were Jewish. Amidst all this, Cole Porter, Andrew Lloyd Webber and Tim Rice seem strangely out of place. It's OK though, non-Jews are allowed in this club. Yet there's no denying that the chosen people were, apparently, chosen to write shows.

There has undoubtedly also been a large gay influence on the art form. Some of the above and dozens of other key figures fell into or hovered around that category. Gay themes surface in many shows – *La Cage aux Folles*, *Kiss of the Spider Woman*, *Cabaret*, *Rent*.

Yet the sheer size of audiences that have flocked to musicals belie my friend's comment. Some statistics – *Cats* has to date purred its way into around 250 cities in more than 20 countries, *Les Misérables* has been seen by more than 51 million people in more than 38 countries, *Phantom of the Opera* by more than 80 million in 25 countries. Not bad going for a genre whose hard-core fan base is supposedly niche.

Musicals, though, should be seen in context. It could be said that they have been gestating since, variously, the musical extravaganzas of the Greek, then Roman Empires, the wandering players Shakespeare would have known (and certainly during this period the development of indoor theatres – with musicians needed to cover lengthy intervals enabling the house candles to be changed – advanced the relationship of music and drama) via the *commedia dell'arte* players from mainland Europe, or early opera. Most would point to the comic *opera buffa* from the likes of Rossini, or the operettas of Offenbach in France and Gilbert and Sullivan in England (and later, Franz Lehár in Austria) as the real starting point.

One can see why. Those forms intermingled speech and song, with the musical moments offering the dramatic high points. Fast forward several decades and, say, the sweet-toned climax of *Show Boat*'s 'You Are Love' sounds clearly a descendant of Nanki-Poo's 'A Wandering Minstrel, I' from G&S's *The Mikado*. But it's hardly that simple. To start with, the first official musical is usually thought to be *The Black Crook*, a play with music that premiered in New York in 1866. Which predates Gilbert and Sullivan's first show by some nine years.

Clearly, the evolution of the musical has taken place alongside that of various other genres. It has constantly learned from, been influenced by and assimilated the best of them. Operetta, most obviously. But then the jazz revolution of the late nineteenth and early twentieth centuries and its effect in turn on popular and folk song had its own impact. Along came musical revues in New York and London – shows such as the Ziegfeld *Follies* and *No, No, Nanette* that spawned or adopted hit songs. In England, the working-class humour of the music-halls was still permeating musicals right up to Lionel Bart and beyond. In the US, shows were shot through with the bawdy flamboyance of vaudeville, which achieved a weird and unsettling synthesis with the spirit of German cabaret in Kander and Ebb's *Chicago*. Kurt Weill and fellow immigrants from a violent Europe brought that Berlin sensibility to the playhouses of New York (witness Weill's at once alienating and absorbing *Lady in the Dark*).

The quantum leap forward for the musical occurred in 1928 with Jerome Kern's *Show Boat*. At once a finely wrought play and a stinging critique of racism, it was a far cry from the all-but-plotless revues that dominated. Kern's lyricist, Oscar Hammerstein II, would pull off the same trick to even finer effect fifteen years later with *Oklahoma!* in the company of the composer Richard Rodgers. If *Show Boat* showed that music could intensify the emotional impact of a play (the baying refrains of 'Ol' Man River' – 'You dare not make the white folk frown' – haunt the show like a leitmotif; the audience's musical conscience), *Oklahoma!* broke new ground in terms of complexity of character and evenness of structure. It also introduced the notion of dance – an element of musical theatre that would grow until choreographers such as Jerome Robbins, Bob Fosse and Gillian Lynne would become as influential as any composer or lyricist.

The 1970s was a fascinating decade for the musical. Blissed out on the free love, rock'n'roll-infused era, shows began to boldly experiment. *A Chorus Line* riffed on the very nature of show business, showing its harshness, the way it can exploit the vulnerable and insecure, cast aside the washed-up and yet be as addictive as any drug. Sex and drugs were the chosen expressions of pacifist dissent in *Hair*, a show so free-flowing as to be at times incoherent – but powerful for all that. And rock powered The Who's *Tommy* and, far more successfully, Andrew Lloyd Webber's *Jesus Christ Superstar*. By the 1980s shows seemed to have finally cut themselves adrift from the ballads and conventions of operetta. Instead audiences endured the thrashing guitar of *Superstar* as Jesus is lashed by Pilot's minions, or thrilled to the driving beats of *Hair*. Some of that spirit fuelled Stephen Schwartz's folk singalong *Godspell*.

So what happened next? The end of the musical – which has been predicted almost as long as the form has existed? The renunciation of structure and move towards anarchy? Amazingly, the opposite. Confident in their new-found musical voices, the rock composers discovered that actually rock can be quasi-operatic in its outsize emotional scale. Through the 1980s Lloyd Webber explored and refined that idea: *Evita* and later *Phantom of the Opera* are rigidly structured, cleverly built and use musical and theatrical devices that reach back to Puccini. *Evita*'s 'Don't Cry for Me Argentina' is as much a diva moment as anything in *Tosca*. In *Phantom*, meanwhile, rock is presented as sexual liberation (who, after all, is the Phantom if not a shadowy rocker, compared to square Raoul?) – but through the prism of grand opera. Along the same lines came Alain Boublil and Claude-Michel Schönberg with *Les Mis* and *Miss Saigon*.

Now, as the first decade of the twenty-first century begins to move to its conclusion, that movement has started to subside, to settle perhaps. Audiences or authors tired of the operatic through-sung shows; someone did, anyway. There was a concerted move to recapture the musical comedy days of the 1940s and 1950s. Cameron Mackintosh, the UK's über-producer of the epic shows, had moved away from them to mount or back musicals with more modest, comic ambitions such as *The Witches of Eastwick* and *Avenue Q* (and simultaneously set himself to reinventing some old favourites, among them *Oliver!*, *Mary Poppins* and *My Fair Lady*). From the US came *The Producers* and *Hairspray*. Audiences learned to laugh again.

There were also financial reasons for all of this (and political too, arguably, as a public emotionally battered by war and terrorism sought escapist fare). Musicals had become expensive – incredibly so for anyone with pretensions to Broadway or the West End. The vast receipts of the handful of phenomenal successes (*Les Mis*, *Saigon*, *Cats*, *Starlight Express*) of the 1980s had driven up costs so that by the mid-1990s it was all but impossible to stage a musical of any scale for less than around 3 or 4 million pounds. A big show could easily cost 7 or 8.

As the risks went up, so producers looked for safe bets. The individuals who would previously risk their houses on a show they believed in for the most part couldn't keep up. To stay in that league they would have to join producing conglomerates – effectively become corporations. And corporations are generally risk-averse. At the same time big businesses were tempted to get in the game, either by the potential rewards or the publicity or both. Results were mixed: Disney's first effort, for instance, was the cynical-feeling *Beauty and the Beast*, but its follow-up, *The Lion King*, was a magnificent celebration of theatrical craft. In any case, finding the sort of person to take a chance on a show about, say, cats, using lyrics by a dead poet, would be an almost-definite no-go now.

There are the breakthroughs, the experiments. *Spring Awakening*, a celebration of love and contemporary rock, or the gloriously subversive and original *Avenue Q*, both from New York, have been breaths of fresh air. And the truth is that talent will out, whatever the financial situation. What is needed now is that talent. Where are the new composers to succeed Andrew Lloyd Webber and Stephen Sondheim, today's most revered talents? There are fine writers around – Adam Guettel (Richard Rodgers's grandson), Jason Robert Brown and George Stiles to name three. But none so far has really seized the imagination of the wider public.

If one person in the entire history of the musical has shown its possibilities, that man is Sondheim. He has stretched himself and the genre, moving adeptly from farce (*A Funny Thing Happened on the Way to the Forum*) to poignant comedy (*A Little Night Music*) to hip relationships drama (*Company*) to nostalgia both bitter (*Follies*) and hopeful (*Merrily We Roll Along*) to Grand Guignol (*Sweeney Todd*) to post-modern fantasy (*Into the Woods*) to a work that grapples with the very limits of what the musical can possibly do – *Sunday in the Park with George*. In this musical, Sondheim strains to create drama from art, a plot from the act of painting. And at the miraculous close of Act I, as his various characters assemble to re-create visually Georges Seurat's pointillist masterpiece *Sunday Afternoon on the Island of La Grande Jatte*, there is that rare sense of art forms swirling together like paint on a palette, to create something utterly new, something riveting. Music, drama and the stage picture fuse in a way that cannot help but leave an audience astonished, and deeply touched. Such is the power and the possibilities of the musical.

If there is not yet a new Sondheim on the horizon, one will undoubtedly surface. And in the meantime, there is an army of musicals already written, many frequently revived, which offer a wealth of material to amuse, charm, shock, move, delight – and have hardy eleven-year-old boys weep like girls at the prospect of revisiting them. (Shall I ever live that one down?) I hope that this book provides a useful guide to the shows you should make a beeline for, as well as a few to avoid like the plague.

JAMES INVERNE
Reading, 2009

MY HUNDRED GREATEST MUSICALS

Annie Get Your Gun

Music and lyrics by Irving Berlin
Book by Dorothy and Herbert Fields
Premiere: 16 May 1946, at the Imperial Theatre, New York

Irving Berlin proved he could pile as many hit songs into one show as his great rivals Rodgers and Hammerstein with this one. Not that the latter pair minded in the slightest. They were *Annie Get Your Gun*'s producers.

With a songlist that includes the likes of 'You Can't Get a Man with a Gun' and 'There's No Business Like Show Business', this was an enormous success. It was also something of a throwback to the pre-*Oklahoma!* days when musicals had relatively two-dimensional stories on which to hang lots of great tunes.

Despite the fine Ray Middleton as Frank in the first cast, the show was really all about Ethel Merman. This was one of her defining roles and to this day it is difficult to hear 'There's No Business . . .' without hearing her voice in the mind's ear.

TRIVIA

Hammerstein's old collaborator Jerome Kern had been slated for this project, but died before he could complete it.

THE PLOT

The tomboyish Annie Oakley impresses the star of the Buffalo Bill show, Frank Butler, when she beats him in a shooting contest. He invites her to join the show, and she agrees. When her prowess threatens to eclipse his, however, he storms off to join a rival Wild West show. Neither can admit their love for the other, but soon they will have to work together again, if only to save their struggling shows.

NUMBERS TO LISTEN OUT FOR

'I'm A Bad, Bad Man'
'Doin' What Comes Natur'lly'

'The Girl That I Marry'
'You Can't Get a Man with a Gun'
'There's No Business Like Show Business'
'They Say It's Wonderful'
'Moonshine Lullaby'
'My Defenses Are Down'
'Who Do You Love, I Hope'
'I Got Lost in His Arms'
'I Got the Sun in the Morning'
'Anything You Can Do'

RECOMMENDED RECORDING

Some people have a problem with Ethel Merman in this role.
I tend to agree. While I love her rendition of certain songs,
especially 'There's No Business Like Show Business' (where
she seems to embody the formidable life force of Broadway
itself), there's no vulnerability in her performance. No sense
that she needs Frank. All that is there, plus a good sense of
bravado and tinges of wildness in Judy Kaye's remarkable performance, for TER. It's a two-CD set that's as complete as it
gets, and features a fine Frank from Barry Bostwick.

Anything Goes

Music and lyrics by Cole Porter
Book by Guy Bolton and P. G. Wodehouse
Premiere: 21 November 1934, at the Alvin Theatre, New York

Which of the *Anything Goes* myths are actually true? We know
that Guy Bolton and P. G. Wodehouse saw much of their book
thrown out just weeks before the first night. But was that, as
common wisdom has it, because they set their story around a
shipwreck and a real-life disaster made it necessary to change
this, or, as some argue, that their work was simply deemed not
up to scratch? Howard Lindsay and Russel Crouse were asked
to supply revisions. When a revival shortly before Porter died
included his songs from elsewhere such as 'De-Lovely', did

he really approve the new version? And did the title actually come from that widely reported conversation when, with opening night looming and no title yet selected, an impresario told everyone to choose anything because so late in the day was it that 'anything goes'?

It doesn't really matter, since we are left with one of the most tuneful and funny of all musicals. And in Reno Sweeney, the great Ethel Merman created one of her most famous roles. So totally did she throw herself into the show, indeed, that during a session of improvisation intended to throw up some good new dialogue, the one-time secretary dutifully took down what everybody said.

All that work was repaid in a fabulously popular show. The ever influential *New York Times* delivered a rave. Calling Bolton, Wodehouse, Porter, Lindsay and Crouse 'supermen', the newspaper's Brooks Atkinson noted in his first-night review that, 'When a show is off the top shelf of the pantry cupboard it is hard to remember that . . . the singers have not composed all those exultant tunes. If Ethel Merman did not write 'I Get a Kick out of You' and also the title song of the show she has made them hers now by the swinging gusto of her platform style.' Since that high-powered night when Broadway once again beamed bright, the lustre of *Anything Goes* has never dimmed.

TRIVIA

Anything Goes producer Vinton Freedley built, with his business partner Alex A. Aarons, the Alvin Theatre where the show was premiered. The theatre's name derives from the beginnings of the names Alex and Vinton.

THE PLOT

Billy Crocker, running an errand for his Wall Street boss on board the s.s. *American* as it floats in harbour, sees the love of his life, Hope Harcourt, also on board. She is engaged, but he stays to try and win her heart. He enlists the support of his friend, the singing evangelist Reno Sweeney (who herself is in love with Billy).

Matters get even more complicated when it transpires that two gangsters are on board and Billy unwittingly accepts a ticket that should have belonged to Public Enemy No. 1, Snake Eyes Johnson – for whom Billy is mistaken. There is trouble at sea.

NUMBERS TO LISTEN OUT FOR

This list uses the 1962 revival order of songs, in which several Porter numbers were imported from elsewhere – as Porter was still alive, it is generally assumed that it was done with his blessing. And it does make a great show even better!

'I Get a Kick out of You'
'You're the Top'
'Friendship'
'It's De-Lovely'
'Anything Goes'
'Let's Misbehave'
'Blow, Gabriel, Blow'
'Be Like the Bluebird'
'The Gypsy in Me'

RECOMMENDED RECORDING

For all that Merman is considered wellnigh iconic in the role, I prefer the more vulnerable yet still feisty and resourceful interpretation of Sally Ann Triplett, in a 2003 revival at London's National Theatre. And this is my preferred version all round, with a great sense of company and comedy from all. There are other lovely individual turns too from John Barrowman's Billy, Mary Stockley's Hope and Martin Marquez as the would-be highly dangerous criminal, Moonface Martin.

Aspects of Love

Music by Andrew Lloyd Webber
Lyrics and book by Don Black and Charles Hart
Premiere: 17 April 1989, at the Prince of Wales Theatre, London

'He couldn't decide whether to take the Puccini route, or the Offenbach route,' a jovial Alan Jay Lerner told fellow lyricist Don Black on the opening night of *Aspects of Love*, referring to its composer Andrew Lloyd Webber. 'He went the Puccini route. But he should have gone the Offenbach route!'

Lerner was not entirely fair, and neither are the theatre historians when they routinely brand *Aspects* a flop. It did run for three years, not great by the composer's previous standards, very good by those of most other shows – but then *Aspects* would never have the crashing chandeliers, rollerskating singers or dancing felines so beloved of the marketeers. It was, in a departure from *Phantom of the Opera*, its immediate predecessor, an intimate chamber piece.

In reply to Lerner's jibe, Lloyd Webber instinctively goes the Puccini route. The big, hit-'em-between-the-eyes tune is in his DNA, and *Aspects* obliges with the heroic 'Love Changes Everything'. Yet the palette is nicely varied – there are introspective little waltz numbers, suggesting a nostalgia for the opulence of years gone by, and in fact the prevailing mood is of elegance and urbanity. If anything the big numbers, good as they are, tend to stick out uncomfortably.

Trevor Nunn directed the first production, which was generally deemed too statuesque for the subject matter. A new, more restrained staging was put in place for 1993 and was liked far better.

The problems did not, however, stop there. If this show had a publicity 'hook', it was in the casting of Roger Moore as the sophisticated uncle, George. Better known for bopping villains as James Bond or the television spy The Saint than singing romantic ballads, this was to be Moore's first musical. When he backed out at the last minute, it caused some bad press the production could well have done without (as if the post-

Phantom pressure wasn't enough), although Kevin Colson stepped in, expertly, at short notice.

The show did not fare well on Broadway, running for just under a year. Yet it seems that time – and distance from *Phantom* mania – are being kind to *Aspects*. It is remembered as a relative flop (notwithstanding Michael Ball reaching number two in the pop charts with 'Love Changes Everything'), but one for which many people have genuine affection. I suspect that history itself will judge it as a fine score, and a fine show.

TRIVIA

Trevor Nunn was insistent that, no matter how good their voices, the cast had to be good actors first and foremost. So when he auditioned Michael Ball – for whom the role of Alex turned out to be a star-making turn – he asked the singer to perform soliloquies from Shakespeare.

According to Lloyd Webber, during one audition for the part of Rose, the very beautiful and talented Catherine Zeta Jones was among the hopefuls. Black patiently explained to his excited colleagues that they couldn't cast her – since the plot finally hinged on Alex leaving Rose, he felt that the audience would never believe that he could turn his back on such an alluring actress! Reluctantly, the others agreed.

THE PLOT

The teenage Alex Dillingham is obsessed with the beautiful actress Rose Vibert. They embark on a romance, which is endangered when Rose meets Alex's charismatic uncle, George. She leaves Alex for George, whom she marries. But this is just the start of romantic complications which span some seventeen years.

NUMBERS TO LISTEN OUT FOR

'Love Changes Everything'
'Parlez-Vous Français?'
'Seeing Is Believing'
'A Memory of Happy Moments'

'Everybody Loves a Hero'
'She'd Be Far Better Off with You'
'Other Pleasures'
'The First Man You Remember'
'Anything But Lonely'

RECOMMENDED RECORDING

The original London cast recording is really marvellous. Ironically, for all Michael Ball's warm and pliant voice – a very natural tenor that easily reaches the highest notes – it is last-minute understudy Kevin Colson who steals the show. Everything with him is considered and, one feels, deeply personal. His George, sung with firm, resonant tones, is every bit as fascinating a character as the story requires him to be. By contrast Ann Crumb, aptly, seems almost a mess of insecurities as Rose – glamorous and desirable, but also vulnerable and even needy. Although on disc the pace eases off rather too much in the inferior second half, it is a subtly intoxicating listen.

Assassins

Music and lyrics by Stephen Sondheim
Book by John Weidman
Premiere: 27 January 1991, at the Playwrights Horizons Theatre,
    New York

Even for Sondheim, a show about the men who have tried to kill American presidents was pretty hard core. The satire was unremitting, the humour less of a relief than in, say, *Sweeney Todd*, with the composer aiming to hit audiences right between the eyes – 'Everybody's Got the Right to Their Dreams' sing the murderers in a twisted vision of the American Dream.

But then, this is not a musical where the guy gets the gal and waltzes off into the sunset carolling happily – it is a show where the guy gets the guy in the head and sings of his justification for doing so. In a word, terrifying. And frighteningly appropriate in an unstable world.

TRIVIA

Sondheim first came across the material when working with the Musical Theatre Lab, an organisation dedicated to encouraging new musicals. One script sent in was called *Assassins*, and depicted a Vietnam veteran who decides to kill the president. Sondheim wished he'd had the idea, and years later tracked down its writer, Charles Gilbert, to ask if he could do something similar with John Weidman.

THE PLOT

At a fairground, the owner of a shooting gallery tries to persuade passers-by, who include a parade of actual and would-be presidential assassins, to kill a president. A succession of scenes deals with the various attempted shootings from various points of view – culminating with Lee Harvey Oswald's decision to assassinate President Kennedy.

NUMBERS TO LISTEN OUT FOR

'Everybody's Got the Right'
'The Ballad of Booth'
'Gun Song'
'Unworthy of Your Love'
'Something Just Broke' (added for London production)

RECOMMENDED RECORDINGS

Honestly, this is a stunning show, but I almost never put on the recordings. It is deliberately so unsettling as to make for a decidedly unpleasant listen. What works as a production is not as powerful purely through an album, so the recordings work best as reminders of the work's effect on stage. Although it omits the not-yet-written 'Something Just Broke', the original New York cast recording on RCA is properly hard-hitting and vividly performed.

Avenue Q

Music and lyrics by Robert Lopez and Jeff Marx
Book by Jeff Whitty
Premiere: 19 March 2003, at the Vineyard Theatre, New York

In Hollywood there's a phrase for a certain type of movie pitch – 'high concept'. It refers to an idea that is very easy to describe, preferably in only one sentence, and is so good it becomes the point of making the film (a classic 'high-concept' idea, for instance, is the film *Phonebooth* – guy takes a random call in a phonebooth, which turns out to be from a sniper who says that if he leaves the booth he will be shot). So how's this for musical-theatre high concept: *Sesame Street* for grown-ups, complete with adult themes and swearing (and puppet sex)?

It didn't quite do the trick for Robert Lopez and Jeff Marx when they were touting the idea as a TV series, perhaps because with the likes of *South Park* and even *The Simpsons* around already it didn't seem quite fresh enough. For musicals though, this was highly original.

And so this offbeat (and occasionally beat-off) tale of the down-at-heel street where human and monster are united by their hang-ups was premiered at the Off-Broadway Vineyard Theatre in New York. It instantly became a cult hit and on its Broadway transfer to the Golden Theatre (outside which punters are invited to pose for photographs with a cut-out of the pornography-loving Trekkie Monster) won the Tony Award for Best Musical.

Among its admirers was the British producer Cameron Mackintosh, who put his money where his heart is and brought it to London's West End, where it has enjoyed similar success. A new song was played on video screens to London preview audiences – the puppet character Nicky was shown sitting on the toilet, and sings the number 'Time', about how he intends to take as long as he wants during the interval. It was cut before the London opening.

TRIVIA

In a World Aids Day benefit in the US, the cast of *Avenue Q* performed a sequel to *Fiddler on the Roof*, entitled *Avenue Jew* – where Tevye and his family arrive in America to live on Avenue Jew. Various parallel story lines to *Avenue Q* include the song, 'What Do You Do with a BA in Yiddish?'

For the Israeli production of the show, the character of Gary Coleman was considered not well enough known, so a local former-child-star-turned-actress Michal Yannai was enlisted, playing herself.

THE PLOT

Unable to afford more expensive accommodation, recent college graduate Princeton arrives in Avenue Q and rents an apartment from the landlord, ex-child-star Gary Coleman. His neighbours include the sweet young teacher Kate Monster, the clientless therapist Christmas Eve and her would-be comedian husband Brian, the co-habiting friends Nicky and (in-denial homosexual) Rod, and the constantly masturbating Trekkie Monster.

Rod is looking for his purpose in life. Kate has an ambition to open a special school just for monsters, and a discussion about racism leads them to acknowledge that 'everyone's a little bit racist'.

Kate's headmistress, Mrs Thistletwat, calls to ask Kate to take a class the next day while she has major surgery. The delighted Kate starts to prepare a subject on the worldwide web, but is interrupted by Trekkie Monster who insists that 'The Internet Is for Porn'. That evening, however, Princeton and Kate get drunk and, despite an attempted seduction by the singer Lucy The Slut, Princeton has very noisy sex with Kate. She oversleeps the next day, misses her class and resigns from her job.

At Brian and Christmas Eve's wedding, Nicky tells of his suspicion that Rod is gay, which Rod angrily denies. The wedding scares the commitment-shy Princeton, who breaks up with Kate, telling her that he must find his purpose. Two weeks later, Princeton sleeps with Lucy The Slut. Monster relationships are clearly just as complicated as the human variety.

NUMBERS TO LISTEN OUT FOR

'It Sucks to Be Me'
'If You Were Gay'
'Everyone's a Little Bit Racist'
'The Internet Is for Porn'
'There's a Fine, Fine Line'
'For Now'

RECOMMENDED RECORDING

An easy one, this, as at the time of writing there is only one recording. And the original Broadway cast is excellent, the humour coming across with zip and clarity. The only weak link is the decision (reversed for London) to cast Gary Coleman with a girl (Natalie Venetia Belcon); it might have worked in the theatre, but becomes irritating on repeated hearing.

Babes in Arms

Music by Richard Rodgers
Book and lyrics by Larry Hart
Premiere: 14 April 1937, at the Shubert Theatre, New York

At this period in their professional relationship, for all the private problems they experienced (not least because of Larry Hart's addictive personality), Rodgers and Hart were churning out marvellous shows with a seemingly inexhaustible supply of hit songs. *Babes in Arms* alone boasts standards such as 'My Funny Valentine', 'The Lady Is a Tramp', 'Johnny One Note' and 'I Wish I Were in Love Again'.

TRIVIA

The cast was not famous at the time, but included the young future star Alfred Drake.

THE PLOT

A group of youngsters is left to their own devices when their show-business parents cannot get work. So the teenagers resolve to put on a show to raise enough money to stop them being sent to a farm to work. The show flops. But life, and showbiz (at least in a musical), is full of second chances.

NUMBERS TO LISTEN OUT FOR

'Where or When'
'Babes in Arms'
'I Wish I Were in Love Again'
'My Funny Valentine'
'Johnny One Note'
'The Lady Is a Tramp'

RECOMMENDED RECORDINGS

There are some excellent recordings, if you can get past the idea that these mega-famous songs should be sung as part of an integrated musical rather than as showpieces by sophisticated performers. Is it OK by you if it isn't Sinatra singing 'The Lady Is a Tramp'? If yes, then I'd go for the splendid 1989 New World recording with Judy Blazer, Jason Graae and Judy Kaye.

Barnum

Music by Cy Coleman
Lyrics by Michael Stewart
Book by Mark Bramble
Premiere: 30 April 1980, at the St James Theatre, New York

If he was really going to capture the spirit of the most famous of all circus impresarios, P. T. Barnum, Cy Coleman must have known he would have to create, at least, 'the greatest show on earth'. He gave it a darn good try and few remember *Barnum* as anything other than a fabulously good time.

Of course, a musical about circus folk was going to require performers who could actually undertake those feats. This was easier said than done. Weeks went by without a satisfactory cast being put together. There were actors who could do head-stands, singers who could do backflips – but walking a tight-rope, strolling upside-down, flying between trapezes? That was an entirely different matter. Eventually, buzz about the show reached the circus world itself, and young circus profes-sionals began showing up at auditions. What was more, many of them could act and sing.

The lead role would be trickiest of all to cast. Where would Coleman find a star who would be prepared to shoulder the very real risks in taking on not only songs but stunts every night? He remembered a Molière-inspired show called *Scapino*, and its leading man who would suddenly run from the back of the stage and leap into the auditorium, landing nimbly on the back of a seat in the front row – and then run on chair backs all the way to the rear of the stalls. Jim Dale was recruited to cre-ate the title role and, with the young Glenn Close as his wife, the New York production lasted a very healthy two years.

Coleman hit gold again for the London transfer. Michael Crawford performed most of his own stunts on his television show *Some Mothers Do 'Ave 'Em*, and had earned his musical spurs in shows such as John Barry's *Billy*. The West End production ran for even longer. For Crawford himself, the rewards were to be even greater – Andrew Lloyd Webber heard him sing and remembered him when he came to cast *Phantom of the Opera*.

TRIVIA

Coleman was classically trained, and composed a piano sonata in his teens – which he promptly lost.

For the original Broadway cast, The Oldest Woman Alive was played by Terri White, who in fact was only twenty-three.

THE PLOT

Phineas Taylor Barnum promises the audience the most amazing sights they will ever see. The audience, however, quickly discovers that his early skill is for 'humbug' – as he persuades a hundred-and-sixty-year-old woman to pose as George Washington's nurse. His acts and stunts grow ever more elaborate and more popular, despite the disapproval of his wife Chairy. A more serious threat to their marriage will emerge, however, when Barnum promotes the great Swedish soprano, Jenny Lind. Meanwhile, despite the call of a more sober life and then politics, a fellow showman comes calling, the circus owner James A. Bailey. And he wants a partnership, so that together they can create the greatest show on earth.

NUMBERS TO LISTEN OUT FOR

'There Is a Sucker Born Ev'ry Minute'
'The Colors of My Life'
'One Brick at a Time'
'Bigger Isn't Better'
'Love Makes Such Fools of Us All'
'Come Follow the Band'
'Black and White'
'Join the Circus'

RECOMMENDED RECORDING

Whilst on stage this show is suffused in spectacle (in what Coleman called 'a birthday cake of a musical'), on record it's all about Barnum himself. Coleman was indeed blessed with two great showmen in Jim Dale and Michael Crawford. Finally, though, it is Crawford who has just that extra ingredient – and it is a gift that he was born with. You just naturally warm to the guy. All of his energy, his drive and his enthusiasm (qualities that Dale also has in spades) are channelled into his own brand of likeability – you want him to succeed. It lifts the London cast version above its American rival, just.

The Beautiful Game

Music by Andrew Lloyd Webber
Book and lyrics by Ben Elton
Premiere: 26 September 2000, at the Cambridge Theatre, London

This may be Andrew Lloyd Webber's most underrated musical. One of the things to be admired about him is the way he continually seeks out new and varied dramatic ground – from the Bible, to the politics of Argentina, to T. S. Eliot, to speeding trains, to Gothic melodrama and, here, the Troubles of Northern Ireland. His lyricist was the comedian and writer Ben Elton, here making a successful debut as a lyricist (before disgracing himself by giving in totally to the forces of crass commercialism with the feeble Rod Stewart musical, *Tonight's the Night*).

The show lasted less than a year in the West End. This was partly to be expected for a show with such a downbeat theme – an Irish youth football team, and its members as they gradually grow up and are split by sectarian loyalties. Partly also, the marketing may have been to blame – which seemed to concentrate on a Roy-of-the-Rovers-style football image, giving little sense that there was considerably more to it. Neither did a Broadway transfer materialise, very unusually for a Lloyd Webber show.

Nevertheless, this is a brave musical – one that seeks to tackle something of contemporary political importance in the tradition of the anti-racism themes of *Show Boat* and *South Pacific*. It also contained some extremely strong numbers, not least the anthemic 'Our Kind of Love'. And compensation of a kind came for the composer when the show was named the year's best musical by the UK Critics' Circle.

TRIVIA

Elton originally wanted this story to form only a single act, with two separate acts focusing on other conflict zones.

For leading lady Shonagh Daly the show had painful memories. She grew up in Northern Ireland, and with one Catholic and one Protestant parent, the family experienced a great deal of abuse.

On a lighter note, Daly started her career as an usher for *Phantom of the Opera* in London. Between one matinee and evening show she and some fellow ushers had too much to drink, and during the late performance she lay down in a quiet corner of the auditorium to sleep it off. 'I'm glad you're enjoying my show,' said a none-too-impressed voice. She opened her eyes to see Lloyd Webber glaring down at her. She did not remind him of the incident when auditioning for *The Beautiful Game*.

THE PLOT

In 1960s Belfast, a youth football team celebrates its triumphs and in particular the on-pitch heroism of its star player, John. As the boys grow up, however, Northern Ireland's sectarian violence pulls the team members onto opposite sides. John himself, after being imprisoned for an accidental crime, is inducted into the IRA. Loyalties, friendships and marriages are tested to the limit.

NUMBERS TO LISTEN OUT FOR

  'The Beautiful Game'
  'Let Us Love in Peace'
  'Our Kind of Love'
  'If This Is What We're Fighting for'

RECOMMENDED RECORDING

Only one to choose from, and it is very good. Josie Walker and Hannah Waddingham steal the show as the suffering footballers' wives.

Billy

Music by John Barry
Lyrics by Don Black
Book by Dick Clement and Ian La Frenais
Premiere: 1 May 1974, at the Theatre Royal, Drury Lane, London

Did the daydreaming Northern hero of Keith Waterhouse's hit comedy *Billy Liar* seem an unlikely subject for the composer John Barry, then in his heyday and installed as the glamorous composer of choice for James Bond? In fact, it was a natural fit. Barry, like Waterhouse's Billy, is a Yorkshireman. If, unlike Billy, he seems down to earth, his childhood was filled with outsize show-business figures – his father owned a chain of cinemas and concert halls and the stars would sometimes come to his house for a meal. To get from Yorkshire to Hollywood, Barry, again like Billy, must have had his dreams. Unlike the fictional character, the composer achieved his.

Barry teamed with his regular collaborator, lyricist Don Black, and the immensely successful television comedy writers Ian La Frenais and Dick Clement (between them, the pair created hit shows including *The Likely Lads*, *Porridge* and *Auf Wiedersehen, Pet*). They came up with a witty script and a sharp, attractive roster of songs.

But this show was always going to hinge on its star, and this is where Barry ran into problems. Michael Crawford was in his first flush of fame from his still-new TV series *Some Mothers Do 'Ave 'Em* and his ego could at times run wild. Barry, not known for being a soft touch, clashed repeatedly with his leading man. One memorable argument during a rehearsal featured Crawford saying, 'You don't realise how important I am to this show!' Barry glowered back at him from the stalls. 'If you're so important,' he taunted, 'then why am I telling you to **** off?'

But Crawford was perfect for the role ('A star is born,' trumpeted one critic, somewhat belatedly), and the show was one of the big hits of its season. Alongside him in a talented cast were Elaine Paige and Diana Quick. There might have been a grain of truth in Crawford's boast, since the show closed not very long after he eventually left, despite a fine successor in Roy Castle. It would be good indeed to have an overdue modern revival to see how another *Billy* fares.

TRIVIA

Another musical shares a title with *Billy*, also a book adaptation – but that American show is of Herman Melville's *Billy Budd* and lasted only one night (possibly because there is already a magnificent English-language opera on that subject by Benjamin Britten).

A big London revival was planned for 1991, but it never transpired.

THE PLOT

Billy Fisher is an undertaker's clerk who dreams of better things for himself. He escapes his everyday humdrum life by living in his own private dream world, which he calls Ambrosia. In real life he has three girlfriends, and spends much of his time inventing excuses to placate them. Eventually he must decide whether he will ever achieve his ambition and board a train to London to try his hand as a comedy writer.

NUMBERS TO LISTEN OUT FOR

'It Were All Green Hills'
'Any Minute Now'
'Is This Where I Wake Up?'
'Billy'
'Ambrosia'
'The Lady from LA'
'I Missed the Last Rainbow'
'Some of Us Belong to the Stars'

RECOMMENDED RECORDING

The original (and so far only) cast album is intermittently available on Sony. It's charming and funny, catching Crawford's imaginative, hugely likeable Billy to fine effect. When he regretfully muses, 'I Missed the Last Rainbow', you cannot help but feel for the daft so-and-so.

Billy Elliot – The Musical

Music by Elton John
Book and lyrics by Lee Hall
Premiere: 11 March 2005, at the Victoria Palace Theatre, London

There's no doubt that Elton John sees some of Billy Elliot – the small-town boy who overcame local prejudice to achieve his dream – in himself. He has said as much in interviews, and it was following the premiere of Stephen Daldry's film at the 2000 Cannes Film Festival that, racked by emotion, he approached Daldry and his screenwriter Lee Hall at the after-screening party and asked to turn the film into a stage musical. He then went to the film's producers, Working Title, and persuaded them to fund the project (which came in at a fairly hefty £5 million).

However, igniting a rock superstar's passion for an idea is one thing. Getting him to engage in the long, arduous process of making a musical is quite another. John was willing but, due to his hectic touring schedule, not able to sit in a room and brainstorm ideas with Hall. A compromise was reached, and the whole of the first half of the show was written with composer and lyricist oceans apart. Hall would write his lyrics, fax them to John in the US and – with a speed that staggered Hall – invariably later that same day John would phone up and play a completed song down the line from his tape recorder. And they were so good hardly anything was changed in any of them.

The rock star did manage to return to the UK to work with Hall face to face on Act II. He insisted that the songs be written chronologically, so that he could feel the musical growing organically. Once the show was written, John declared that he could contribute nothing to the rehearsal process so, leaving his baby in the hands of Daldry and Hall, he left. The first time he saw Billy Elliot complete was the opening night.

And in truth, even more than *Cats* reflected the sensibilities of its director Trevor Nunn and choreographer Gillian Lynne, this is Stephen Daldry's show. John's score, mixing pounding rock numbers, stoical anthems and wistful ballads, is highly effective. As are Lee Hall's unsentimental, sharp-witted book and lyrics. But it is Daldry's brilliant production that lifted this musical into the realms of the greats.

Daldry's understanding of the characters and their context is so deep – and not just, one feels, because he worked on the film – that he is able to go beyond mere storytelling and start playing with the very idea of what a stage show can do. In one breathtaking sequence, for instance, a baying stand-off between striking miners and riot police is literally intersected by a parallel scene of a ballet class. Daldry lets the audience absorb the strange and scary sight of adults swearing and screaming over the heads of the little ballerinas, before brilliantly merging the scenes – and gasps turn to laughter as the burly men twirl the girls over their heads, still swearing at each other all the while. There you have the whole thing. The fury and desperation of the strike, the image of the new generation yearning for better things, and even the tough humour of Northerners under stress.

And so, just as another Elton John show, *The Lion King*, had done, *Billy Elliot* actually improved on its cinematic source material. The *Daily Telegraph* called it 'the greatest British musical yet written' – I'd refine that. Musically it doesn't distinguish itself as individually as one or two of the Lionel Bart scores but musicals are written to be put on stage. And this is one of the finest British musicals yet produced.

TRIVIA

Billy Elliot bedded in for a long run in London, and at the time of writing an international roll-out is under way, with stagings already in New York and Sydney. Such was the anticipated demand for child actors for the show (by law they can work far fewer hours than adults) that Daldry and Co. created an entire school to groom young cast members. The Billy Elliot School

is in Leeds, and is run on Saturdays at that city's Girls' High
School. Students work with top West End choreographers,
vocal coaches and movement experts.

THE PLOT

In the dark days of the 1984 coal miners' strike in County
Durham, Billy Elliot's father and brother are fighting daily
battles with riot police shielding workers defying the strike.
Billy joins a girls' ballet class and his potential is soon spotted
by the instructor, Mrs Wilkinson. She wants Billy to try out
for the Royal Ballet School in London, but he knows he will
never get his family to agree. Mrs Wilkinson's daughter
Debbie becomes his friend and accomplice, but Billy is not
the only one with secrets. His other friend, Michael, confesses
that he likes dressing up in women's clothing.

Eventually Billy's father allows him to audition and breaks
the strike himself to help him raise the money for the journey. Much is at stake, as Billy realises that ballet – by now his
consuming love – is the only way he will ever escape the
poverty of his surroundings. Asked to explain to the panel why
he wants to be a dancer, he responds with passion, in the song
'Electricity'. He is accepted, and prepares to move to London.
Meanwhile, the great days of the mining communities appear
to be over.

NUMBERS TO LISTEN OUT FOR

'Shine'
'Grandma's Song'
'Angry Dance'
'Merry Christmas Maggie Thatcher'
'Electricity'
'Once We Were Kings'

RECOMMENDED RECORDING

The original London cast album is excellent, with a wonderful, committed cast – and you get a bonus turn from Sir Elton
himself. But, as mentioned above, the production is so much

the thing here. One wonders hopefully if Stephen Daldry might follow the Mel Brooks path and turn the musical of his film back into a movie. Now that would be worth seeing.

Blitz!

Music, lyrics and book by Lionel Bart
Premiere: 8 May 1962, at the Adelphi Theatre, London

Given that the Blitz was largely about Britain's buildings being bombed, it is perhaps ironic that the one thing people tend to remember about *Blitz!* is the awe-inspiring sets. This is the show generally credited with ushering in the age of the musical spectacular. Its enormous and complex mechanical sets were by Sean Kenny, who would go on to design the then state-of-the-art New London Theatre (whose versatile stage machinery was used to such advantage for many years by Andrew Lloyd Webber's *Cats*).

The show was produced while Bart's most popular musical, *Oliver!*, was still playing the West End. The exclamation marks seemed appropriate, as Bart was at this point the most successful British writer of musicals in a long time, and that title was not really challenged until Andrew Lloyd Webber came along. But as boisterous and humane as his shows were (suffused with the spirit of the music-hall with which Bart grew up), he was also determined to become an ever bigger noise. He assumed not only writing and composing duties on *Blitz!* but directed it too. It worked here, but the erosion of Bart's willingness to accept collaborators would shortly prove his undoing with the personally and professionally disastrous *Twang!!*

TRIVIA

One number, 'The Day after Tomorrow', designed to sound like a Vera Lynn wartime standard, was actually sung on stage by Dame Vera Lynn's recorded voice as the characters listened to her on the radio.

THE PLOT

Two families who hate each other, the Blitzsteins and the Lockes, happen to own neighbouring stalls in the local London market. When the Blitz erupts around them, they are all forced to make drastic changes to their way of life. At the same time, they must deal with the fact that their children are falling in love – with each other.

NUMBERS TO LISTEN OUT FOR

‘Our Hotel’
‘I Want to Whisper Something’
‘Be What You Wanna Be’
‘Petticoat Lane’
‘Far Away’
‘The Day after Tomorrow’

RECOMMENDED RECORDING

The irrepressible cockney spirit of the Blitz is alive and vibrant in the 1962 original London cast recording, featuring Toni Palmer and Grazina Frame.

Blood Brothers

Music, book and lyrics by Willy Russell
Premiere: 11 April 1983, Lyric Theatre, London

This musical has come back from the dead at least twice. Known for writing strong, memorable female characters – especially in his plays *Educating Rita* and *Shirley Valentine* – Russell delivered another in the person of Mrs Johnstone, the unfortunate mother of twin boys, one of whom she gives away only to find that the boys become friends, with tragic results. The difference here was that he resolved to write the music.

A child of 1960s Liverpool, Russell had been, almost inevitably, in a band and still had dreams of making it in music. When one day he heard his son humming one of Russell's own songs (the son wasn't aware of that fact) he was inspired to write a musical.

The opening was not auspicious. The first run, in Liverpool, was deemed to have gone OK and a London transfer was secured. But even with the excellent Barbara Dickson as the lead, *Blood Brothers* only managed to limp on for a matter of months in the West End.

It would take a producer of vision and tenacity to make the show a success – Bill Kenwright, a man known for standing by his enthusiasms. He loved the show, but ordered fairly major changes during a UK tour (in fact, he had to tour it three times before he could persuade a bruised Russell to risk another London outing). By the time he brought it back to the capital, to the Phoenix Theatre in 1988, it was a more commercial show – with Kiki Dee in the lead and the emerging star Con O'Neill in the pivotal role of Mickey. At the time of writing, it is still at the Phoenix nearly twenty years later.

That was *Blood Brothers*' first resurrection. The second took place in New York, where Kenwright opened it in 1993. Neither box office nor the reviews were good, despite a standing ovation every night. The theatre's owner told Kenwright that the show was dead and had to come off. Desperate to protect the musical he loved, Kenwright quickly lied, saying that he had arranged for two stars to join the show – Petula Clark and David Cassidy. A stay of execution was granted, and luckily the stars in question agreed (although with Cassidy in New York and Clark in Australia they rehearsed together only four days before their first performance). Gradually the demand built, the show ran for two years and bagged seven Tony Award nominations. *Blood Brothers* had been saved again.

TRIVIA

On the first night at the Phoenix, a mechanised bridge got stuck in mid-air and crashed to the ground, bringing part of the set with it. Many of the audience apparently thought it was a heavily symbolic part of the production.

THE PLOT

Liverpool single mother Mrs Johnstone is devastated when she finds out she is expecting twins – she knows that she will never be able to afford to look after two more children. So when her wealthy but childless employer Mrs Lyons asks to have one of the babies, Mrs Johnstone agrees. Mrs Lyons names her new baby Eddie, while the brother left with his mother is named Mickey. Fate seems to dog the boys' childhoods, as they meet by chance and become best friends – even when both mothers move away, they move coincidentally to the same town. Eddie and Mickey are inseparable, and are equally close to a third friend, Linda, whom years later Mickey marries.

Unable to escape the privations of his poor background, Mickey eventually goes to prison for a robbery that goes tragically wrong. When he gets out he is dogged by depression. Linda, unable to cope any more, enters into an affair with Eddie (who has long secretly loved her). Mickey finds out and goes in search of Eddie with a gun. Linda warns his mother, who intercepts Mickey just as he finds his one-time friend. She tells them both the truth, and Mickey is even more outraged, knowing that it was only chance that kept him from Eddie's privileged upbringing. As he shoots Eddie, he himself is gunned down by police. The distraught Mrs Johnstone kneels over the bodies of her children, begging for someone to tell her that this is all just make-believe.

NUMBERS TO LISTEN OUT FOR

'Tell Me It's Not True'
'Marilyn Monroe'
'The Devil's Got Your Number'
'My Friend'
'Living on the Never-Never'

RECOMMENDED RECORDINGS

For all the glitzy orchestrations of the 1988 London cast, there's something truer, more gritty about the original. Neither Barbara Dickson nor Kiki Dee is a great actress, but Dickson delivers the more haunting, melancholy performance. Honours are shared evenly elsewhere – Con O'Neill is touching as Mickey on the newer set, Andrew C. Wadsworth similarly affecting as the older cast's Eddie. But Andrew Schofield's original narrator is far tougher, more frightening than his rival.

The Boy Friend

Music, lyrics and book by Sandy Wilson
Premiere: 14 January 1954, at Wyndham's Theatre, London

Originating at the Players' Theatre Club in April 1953, before a tremendously successful West End transfer, *The Boy Friend* became one of the most popular of all British musicals. Crafted with love and evident affection for the song-and-dance styles of the 1920s to which it pays tribute, the phrase 'feel-good show' might have been invented for this musical.

TRIVIA

Wilson hated Ken Russell's film version. Russell, for his part, reasoned in a newspaper article, 'Maybe he found my version of his twee little seaside trifle just too rich . . . offering as it did a veritable banquet of Busby Berkeley delights.'

Julie Andrews, whose New York turn in the show was reportedly instrumental in landing her the lead in *My Fair Lady*, loved the show so much she chose it for her directing debut, in 2003.

THE PLOT

At a school for young ladies, Polly Brown pines for a boy-friend – especially as all her friends seem to have them. Meanwhile her father is amazed to find out that Polly's headmistress is an ex-girlfriend. As Polly is romanced by the serving boy Tony, love and dancing all around prevail.

NUMBERS TO LISTEN OUT FOR

'The Boy Friend'
'Won't You Charleston with Me?'
'Fancy Forgetting'
'I Could Be Happy with You'
'A Room in Bloomsbury'
'It's Never Too Late to Fall in Love'
'Poor Little Pierrette'

RECOMMENDED RECORDINGS

Thank heavens the 1954 London cast album (albeit not quite complete) is available again. It catches, in a way that no other recording quite does, the seriousness of purpose that all great parodies must have. Annie Rogers, Anthony Hayes and Maria Charles are pitch perfect among a cast without a weak link. Julie Andrews fans will not want to be without the also-good-only-not-quite-on-the-same-level 1954 Broadway cast album.

The Boys from Syracuse

Music by Richard Rodgers
Lyrics by Larry Hart
Book by George Abbot
Premiere: 23 November 1938, at the Alvin Theatre, New York

As musicals based on Shakespeare go, this isn't in the league of Cole Porter's *Kiss Me, Kate*, but then very little is. *The Boys from Syracuse* is a fairly faithful version of the original play, *The Comedy of Errors*, with a laugh-a-little-groan-a-little script and some terrific musical numbers.

TRIVIA

Larry Hart's brother, the comedian Teddy Hart, created the role of Dromio of Ephesus – he looked very similar to the actor Jimmy Savo, who played Dromio's twin brother.

THE PLOT

When Antipholus and his servant Dromio arrive in Ephesus, from their home in Syracuse, they are baffled to discover that the citizens there already seem to know them. Confusion upon confusion ensues until it transpires that the twin brothers that both master and servant have not seen since a shipwreck many years previously are alive and living in Ephesus.

NUMBERS TO LISTEN OUT FOR

'What Do you Do with a Man?'
'Falling in Love with Love'
'The Shortest Day of the Year'
'This Can't Be Love'
'Sing for Your Supper'
'Oh, Diogenes'

RECOMMENDED RECORDING

Davis Gaines and Debbie Gravitte star in a 1997 New York concert cast album on DRG that is at once more complete than its predecessors and bubbling with wit and charm.

Brigadoon

Music by Frederick Loewe
Book and lyrics by Alan Jay Lerner
Premiere: 13 March 1947, at the Ziegfeld Theatre, New York

Considering that it is the least known of Lerner and Loewe's major works – with the trio of *My Fair Lady*, *Camelot* and *Gigi* far outstripping it in fame – there are those who make a strong case for *Brigadoon* as being every bit the equal of those three (and some would say better than the last two). Its offbeat story certainly drew some superb work from its writers.

The tale of a village that appears only once every century and is open only to newcomers who will stay there for love of one of its inhabitants, never to leave, sounds more like meat for a ghostly opera by Wagner or Bartók. But in Lerner and

Loewe's hands, it is a beautiful, poignant romance. The 1954 film starred Gene Kelly, Van Johnson and Cyd Charisse but, as with *My Fair Lady*, the movie uses less-than-convincing studio sets rather than location filming.

TRIVIA

The story was modelled on the German legend of Germelshausen. But in the mid-1940s it was considered too risky to brave Broadway with a musical set in Germany, so Scotland was substituted.

THE PLOT

Tommy and Jeff, New York tourists in Scotland, lose their way and happen upon the village of Brigadoon. Tommy falls for one of its inhabitants, Fiona. Even when he discovers the truth about the village – that, to protect it from a changing world, it appears only once every hundred years (but each century feels like a day to the villagers) and that the 'miracle' will be undone if anyone ever leaves – he still wants to stay with Fiona. When Jeff accidentally causes the death of a villager, he persuades Tommy to leave with him, but his friend will not quickly forget Brigadoon, or Fiona.

NUMBERS TO LISTEN OUT FOR

'Brigadoon'
'Waitin' for My Dearie'
'I'll Go Home with Bonnie Jean'
'The Heather on the Hill'
'The Love of My Life'
'Come to Me, Bend to Me'
'Almost Like Being in Love'
'There But for You Go I'
'From This Day on'

RECOMMENDED RECORDING

I'm very fond of the 1988 London cast recording, beautifully done with Jacinta Mulcahy, Robert Meadmore and Lesley

Mackie. If there are no star turns, well, it's not really that kind of show – and it's a most satisfying listen.

Cabaret

Music by John Kander
Lyrics by Fred Ebb
Book by Joe Masteroff
Premiere: 20 November 1966, at the Broadhurst Theatre, New York

For their story set in Berlin immediately pre-World War II, Kander and Ebb needed to supply a *faux* Nazi anthem. They came up with the beautiful yet chillingly purposeful 'Tomorrow Belongs to Me'. When *Cabaret* opened, its writers received many letters condemning them for using a real Nazi song (according to Mark Steyn, in his history of musicals *Broadway Babies Say Goodnight*, one audience member even swore blind he remembered hearing the song in a Nazi death camp, as victims were herded off to the gas chambers). The song was a pure invention, but it hit a nerve. It was intended to.

There are few more important musicals than *Cabaret*. Important, yes, because it was a big hit, spawned a great film and incorporated a clutch of famous songs, but more so because of what it can tell us about ourselves. Kander and Ebb's masterstroke was to realise the supreme irony that, while the Berlin cabarets were nightly filled with laughter, with indulgence and decadent pleasure-seeking – frighteningly out of place in a city that was engineering one of the most horrific campaigns of genocide the world has known – actors are almost always free to show what they like on stage. So, under the thin disguise of entertainment, the performers in the cabaret could satirise the Nazis almost as much as they wished. The show's great question would then become: how long will the audience, and in some cases the performers themselves, ignore what they are actually being shown?

Basing their work on Christopher Isherwood's 1935 memories of Germany, *Berlin Stories* (later becoming the play and then film *I Am a Camera*), Kander and Ebb underlined the warped reflection that is their Kit Kat Club, with its odd and unsettling MC, by having a 'real-life' plot whose episodes directly correspond to songs in the club. So Sally Bowles's landlady is worried about her love affair with a Jewish man (characters all but expunged from the very different film version) – and the club's MC introduces a flamboyant number in which he complains that nobody approves of his own romance with a gorilla. That song ends with the suddenly brutal pay-off line, 'If you could see her through my eyes, she wouldn't look Jewish at all.'

But in 'Tomorrow Belongs to Me' the louring threats outside the club suddenly seem real and direct. As more and more drinkers at a beer garden join in the impromptu anthem, it is terrifyingly clear that an entire society has been brainwashed. Anyone doubting that this song still touches nerves should surf the web – browsing the video-sharing site YouTube I came across a recording of this song, and was shocked to see fellow users' comments below filled with anti-Semitic diatribes as well as passionate condemnations of racism. At the close of Hal Prince's original production of *Cabaret*, a mirror was lowered until the audience found themselves staring at their own reflection, somehow implicated in the violence. Clearly, with or without a mirror, the musical still has that effect.

TRIVIA

The play *I Am a Camera* had previously been optioned as a musical for the British show-writer Sandy Wilson. He actually went so far as to write a version, which has never been successfully produced.

The spiky music and lyrics are stylistically not dissimilar to the work of the great German songwriter Kurt Weill (not surprising given the subject matter), and Weill's wife Lotte Lenya created the role of Sally's landlady, Fräulein Schneider. There were even some suggestions after the opening that Kander might have plagiarised some ideas from Weill – accusations to which Lenya quickly put paid, pointing out that both composers were simply being true to the period.

THE PLOT

As the Nazis come to power in Berlin, the aspiring American writer Cliff Bradshaw arrives in the city and takes lodgings at the house of Fräulein Schneider. He soon discovers the Kit Kat cabaret club, where he meets its English star, Sally Bowles. When Sally appears in Cliff's room and asks to stay after a fight with her boyfriend, he reluctantly agrees. Gradually, Sally and Cliff fall in love, as at the same time do Fräulein Schneider and the Jewish fruit-seller Herr Schultz. As both couples try to make their relationships work, the Kit Kat club satirically underlines both their personal difficulties, and the gathering political clouds. For how long can they all ignore a world gone mad?

NUMBERS TO LISTEN OUT FOR

'Willkommen'
'So What?'
'Don't Tell Mama'
'Perfectly Marvellous'
'Two Ladies'
'Tomorrow Belongs to Me'
'Why Should I Wake up?'
'The Money Song'
'Meeskite'
'If You Could See Her'
'Cabaret'

RECOMMENDED RECORDINGS

You can't go too far wrong with any of the major *Cabaret* recordings. But it's worth knowing that the famous 1972 film is so different from the stage show as to be almost another musical. It is arguably no less great, although its major flaw is also its strongest asset – the casting of Liza Minnelli as Sally Bowles. This has come to be the role that has defined Minnelli's career. Her idiosyncratic vocal style in most ways perfectly suits the scabrous writing, and she seizes her big numbers like a true star, shining at the highest possible wattage. And there's the problem. Sally is a small-time singer who will never reach the top. In terms of character, Minnelli is just too good an entertainer.

The original Broadway cast remains a favourite, with a sense of freshness and genuine daring. Jill Haworth is not nearly so talented a singer as Minnelli, and here that's all to the good – her soft-grained voice may not be as stylised as might be expected in this music, but she sounds exactly as Sally should, a good-time London girl abroad. Alongside her Joel Grey's offbeat MC (though he's even better in the film, for which he won an Oscar) and Lotte Lenya's gravel-voiced Fräulein Schneider more than supply the requisite acidity. At the time of writing, this release comes with some fascinating original workshop sessions featuring Kander and Ebb.

Of more modern versions, my vote goes to TER's two-CD set, billed as the first complete studio recording. A fabulous cast includes Maria Friedman (a Sally in the mould of Haworth, slightly less vividly acted but better sung) and Jonathan Pryce as a dangerous-sounding MC. Judi Dench, London's first Sally, is a rather wistful Fräulein Schneider. Her sweet Herr Schultz is none other than Fred Ebb.

La Cage aux Folles

Music and lyrics by Jerry Herman
Book by Harvey Fierstein
Premiere: 21 August 1983, at the Palace Theatre, New York

Given that musicals are widely stereotyped as deriving a large sector of their audiences from the gay community (not untrue, and certainly many leading ladies of the tuners have become gay icons – most famously Judy Garland had her 'friends of Dorothy'), it took until 1983 for there to be a major musical around the subject of homosexuality. There had been some fringe musicals with colourful names like *Boy Meets Boy* and *The Faggot*. Yet as far as mainstream Broadway or the West End were concerned, before Jerry Herman's *La Cage aux*

Folles, there had been only hints, and peripheral characters such as Mama Morton in Kander and Ebb's *Chicago*. Herman and his book-writer Harvey Fierstein forged a traditional musical-comedy romance with two leading men who were in love, around the setting of a drag-cabaret club. After *Cage* others followed, like *Kiss of the Spider Woman*, *The Boy from Oz* and *Taboo*.

The story was already familiar to cinephiles, as a 1978 French film. It would later become known to millions more as a Hollywood remake starring Robin Williams and Nathan Lane, *The Birdcage*. And Herman kept his version very much in an Establishment tradition – there were few nods to any counter-culture here. Of course there were big song-and-dance routines with men dressed as women, but at heart there was nothing really to shock the typically genteel Broadway audiences. The score is firmly in Herman's trademark style, with tap-along numbers alternating with sweeping torch songs. Whether its adherents approved or not (they did), gay culture was being officially welcomed on to the stages of the Great White Way – it had always been an intrinsic part of musical-theatre traditions in any case, and this simply made that explicit.

The show enjoyed a very long run in New York and similar success in London and elsewhere. George Hearn, one of its two leading men, won the Best Actor Tony. It also beat Sondheim's *Sunday in the Park with George* for the Best Musical prize. And its big Act I closer, 'I Am What I Am', has become one of the best loved of all gay anthems (and a Shirley Bassey signature tune).

TRIVIA

Twenty years later, Harvey Fierstein himself created one of the most popular of Broadway drag roles – that of Edna Turnblad in *Hairspray*. The road for that role was arguably paved by *La Cage aux Folles*.

THE PLOT

The popular La Cage aux Folles nightclub in St Tropez is run by Georges, and his partner, Albin, is its 'leading lady'. Matters get distinctly confused when Georges's son Jean-Michel announces his intention to get married – to the daughter of a prominent member of a far-right political party that aims to close drag clubs such as La Cage. Jean-Michel asks the very camp Albin to leave when his prospective in-laws visit, and for Georges to pretend to be a straight diplomat. Albin, deeply upset, comes up with a better plan. He will pass himself off as Jean-Michel's straight uncle. There should be nothing to it.

NUMBERS TO LISTEN OUT FOR

'A Little More Mascara'
'With You on My Arm'
'La Cage aux Folles'
'I Am What I Am'
'Song on the Sand'
'Masculinity'
'Look Over There'

RECOMMENDED RECORDINGS

The Broadway cast on RCA is led by consummate artists George Hearn and Gene Barry, and their level of commitment and talent filters down through the company. If Hearn gets the big number, Barry yields nothing in wit and charm. There is, though it might be difficult to find, also a very decent Australian cast version with Keith Michell and Jon Ewing – but in any case the Broadway album wins out.

Call Me Madam

Music and lyrics by Irving Berlin
Book by Russel Crouse and Howard Lindsay
Premiere: 12 October 1950, at the Imperial Theatre, New York

It might not have maintained its reputation as one of Irving Berlin's finer works – a situation not helped when the film version had to be withdrawn from circulation due to rights issues (it has now had a limited release on DVD) – but *Call Me Madam* was a great hit in its day. True, having Ethel Merman in the lead (a role she repeated on screen) in those days seemed enormously to increase your chances of success (she had just scored a triumph in Berlin's *Annie Get Your Gun*), but Berlin had a superb team around him. That great architect of so many great musicals, George Abbott, directed, with Jerome Robbins as choreographer (even though in *Call Me Madam* dance never threatened to become as central as it was in other Robbins shows such as *West Side Story* and *On the Town*).

A high-profile first-night audience included ex-President Eisenhower (who would have been especially pleased with the complimentary number 'They Like Ike'), and they were not disappointed. They were not to know the extravagant headaches the cast and creative team had endured to get to that stage.

The general verdict in the out-of-town try-outs was that the first half was great, the second half was non-existent. Berlin started to cut songs – reluctantly in the case of 'Mr Monotony', a number he loved but that had been elbowed out of several of his shows. He swapped, added, cut, anything to get the show right before they hit New York.

It was Merman who supplied one of the best ideas. The back end of the show was petering out, obstinately refusing to catch fire. Merman was the one who suggested a duet for her and the young male lead, which became one of the score's loveliest songs, an example of Berlin's art at its finest as a mooning love song picks up pace and patter for Merman's interjections, 'You're just in love'. There was an end to the leading lady's patience, however. When Berlin approached her for yet another change – a new lyric for 'The Hostess with the Mostess' – she gave him the full imperious force of her displeasure. 'Call me Miss Birds Eye of 1950,' she instructed. 'This show is frozen!'

TRIVIA

When recording the film's soundtrack, Merman's co-star Donald O'Connor was so daunted by the sheer volume she could produce that he reportedly recorded his side of their big duet in a separate booth.

THE PLOT

In real life, a society hostess from Washington was appointed America's Ambassador to Luxembourg. This provided the premise for *Call Me Madam*, in which 'hostess with the mostess' Sally Adams is sent as Ambassador to the small state of Lichtenburg, where she exercises her own unusual form of diplomacy – an affair with Lichtenburg's Prime Minister. At the same time, her press secretary falls for a local princess.

NUMBERS TO LISTEN OUT FOR

'The Hostess with the Mostess'
'Can You Use Any Money Today?'
'Marrying for Love'
'It's a Lovely Day Today'
'The Best Thing for You'
'Something to Dance about'
'They Like Ike'
'You're Just in Love'

RECOMMENDED RECORDINGS

This is not as straightforward as one might think. Following an almighty battle between Decca – who had Merman on exclu--sive contract – and their rivals RCA, who won the rights to the original-cast album, Merman was forced to withdraw from the RCA recording. Dinah Shaw substituted for her, and was really no substitute. The show had been built around Merman's unique style and Shaw simply didn't fit in. You simply cannot imagine her pushing her way into the highest political circles. The London cast album is better (with Billie Worth) but still not ideal.

As for Merman, she was somewhat placated by Decca's allowing her an album where she could sing songs from the show. Which is good as far as it goes; it just isn't very far. So the film is the best option, with Merman back *in situ* and Donald O'Connor opposite her. The soundtrack was an LP release so, given that few of us have record-players any more, the DVD is the best choice. If you can get it. This might be a good moment to issue a plea for a revival and new recording – perhaps with Sally Ann Triplett, who followed Merman so very adeptly in the National Theatre's *Anything Goes*?

Camelot

Music by Frederick Loewe
Book and lyrics by Alan Jay Lerner
Premiere: 3 December 1960, at the Majestic Theatre, New York

Camelot is best known for its four closing lines:

> Don't let it be forgot,
> That once there was a spot,
> For one brief, shining moment,
> That was known as Camelot.

Thus the dying King Arthur to a young boy, who is charged with the responsibility of spreading the word of what Camelot had once, fleetingly, represented. These words echoed around the world shortly after the assassination of President Kennedy. The President, it was revealed, had often listened to the show's soundtrack recording in the White House and – with Kennedy's administration quickly assuming a glow of idealism, an image of aspiration towards nobility of spirit, and the man himself cast as a hero cut down in his prime – that verse and the musical itself became inextricably linked with the iconic world leader of the age. His administration would for evermore be known by the collective nickname Camelot.

True enough, the King Arthur tales have all of that – the struggle for greatness against the odds (namely, human nature). And Lerner and Loewe's musical has that about it as well. Because repeating the phenomenal success of *My Fair*

Lady, which was still running when *Camelot* opened, was a near-impossible task. That it succeeded at all owes much to bullish determination and a great deal to the idealistic, even heroic, force that was its leading man, Richard Burton.

Adapting T. H. White's book about Arthur, *The Once and Future King*, was Lerner's idea and his partner took some persuading. This time, though, the lyricist did not have George Bernard Shaw providing most of the script, and Lerner's own early efforts were messily structured and overlong. So long, in fact, that at the Toronto try-out the director Moss Hart started the evening by warning the audience that *Camelot* was 'glorious . . . but long' and that they would walk out of the theatre much older than they had been when they walked in.

Around an hour and a half needed to be cut for New York. Moss Hart had a heart attack. Loewe had ulcers. The show had technical issues. And here, with tension between Lerner and Loewe mounting, Burton showed his character. Once the Welshman was persuaded that he should risk a musical, he threw himself into the task of ensuring that the show would be a triumph – calming everyone's nerves, helping out where he could and even rehearsing the understudies for the harassed creative team. Meanwhile his leading lady, Julie Andrews, no longer the inexperienced ingénue of *My Fair Lady*, made everyone endless cups of tea.

With mixed reviews, *Camelot* did succeed, just – but it probably would not have done without help from the immensely popular TV show *Toast of the Town* and its host Ed Sullivan. *My Fair Lady* had been running for five years and, to celebrate, Sullivan invited its writers to have excerpts performed on the show. In a brilliant piece of marketing, they offered Sullivan some of their new show instead. What was good for the influential Ed Sullivan was good for millions of Americans, and success was snatched from the jaws of defeat. The Broadway run neared 900 performances, there was a London opening and a film, and one or two of the numbers have become standards.

Is *Camelot* flawed? Undoubtedly. Is it a great musical? For me, yes, because of what it represents – it aims for something unusual, a musical comedy that gradually darkens to tell us something about human nature. But there remains that sense of concerned idealism about it which, in retrospect, sums up the era of its writing. And there are some terrific songs.

TRIVIA

In one performance, Burton reportedly accepted a challenge from another great actor, Robert Preston, to drink as much vodka as he could without it showing on stage. When he asked the unwitting Julie Andrews her opinion of his performance that night, she innocently replied that he was better than usual!

THE PLOT

Preparing to fight his last great battle, Arthur muses back over his life – the pulling of the sword from the stone, then nervously meeting and later marrying Guinevere. The wizard Merlin teaches him about brotherly peace, before Merlin himself is interred in a magic cave.

Arthur decides to create the Round Table and the idea attracts knights from far and wide. It also inspires the young Lancelot to journey from France. He is introduced to Guinevere who, finding him insufferably arrogant, arranges for three knights to joust with him (much to Arthur's dismay). Lancelot defeats them all, and realises that he is in love with Guinevere. He leaves Camelot in despair, resolved to seek glory for Arthur elsewhere.

Two years pass before Lancelot's return, upon which Arthur knights him. Lancelot proclaims his love to the queen, but she remains devoted to helping Arthur. The king, for his part, has realised that his wife is attracted to Lancelot, but for the sake of peace remains silent. Rather, it is his illegitimate son, Mordred, who interrupts a night of passion between the illicit lovers. Lancelot escapes prison, but Guinevere is sentenced to be burned at the stake.

Arthur is agonised, unable to decide between the rule of law (by which his wife must die) and his love for her. Lancelot, however, rescues her at the last moment, taking her to France. Honour now demands that Arthur must declare war on France and on his friend. Many knights are killed. This, Arthur knows, will be the end of the Round Table – however, before the final day of fighting, he once again sees Lancelot and Guinevere, who has now become a nun, and forgives them. A young boy tells Arthur of his wish to join the Round Table. The king sends him home to spread the tales of Camelot.

NUMBERS TO LISTEN OUT FOR

'How to Handle a Woman'
'I Wonder What the King Is Doing Tonight'
'The Lusty Month of May'
'C'est Moi'
'If Ever I Would Leave You'

RECOMMENDED RECORDING

Richard Harris's Arthur has its fans, but Burton is the king as Arthur. Arrogant yet touching and vulnerable, he never hams, and at the end he declaims those famous four lines with a sense of real poignancy. Julie Andrews is a little generalised as Guinevere, but Robert Goulet is a fine Lancelot – preening but strangely likeable.

Candide

Music by Leonard Bernstein
Lyrics and book by Lillian Hellman
Premiere: 1 December 1956, at the Martin Beck Theatre, New York

Well, the overture is terrific – fizzing, tuneful, exciting. Everyone agreed? Good, because generally that's where agreement stops over *Candide*. There are some brilliant things about this musical – who can easily forget, for instance, the jolly burn-the-heretics knees-up 'What a Day for an Auto-da-fe', or the happily contorted philosophy of Dr Pangloss?

But the book is convoluted and famously difficult to make

work on stage, the original libretto considered so haphazard that a clutch of successors have added their efforts to Lillian Hellman's original (even though the show was her idea in the first place). Richard Wilbur and Hugh Wheeler were later drafted in to save the show, and among those to have tried their own improvements have been Bernstein himself, Dorothy Parker, Stephen Sondheim and John Latouche.

What *Candide* did have was a marvellous first cast, with the great Barbara Cook sparkling in her wonderful coloratura number 'Glitter and Be Gay'. The show flopped, the album was a hit – and so began the show's career as, by and large, a cult failure. Which, strangely, makes it a success.

Perhaps the best performing version was that prepared for the National Theatre's London revival in the late 1990s, by John Caird – who went back to Voltaire's original satire for his inspiration. Finally, felt critics and audiences alike, here was a version that worked as theatre. But the arguments will probably continue as long as it continues to be performed.

TRIVIA

Just as *Candide* was originally a sharp satire by Voltaire, so Bernstein intended it as a criticism of America's darker corners, not least McCarthyism.

THE PLOT

Candide, illegitimate nephew of the Baron of Westphalia, pines for the beautiful Cunegonde. Still, he is happy, as are many people in Westphalia thanks to the unfailingly optimistic teachings of the tutor Dr Pangloss. But Candide's love attracts the ire of the Baron and he is banished and eventually made to join the Bulgarian army. When war is declared, the Baron and his family are killed and Cunegonde meets a very nasty end. Still, says Dr Pangloss when he is reanimated with a tin nose (don't ask), things are still all for the best. Their adventures are just beginning.

NUMBERS TO LISTEN OUT FOR

Overture
'The Best of All Possible Worlds'
'Candide's Lament'
'What a Day for an Auto-da-fe'
'Glitter and Be Gay'
'You Were Dead, You Know'
'My Love'
'Eldorado'

RECOMMENDED RECORDING

Not an easy choice with so many different versions of the text
around. But a good, solid buy would be the two-CD set on DG,
resplendently conducted by the composer. The operatically
inclined but characterful cast includes Jerry Hadley, June
Anderson, Christa Ludwig, Nicolai Gedda, Kurt Ollmann and
sometime Bernstein librettist Adolph Green with the London
Symphony Orchestra.

Carmen Jones

Music by Georges Bizet
Lyrics and book by Oscar Hammerstein II
Premiere: 2 December 1943, at the Broadway Theatre, New York

Bizet's opera *Carmen* has been subject to many adaptations –
most recently a notable South African *Ur-Carmen*, set in the
townships and using the African 'click language'. Oscar
Hammerstein decided it would make a rather good musical,
although in fact the original already uses what would become
the musical-theatre format, with speech interspersed with
songs (complicating the issue, many opera houses at the time
sought to aggrandise the work with the speech sung as recitative rather than spoken).

Had he been alive, the composer might have said to
Hammerstein what Billy Wilder later said to Andrew Lloyd
Webber when the Englishman adapted his film *Sunset Boulevard*:

'You were very clever. You didn't change a thing.' In fact, Hammerstein did change the setting, with a parachute factory in southern America substituted for the traditional cigarette factory in Seville. He also delivered a sharp, witty script and some fabulous new names (Escamillio the bullfighter here becomes Husky Miller the prize-fighter, Micaela is now Cindy Lou). And, following in the footsteps of Gershwin's *Porgy and Bess*, Hammerstein wanted it all cast with black actors. Robert Russell Bennett was drafted in to provide new orchestrations.

It ran for more than a year, and was enough of a hit to be turned into a 1954 film starring Dorothy Dandridge (whose singing voice was dubbed by Marilyn Horne) and Harry Belafonte (with his songs provided by Le Vern Hutcherson). The show is not revived very often, perhaps because the opera is, and it wasn't until 1991 – nearly fifty years after its premiere – that the West End received its first, very successful, production, directed by Simon Callow.

TRIVIA

Cliff Richard had a UK pop hit with a number from the show, 'Beat Out Dat Rhythm on a Drum' (in the opera, the big song-and-dance number that begins Act II).

One of the dancers in the film version, not listed in the credits, is the great choreographer Alvin Ailey.

THE PLOT

Joe is distracted from his Air Force career and his budding love affair with Cindy Lou by the seductive, wilful parachute-factory worker Carmen Jones. When she is arrested, she persuades him not to turn her over to the military police in exchange for her love. He succumbs and lets her escape, knowing that a gaol sentence will follow. On release, they are reunited at Billy Pastor's café, but after a fight with an officer, Joe is doomed to live his life on the run. When Carmen begins to seem more interested in the famous boxer Husky Miller than in Joe, his temper flares.

NUMBERS TO LISTEN OUT FOR

'Dat's Love'
'Dere's a Café on de Corner'
'Beat out Dat Rhythm on a Drum'
'Stan' Up and Fight'
'Dis Flower'

RECOMMENDED RECORDING

I must admit, I do like the soundtrack to the Otto Preminger film (and the film itself, for that matter). It benefits from the full orchestra, and Horne is a magnetic Carmen Jones (just as she's a magnificent Carmen in the Leonard Bernstein recording of the opera – but there you have to cope with Lennie's sometimes bizarre conducting).

Carousel

Music by Richard Rodgers
Lyrics and book by Oscar Hammerstein II
Premiere: 19 April 1945, at the Majestic Theatre, New York

Of all of his own musicals, *Carousel* was Richard Rodgers's favourite. 'Oscar never wrote more meaningful or more moving lyrics,' he wrote in his autobiography *Musical Stages*, 'and to me, my score is more satisfying than any I've ever written. But it's not just the songs; it's the whole play. Beautifully written, tender without being mawkish, it affects me deeply every time I see it performed.'

It was one he and Hammerstein had begun reluctantly. *Oklahoma!* had been such a success that they felt the pressure of delivering a follow-up. To try to adapt Ferenc Molnár's play *Liliom* seemed needlessly to add to those pressures. To start with, *Liliom* was an often revived classic and they ran a very real risk of being accused of adding songs where songs weren't needed. Then there was the fact that *Liliom* was set in Budapest, a place that neither Rodgers nor Hammerstein had the slightest empathy with. And the play ended with just about the least crowd-pleasing scene for a musical possible, where a brutish father's spirit returns to see his daughter and slaps her – which she feels as a kiss. Added to all this, even if they did decide to take it on, there was no guarantee that the Hungarian playwright would approve. This was, after all, the man who had turned down both Gershwin and Puccini.

As it turned out, Molnár was an *Oklahoma!* fan and happily gave them the rights to *Liliom*. The Budapest setting was got over by relocating the story to New England, and as for that final slap, the writers took a deep breath and simply came up with something new and more uplifting. The clincher was the husband's 'Soliloquy' where, having learned that his wife is pregnant, he resolves to make himself a new man for his child. 'That broke the ice,' recalled Rodgers. 'Once we could visualise the man singing, we felt that all the other problems would fall into place.'

Much to everyone's trepidation, the famously stern Molnár turned up to rehearsals one day. Convinced he would hate it, the writers nervously introduced themselves. He was ecstatic with what they had done, especially the new ending. His only, icily delivered, complaint was that the director smoked too much in rehearsal.

Carousel was a smash, consolidating the joint reputations of Rodgers and Hammerstein who, by this time, had decided to become a formal working partnership. It pushes the theatrical integrity of *Oklahoma!* further, introducing in Billy Bigelow a character even more complex than the previous show's Jud. Billy is a mass of contradictions, bullying and beating the woman he loves, loyal to her and to that love despite his feeling that it makes him a weaker man. By having the dead Billy review his life as he tries to enter heaven, the show can end on an up-note, as Billy realises his mistakes and tries to make amends. The result, for all the happy singalongs about June bustin' out, is a warts-and-all portrait of flawed humanity.

TRIVIA

Rodgers and Hammerstein wanted to follow their *Oklahoma!* model by bringing in another largely unknown cast for *Carousel*. Word reached them of a magnificent baritone named John Raitt – so to avoid anyone else discovering him before the new show was ready, they cast him in a touring production of *Oklahoma!* When he opened in *Carousel* he was a sensation.

The climactic number, 'You'll Never Walk Alone', has become a regularly sung anthem at Liverpool Football Club, sung by fans in the stands. (When I asked the Broadway singer Barbara Cook, who knew Rodgers well, whether he would have approved, she raised an eyebrow and replied, 'Well, Dick was always very fastidious about how his songs were performed.')

THE PLOT

Julie Jordan and Carrie Pipperidge, who work in a New England mill, visit a carousel one evening for relaxation. There, Julie immediately strikes up a rapport with the handsome, brooding barker, Billy Bigelow. Julie and Carrie get into an argument with the carousel's owner, Mrs Mullin, and Billy defends them. He is fired, and Julie stays to talk to him despite the warnings from Carrie that if she is late back she will lose her job, and from the mill owner that Billy uses women to his own advantage.

Billy and Julie muse about how things would be if they loved each other. It is clear that this is more than idle chat, and Billy seems genuinely shaken by his new feelings.

A month later, Billy and Julie are married and living with her cousin, Nettie. He, however, is frequently absent and, Julie tells Carrie, is so unhappy at being unemployed that he takes it out on her, on occasion slapping her. Carrie cheers her friend by revealing the news of her own marriage, to the fisherman Mr Snow.

Billy is visited by Mrs Mullin, who offers him his old job back (and her own amorous attentions). He considers the offer, but Julie arrives to tell him that she is pregnant. Billy is thrilled.

He turns down Mrs Mullin and considers how much fun he will have with his son – until it dawns on him that the child might be a girl. This impresses on him the need to provide for his family, and he resolves to get money one way or another – even if he has to take it.

NUMBERS TO LISTEN OUT FOR

'The Carousel Waltz'
'You're a Queer One, Julie Jordan'
'Mister Snow'
'If I Loved You'
'June Is Bustin' Out All Over'
'When the Children Are Asleep'
'Soliloquy'
'Stonecutters Cut It on Stone'
'What's the Use of Wond'rin'?'
'You'll Never Walk Alone'

RECOMMENDED RECORDINGS

Difficult. The Broadway cast recording is fabulously sung, not least by John Raitt's glowing Billy, but it all feels a touch too glamorous for this dark tale. The vocal quality might not be on the same level, but I'd go for the First Night Records album from the National Theatre's 1993 revival. There's a real sense of the drama there, and Joanna Riding's Julie and Michael Hayden's Billy really make you care about the characters. Nothing wrong, either, with the enjoyable 1956 film starring Gordon McRae, but again there's rather more light than shade.

Cats

Music by Andrew Lloyd Webber
Lyrics by T. S. Eliot
Premiere: 11 May 1981, at the New London Theatre

By the 1980s, Andrew Lloyd Webber had a lyricist problem – the first of many (there would later be that famous barbed comment that the composer changed his lyricists as often as he changed his underwear). Tim Rice was a brilliant writer, and a perfect match for the composer in all but personality. Both men deny that they ever fell out *à la* Gilbert and Sullivan, but Lloyd Webber has suggested that Rice's appetite for work was less than his own, while the lyricist in turn has hinted that their characters are not ideally suited (that said, they have occasionally worked together since, on show revivals, and rumours of a re-forming of the partnership resurface every so often).

While he hunted for a new long-term partner, Lloyd Webber turned to a lyricist that surprised everyone. T. S. Eliot was, first of all, dead. Secondly, his *Old Possum's Book of Practical Cats*, while a charming selection of poems, was hardly the kind of dramatic meat on which the composer's previous successes had fed. Joseph, Jesus, Eva Perón and, er, a bunch of cats?

Producer after producer turned the idea down and by the time Lloyd Webber asked Cameron Mackintosh, the young impresario (whom Lloyd Webber had chased around the Café Royal during an argument several years earlier) was almost the composer's last hope. Neither was Lloyd Webber quite sure about how he wanted to tackle it at the time. What he did have was a collection of wonderful songs. He played them to Mackintosh, and had his producer.

Initially, the pair wanted to develop the show as part of a double-bill for a ballet company. The first half would be all dance, set to Lloyd Webber's *Variations on a Theme of Paganini*, while the second, *Cats*, would consist of a song-cycle for solo singer with dancers in the background. Only they couldn't find a dance company to take them seriously (in fact that double-bill idea eventually did come to successful fruition under a somewhat different guise, *Song and Dance*).

Mackintosh had recently seen a fabulous musical version of Shakespeare's *The Comedy of Errors* by the Royal Shakespeare

Company and suggested recruiting its director, Trevor Nunn. After six long months of persuasion, they got their man – crucially, as it turned out. It was Nunn who suggested the framing story of an outsider who is finally accepted by her fellow felines. He also brought with him the great choreographer Gillian Lynne, whose signature is stamped so clearly on the show. And it was Nunn, after several tries by more august lyricists, who came up with the words to the only number in *Cats* not to be set to T. S. Eliot – its most famous song, 'Memory'.

A sterling cast was recruited. Paul Nicholas, Lloyd Webber's original Jesus; Elaine Paige, his greatest Evita; the dazzling Wayne Sleep (soon to become a huge UK star thanks to *Song and Dance*) and the veteran film actor John Mills. Also in that original cast was the composer's future wife, Sarah Brightman.

To say the show was a hit is an understatement. Awards, of which it won plenty, are one thing. *Cats* became the world's longest-running musical (until it was beaten by another Mackintosh production, *Les Misérables*), running 21 years in London. It opened in New York in October 1982 and became Broadway's longest runner – until overtaken by *Phantom of the Opera* (another smash for the Lloyd Webber–Mackintosh hits factory) – closing in 2000.

The success did not stop there. Although the producer Robert Stigwood had already established the practice of exporting shows internationally, it was Mackintosh and *Cats* that began the trend for replicating shows lock, stock and production. The musical to date has been produced in 124 cities, many of them in that same Trevor Nunn staging. Of course, the casting varied and there were some new productions, but across the world audiences were able to see the authentic *Cats* experience. It was not merely a trend in musical theatre. It was the beginning of a phenomenon.

TRIVIA

The first actress to play Grizabella in London was Elaine Paige, and in New York it was Betty Buckley. The two assumed similar roles for Lloyd Webber years later when Paige starred in *Sunset Boulevard* in London and Buckley in New York (although admittedly that is a bit of a cheat, as Paige did later take over the role on Broadway as well).

THE PLOT

The Jellicle tribe of Cats introduce themselves and explain how they each are named. Among those introduced is the rather macho Rum Tum Tugger, independent and fiery. Grizabella's entrance causes a general bristling of the fur – she is an outcast. Even more troubling to them though are the rumblings and crashes of the wicked cat Macavity. The leader of the cats' tribe is Old Deuteronomy. The cats enjoy a celebration – The Jellicle Ball – from which the miserable Grizabella is excluded.

More cats are introduced, including the aged theatre cat Gus. The criminal cat Macavity suddenly appears, captures Old Deuteronomy and disguises himself as the Jellicles' leader. Demeter exposes him, but Old Deuteronomy is still missing. Rum Tum Tugger suggests that they find the magical cat Mr Mistoffelees, who, sure enough, restores Old Deuteronomy to his tribe.

Now their leader must decide who will make the privileged journey to the Heaviside Layer. Grizabella returns and sings 'Memory', a song of such heartfelt emotion that she is the chosen one.

NUMBERS TO LISTEN OUT FOR

'The Jellicle Ball'
'Memory'
'Magical Mr Mistoffelees'

RECOMMENDED RECORDING

Of all musicals, *Cats* is the one that needs to be seen more than merely heard. Its sense of theatrical adventure and daring comes from the combination of music, dance and – if you're lucky enough to catch it – Nunn's clever playing-with-perspective production. Unfortunately, the DVD film, which features that production and original cast member Paige, is strangely dry and wanting in atmosphere. Perhaps it's the absence of a live audience, or perhaps you just needed to be there. So the original London cast recording is still the best, giving at least a hint of the energy and dynamism that exploded onto that stage back in 1981.

Chicago

Music by John Kander
Lyrics by Fred Ebb
Book by Fred Ebb and Bob Fosse
Premiere: 3 June 1975, at the 46th Street Theatre, New York

The year 1975 was a good one for musicals in New York. Barely two weeks after *A Chorus Line* opened came Kander and Ebb's – and, as much to the point, choreographer Bob Fosse's – *Chicago*. It was as revolutionary in its way as Marvin Hamlisch's enduring crowd-pleaser.

In their earlier hit, *Cabaret*, Kander and Ebb had used the decadent, dead-eyed atmosphere of the Berlin cabaret clubs to mirror the moral decline of Nazi Germany. Here, they managed to retain that highly stylised sense of detachment but liberated it from its Berlin setting. Their unique brand of acid-dipped, angular melodies was brought to bear on a Chicago murder case.

The 1920s trial of the killers Beulah Annan and the singer Belva Gaertner had so transfixed crime reporter Maurine Dallas Watkins that she wrote a play about them. Only after her own death, however, did she (in her will) finally acquiesce to Fosse's request to use the material as a basis for a new musical.

Fosse cast his wife Gwen Verdon (who had first brought the play to his attention) as the lethal would-be singing sensation Roxie Hart, and Chita Rivera as her idol, the equally fatal cabaret star Velma Kelly. He then set about creating choreography that would set the performers even further from real life – at times they pinioned about like marionettes (literally in one song, where Roxie acts as a ventriloquist's dummy for her lawyer, Billy Flynn). Kander and Ebb sealed the device by having each number introduced by a master of ceremonies.

It was brilliant, and wicked and wickedly sexy. On a television talk show of the time, Gwen Verdon confessed that she had seen at least one wife hit her husband, who had apparently been leering too intently at the shapely Chita Rivera, 'with a backhand right across the face'. It was, however, deliberately uncomfortable entertainment and, although it enjoyed a decent run (bolstered by a spot of star understudying from Liza Minnelli when Gwen Verdon became ill for a time), it could not stand up to the onslaught of *A Chorus Line*.

Ironically for a show written in the 1970s, with a musical and dramatic style that harked back some forty years earlier, it finally found its time with the 1996 revival. A public made cynical by the trials-as-mass-entertainment of O. J. Simpson and Louise Woodward saw their own age reflected in Kander and Ebb's reborn musical, and the show became a smash around the world (cleverly kept alive by continual star casting).

Not everyone is a fan of the revival, which is close to a semi-staged concert version (the cast are all in black, the orchestra is placed centre stage). Director Gary Marshall far preferred Fosse's original staging which, he insisted, told the story better despite the cabaret-style structure. After decades of discussion about the right approach (producer Martin Richards held the movie rights for many years, with Fosse telling him excitedly over the phone at one point that 'he finally knew how to film *Chicago*' – before dying shortly afterwards, having revealed his secret to no one), it was Marshall who directed the 2002 film. His big idea was to have all the songs happen in Roxie's head, and it worked splendidly. The film, starring Renée Zellweger, Catherine Zeta Jones and Richard Gere, was a smash, bagging six Oscars including Best Picture.

TRIVIA

Stars to have played the 1996 production since it opened have included David Hasselhoff, Sacha Distel, Joel Grey, Kelly Osbourne, Brooke Shields, Marti Pellow, Denise Van Outen, Melanie Griffith and Alison Moyet.

Ron Orbach, who has played Amos Hart in the Broadway revival of *Chicago*, is the cousin of the late Jerry Orbach, who created the role of Billy Flynn.

THE PLOT

Roxie Hart, a slightly psychotic housewife who dreams of success as a singer, is ditched by her lover. Offended, she shoots him dead. Much to her annoyance, her ever loyal husband Amos decides to give her up to the police. Once in prison she meets the other female inmates of Death Row, and is deeply excited to meet the legendary star Velma Kelly, who is accused of killing the other half of her sister act.

With the help (for cash) of Matron 'Mama' Morton, both women turn to the lawyer Billy Flynn to get them off the hook. For a substantial amount of money, Billy agrees, and tutors the inexperienced Roxie in the ways of wooing the press and, through them, the public. Velma soon becomes jealous, though, and what is already a fight for their lives becomes a battle for – perhaps even more important to them – celebrity.

NUMBERS TO LISTEN OUT FOR

'All That Jazz'
'Funny Honey'
'Cell Block Tango'
'When You're Good to Mama'
'All I Care About'
'We Both Reached for the Gun'
'Roxie'
'Mr Cellophane'
'Razzle Dazzle'
'Class'

'Nowadays'
'Hot Honey Rag'

RECOMMENDED RECORDINGS

The 1998 London cast is dominated by the Velma of Ute Lemper. She is the stylistic linchpin of this recording, vamping it up Berlin style. When the 'z' of jazz threatens to cut into the orchestra like a drill, you know you're listening to a singer who understands this show. Ruthie Henshall's mad drama queen Roxie is a delight and very funny (not that you'd ever want to meet this woman!). Henry Goodman's matinee idol Billy could perhaps do with a touch more sleaze beneath the carefully cultivated exterior, but it's a fine, calculating portrayal, while Nigel Planer is splendidly lost as Amos.

That production's Broadway cast album is still impressive, but almost every cast member pales beside the London equivalent. The exception is Joel Grey's softly sung Amos, even more sympathetic than Nigel Planer. No, this set's great asset is its band – which pays far more attention to texture and detail without neglecting the sheer swing of the thing than we are used to from cast albums. This pit provides a musical masterclass in comedy and in how to play Kander and Ebb. For that alone this recording should be heard. There is, incidentally, a tenth-anniversary edition which includes not only this Broadway cast album but a second CD made up of the production's protagonists around the world (and a 'making of' DVD). There are some real finds here, but it's not the ones you would expect (although Brooke Shields acquits herself rather better than might have been predicted as Roxie).

The film soundtrack showcases more than capable turns from Hollywood's finest but numbers like 'Cell Block Tango' bludgeon you into submission rather than getting inside your head. Catherine Zeta Jones and Renée Zellweger are accomplished as Velma and Roxie but don't have enough of that Weillesque spite in their voices. Richard Gere is a smooth Billy, John C. Reilly a slightly miscast Amos. Not a soundtrack to collect, then, but the flamboyant film itself – the prison increasingly hellish – is a marvellous achievement and belongs on every show-lover's DVD player.

A Chorus Line

Music by Marvin Hamlisch
Lyrics by Edward Kleban
Book by James Kirkwood Jr and Nicholas Dante
Premiere: 21 May 1975, at the Public Theatre, New York

A stage. That's it. No extravagant set, no stars, just – possibilities. It sounds more like the kind of spare production favoured by the pioneering theatre director Peter Brook than a Broadway – well, off-Broadway originally – musical. And commercial shows don't have much more experimental roots than a group of real-life dancers, or 'gypsies' as they're known in the biz, sitting around discussing their experiences.

And yet, *A Chorus Line* had its own theatrical guru, in the director-choreographer Michael Bennett. There has been much discussion about whether the original, taped workshop sessions were Bennett's own idea or not, but there is no doubt that it was his driving concept that shaped the show. From those recorded discussions came the substance – a show framed by an audition. Song, dance and speech were fused to riveting, poignant effect as Zach the director insists on hearing his desperate hopefuls' innermost fears, their overriding dreams.

It turned out that you don't need stars to have a hit. You don't need to come out humming the sets. You don't need a recognisable movie title. Great stagecraft can work wonders (and bag you multiple awards including a Pulitzer Prize), and on its transfer two months later to Broadway's Shubert Theatre, *A Chorus Line* high-kicked its way to become the longest-running show in Broadway history. The night it achieved that record, Bennett called in hundreds of current and previous cast members so that the final number, 'One', was performed by a chorus line of 338. It had run for nearly fifteen years, surely the longest audition in the world, by the time it closed in 1990. That record stood until *Cats* pounced in 1997.

TRIVIA

Robert LuPone, who created the role of Zach, is the brother of the more famous Patti LuPone.

Some of the sardonic humour that runs through the piece was actually written by an uncredited Neil Simon.

The show's lyricist Edward Kleban has said that he thinks *A Chorus Line*'s hit number, 'What I Did for Love', is 'dreadful'.

In the original workshops, the successful auditioners were picked at random, so that they would genuinely express surprised pleasure. Once the show opened, the results were set in stone.

THE PLOT

At an audition for the chorus of a Broadway show, the director, Zach, coaxes his dancers to reveal to him who they really are. It becomes the most challenging audition they have ever faced, and not only do they have to endure hours of strenuous dancing – they must come face to face with their own lives.

NUMBERS TO LISTEN OUT FOR

'I Hope I Get It'
'I Can Do That'
'At the Ballet'
'Sing!'
'Hello Twelve, Hello Thirteen, Hello Love'
'Nothing'
'Dance: Ten; Looks: Three'
'The Music and the Mirror'
'One'
'What I Did for Love'

RECOMMENDED RECORDING

First, and most important, never, *ever* watch the film version if you have never seen this show before. In one of those dreadful show-business ironies, one of the boldest and most experimental of musicals is given a tired and unimaginative reading by director Richard Attenborough. With heavy-handed acting, not least from Michael Douglas's turn as Zach (more gangster than director), any sense of spontaneity or love of the theatre is killed stone dead. OK, so now I've got that out of my system, other options. In fact, with the 2007 Broadway cast weighed down by elaborate orchestrations and some indifferent singing, the choice is clear.

The original Broadway cast album is one of the great show recordings. All the breathless excitement of opening night is there which, given the subject matter, serves the show admirably. The whole thing pulses along with nervous energy – and the great torch songs are filled with urgent need as well as passion. It almost seems like everything you need to know about the dancer's life.

City of Angels

Music by Cy Coleman
Lyrics by David Zippel
Book by Larry Gelbart
Premiere: 11 December 1989, at the Virginia Theatre, New York

City of Angels was not the West End's finest hour. Not that there was anything at all wrong with the show – quite the opposite. It was witty, pacey, involving and clever. Exactly the sort of show that deserved to play for years. Except that it closed within months.

London's theatre commentators were aghast, and ashamed. The influential critic of the *Daily Mail*, Jack Tinker, wrote a spirited attack on a Theatreland that could sustain long runs for second-raters such as *Buddy* (an efficient but faintly heartless tribute show to Buddy Holly) and hardly give house room to a genuinely original musical that was as satisfyingly cerebral as it was entertaining. *City of Angels*'s London adventure was left panting with, reportedly, losses exceeding £2 million.

That *City of Angels* should have been as good as it is is hardly a shock – it had the finest of pedigrees. As composer, Cy Coleman, the Broadway veteran behind such successes as *Little Me*, *Sweet Charity* and *Barnum*. On the book, a comedy writer to match Coleman's achievements, Larry Gelbart – one of the legendary team of writers (alongside Woody Allen, Neil Simon and Mel Brooks) for the comedian Sid Caesar, and architect of a string of hits including the TV series *M*A*S*H*, the film *Tootsie* and, not least, the Stephen Sondheim musical *A Funny Thing Happened on the Way to the Forum*. And the brilliant David Zippel as lyricist.

To rub salt into London's wounds, the show had done just fine in New York. Better than fine, it had been the toast of the town. It was credited with bringing the great traditions of the American musical back to the Great White Way (this at a time when Broadway was all but dominated by imports from London, courtesy of Andrew Lloyd Webber and Cameron Mackintosh, and was not feeling too happy about the fact).

The triumphant American production, directed by Michael Blakemore, ran for more than two years. Along the way it garnered six Tony Awards, including those for Best Musical, Best Original Score, Best Actor in a Musical and Best Book of a Musical. London was at least partly redeemed by gifting *City of Angels* the Olivier Award for Best Musical.

TRIVIA

Composer Cy Coleman won the Tony Awards for Best Musical and Best Original Score with *City of Angels*. The following year he won the same two prizes again, for his show *The Will Rogers Follies*.

THE PLOT

Set in 1940s Hollywood, the talented young novelist Stine agrees to write a detective film for the producer Buddy Fidler.

While Stine struggles with the pressures of Fidler's ever more infuriating demands, his hero, Stone – in scenes that are usually played with all the 'fictional' characters wearing black and white – grapples with the case of his life. Not only that but, as the line between real life and fantasy blurs, Stone is deeply unimpressed with Stine's compromising and tells him so. Stone and Stine realise they must work together so that they can each win out.

NUMBERS TO LISTEN OUT FOR

'You Can Always Count on Me'
'Double-Talk'
'The Tennis Song'
'What You Don't Know about Women'
'With Every Breath I Take'
'It Needs Work'
'Stay with Me'
'You're Nothing without Me'

RECOMMENDED RECORDINGS

Further underlining the unfairness of its failure in London, the UK cast recording – cast from strength with the likes of Roger Allam and Henry Goodman – has the edge over its US revival in terms of character presence. Where the American cast scores is in its jazz 'sheen', that seemingly genetic ability to swing, seemingly without effort. It conjures up all the fun and the fears of 1940s Hollywood. A very good cast includes Gregg Edelman and James Naughton, but it's for the general atmosphere and storytelling sweep that you should get the Broadway cast on Sony (though real fans must have both!).

The Comedy of Errors

Music by Guy Woolfenden
Lyrics by Trevor Nunn (after William Shakespeare)
Book by William Shakespeare

Premiere: 29 September 1976, at the Royal Shakespeare Theatre,
  Stratford-upon-Avon

Clearly Rodgers and Hart's *The Boys from Syracuse* was not
enough. Trevor Nunn, then Artistic Director of the Royal
Shakespeare Company, decided that Shakespeare's *The Comedy of Errors* could usefully do with an even closer adaptation.
As such, its strengths as a musical have been vastly underrated
over time, with Nunn's own magnificent production almost
forgotten (thankfully a film of it has been available on video,
and one prays that a DVD issue is not far off).

As infused with the spirit of the great Broadway musical
comedies and even silent slapstick masters like Chaplin as it is
the poetry of Shakespeare, this *Comedy of Errors* extends the
Bard's lines to create songs – almost as if he were a living
writer who had workshopped with Nunn and composer Guy
Woolfenden, and composer and librettist had routinely yelled,
'Stop there, Will – cue a song!'

All of the songs are witty, with some extremely attractive
melodies – I love the patter of 'There's a Rhyme and a Reason' and the sheer zaniness of Mr Pinch's exorcism song. The
Nunn production, coming at the same time as his great *Macbeth* (Judi Dench starred in both), helped to establish him as
one of the great British directors. It also got him noticed by the
young producer Cameron Mackintosh, who then asked him to
come on board for Andrew Lloyd Webber's *Cats*, and soon
Nunn was also the most successful English director of musicals, with a résumé that so far includes, as well as *Cats*, *Les
Misérables*, *Oklahoma!*, *My Fair Lady*, *Starlight Express*, *Sunset
Boulevard* and *Aspects of Love*.

TRIVIA

Judi Dench is partnered in the cast by Michael Williams, who
was her real-life husband.

It was not only Nunn who went from this production to
Cats. Both shows were choreographed by Gillian Lynne.

THE PLOT

See *The Boys from Syracuse*!

NUMBERS TO LISTEN OUT FOR

'Beg Thou or Borrow'
'A Man Is Master of His Liberty'
'There's a Rhyme and a Reason'
'Exorcism'
'Let's Go Hand in Hand'

RECOMMENDED RECORDING

Alas, the only one available to date is the RSC video and that is hard to get hold of. We live in hope for a DVD. If you do see it on the internet or somewhere, don't hesitate. With a cast that includes Dench, Williams, Nicholas Grace, Roger Rees, Francesca Annis, the marvellous Mike Gwilym, as well as Richard Griffiths in a supporting role (talk about luxury casting!) it's an unalloyed treat.

Company

Music and lyrics by Stephen Sondheim
Book by George Furth
Premiere: 26 April 1970 at the Alvin Theatre, New York

If glimpses of Sondheim's very personal style can be heard in *A Funny Thing Happened on the Way to the Forum*, that style came into its offbeat own with his next show, *Company*. Now the composer placed his audience at one remove from the action – slice-of-life musings about a bachelor and his mostly married friends. A number such as 'The Little Things You Do Together' commented on a relationship in a way that allowed the audience to understand more than the characters themselves.

Sondheim also found a way to marry the pop rhythms of an urban metropolis with the more traditional musical forms, making musicals trendy for the show's many fans. Neither was there a plot, in any typical sense. The main character simply wanders between friends and romantic encounters.

Company ran for twenty months on Broadway, but its impact has been enormous. Not least on the composer himself, who followed this with more concept musicals, among them *Into the Woods*, *Sunday in the Park with George* and *Assassins*.

TRIVIA

Dean Jones, who created the role of Bobby on stage, left the production soon after the opening. He was in the process of separating from his wife, and consequently found acting out Bobby's relationship troubles each night too painful. He was, however, persuaded to return for the cast recording.

THE PLOT

On Bobby's thirty-fifth birthday, his friends make him a surprise birthday party (which he has found out about) and wish him many happy returns and commiserate that he is still single. Bobby's various encounters with his friends after that include the possibly playfully sparring couple Sarah and Harry; Peter and Susan – the ideal couple who announce their divorce; the pressuring David and Jenny and the terrified-of-getting-married Amy and her fiancé Paul.

Bobby goes on several dates but none of them results in any meaningful relationship. And his friends are not exactly perfect examples – one of them, Joanne, reveals in the show's most famous number, the coruscating 'The Ladies Who Lunch', that she knows that she is wasting her life. Yet Robert is rapidly coming to the conclusion that perhaps he might have been wrong all these years.

NUMBERS TO LISTEN OUT FOR

'Company'
'The Little Things You Do Together'
'Sorry-Grateful'
'You Could Drive a Person Crazy'
'Another Hundred People'

'Marry Me a Little'
'Side by Side by Side'
'Barcelona'
'The Ladies Who Lunch'
'Being Alive'

RECOMMENDED RECORDING

In his book *Musical Theatre on Record*, Kurt Gänzl felt that *Company* was a strange, unique show where the brilliant songs managed to 'wipe out' the performers and indeed the characters singing them; that one admired the songcraft without caring about the people. I disagree totally. The original Broadway cast recording is given a strong focal point by Dean Jones's Bobby. In his hands the character builds to a climax of pain, where his conclusion seems temporary and no real solace (knowing Jones's own marital situation at the time adds an unexpected, rather voyeuristic layer to the pathos).

A Connecticut Yankee

Music by Richard Rodgers
Lyrics by Larry Hart
Book by Herbert Fields
Premiere: 3 November 1927, at the Vanderbilt Theatre, New York

Initially worried that they might provoke outrage by musical-ising the classic Mark Twain novel *A Connecticut Yankee in King Arthur's Court*, Rodgers and Hart scored their biggest success to date with this show. It also showcased some of their most enduring songs, namely 'Thou Swell' and 'My Heart Stood Still'. Aping the language of the show, one critic memorably wrote, 'Go, thou sluggard, and enjoy *A Connecticut Yankee* and tell ye cock-eyed worlde thou has had ye helluva time.'

A sad postscript to this show occurred in 1943. Hart, an alcoholic, was on a downward spiral and Rodgers proposed a rehaul of *A Connecticut Yankee*, complete with new songs, to give his friend an incentive to stop drinking. Hart did, and the revival was a success, but as soon as it opened he hit the bottle again. He was dead by the year's end.

TRIVIA

The song 'My Heart Stood Still' was already a hit in London as part of the London revue show *One Dam Thing After Another*. It ended up in *A Connecticut Yankee* only because the singer Beatrice Lillie wanted to introduce it to Broadway. Rodgers didn't trust her to do it well and so pretended that the number was already promised for the New York show. He then hastily negotiated with the revue's producer to be able to include it for Broadway.

THE PLOT

Martin is about to get married in his home town of Hartford, Connecticut, and has been given among his presents a suit of armour. When he is hit with a champagne bottle by his fiancée for flirting with Alice Carter, he is knocked unconscious and dreams that he is one of King Arthur's knights. Martin proceeds to modernise the court. When he comes to he must decide with which girl he really wants to ride off into the sunset.

NUMBERS TO LISTEN OUT FOR

'My Heart Stood Still'
'Thou Swell'
'On a Desert Island with Thee'
'To Keep My Love Alive'
'I Feel at Home with You'

RECOMMENDED RECORDING

This *Yankee* has been poorly served in the recording studio. Decca caught the 1943 cast, headed by the pleasant but uncharismatic Dick Foran. The 1949 film with Bing Crosby is similarly pleasant but uninspired.

Damn Yankees

Music by Richard Adler
Lyrics by Jerry Ross
Book by George Abbott and Douglass Wallop
Premiere: 5 May 1955 at the 46th Street Theatre, New York

This baseball musical was strike two for the pitching of Adler and Ross. Unfortunately, this and its predecessor *The Pajama Game* were all the outstanding work done by the duo, since Ross died aged twenty-nine. But *Damn Yankees* is a darn good show – a really fine example of the kind of amiable, genuinely funny musical comedy that was being churned out in the 1950s.

Douglass Wallop, on whose novel *The Year the Yankees Lost the Pennant* the musical is based, was partnered with the experienced George Abbott to write the book. But this show carved out its special corner of Broadway history when Bob Fosse was brought in to choreograph. Not only was it a hit, marking Fosse's entry into the showbiz major league (he would become perhaps the most fêted choreographer in Broadway history, notwithstanding stiff competition from the likes of Jerome Robbins), it also introduced him to the love of his life, Gwen Verdon. Renowned more as a dancer than as an actress and singer, she was selected to play a demonic temptress because of her physical presence. Although they did not stay married for ever, she and Fosse had a profound effect on each other and it was Verdon he was with when he died.

TRIVIA

Fosse's early dancing and choreographic experience was in nightclubs and burlesque houses – the sexually laid-back atmosphere he encountered there was to have a great effect on him and his work.

THE PLOT

There is little more soul-destroying for the genuine, long-term baseball fan than for the team he supports never to win.

Such is the lot of Joe Boyd, a salesman beginning to get along in years. He is offered the deal of a lifetime by a fellow salesman, Mr Applegate – or the devil – who promises to imbue Joe with youth and baseball brilliance in return for his soul.

Joe signs, and duly becomes the saviour of his beloved team, the Senators. But there is a get-out clause in his contract – if he asks to go home before time, all bets are off. And as Joe begins to miss his abandoned wife more than he expected, Mr Applegate enlists the help of the seductive Lola to ensure that the contract still stands.

NUMBERS TO LISTEN OUT FOR

'Heart'
'Shoeless Joe from Hannibal, Mo'
'A Man Doesn't Know'
'A Little Brains, a Little Talent'
'Whatever Lola Wants, Lola Gets'
'Near to You'

RECOMMENDED RECORDING

There's no competition among recorded versions for Gwen Verdon and Ray Walston in the original Broadway cast on RCA – something of a Broadway classic. The 1990s revival, also recorded, isn't on the same level. And the film soundtrack, also with Verdon and Walston, doesn't quite measure up either.

Evita

Music by Andrew Lloyd Webber
Lyrics by Tim Rice
Premiere: 21 June 1978 at the Prince Edward Theatre, London

The opening of *Evita* was a red-letter day in the history of the musical. Having moved from jolly biblical jamboree (*Joseph*) to intense drama flecked with rock'n'roll extravagance (*Jesus Christ Superstar*), Rice and Lloyd Webber now turned to explore – as deeply and at times as densely as any good play – the character of a recent political figure, Eva Perón. This had never been done before in any major way by musical theatre which, although often preaching an earnest message right from its early days with *Show Boat*, usually felt compelled to exhibit the trappings of traditional musical comedy. *Evita* was different. It used a variety of musical styles, from the seductive, calculating rhythms of tango to rock'n'roll polemics, to evoke a complex Argentina and its anti-heroine.

What is more, the show was immensely successful. Its writers cannily revisited their *Superstar* formula of releasing a concept album first (starring Julie Covington) to build word of mouth and prepare the ground for their new approach. So before it opened they already had a hit song, 'Don't Cry for Me Argentina' (much to the pair's surprise: 'Who wants to buy a song about a country you've hardly even heard of?' said Rice later). When *Evita* finally broke over the West End like a tidal wave, and achieved a similar feat at New York's Broadway Theatre, it established London as the gravitational centre for musicals for two decades. High ticket prices and a reluctance to experiment meant that Broadway was in decline, just as the West End was in its creative pomp. *Evita* also, of course, firmly established the through-sung musical as the form of the moment (and London's pre-eminence did not begin to fade until that form began to drop out of fashion during the 1990s – at which point Broadway bounced back with a batch of new musical comedies).

Unluckily for Julie Covington, but happily for Elaine Paige, Covington recorded the title role on the concept album but was not to create it on stage. And so Paige's career was made, in a role that showed off all her formidable acting as well as vocal prowess. Similarly, David Essex played the sardonic narrator (who was eventually named as Che Guevara) rather than the album's Colm Wilkinson – he, however, did eventually find his own star-making part, in another of this period's great through-sung shows, *Les Misérables*.

TRIVIA

Appropriately, for a musical about a character who frequently staked everything on her chosen path, the Prince Edward Theatre used to be a casino.

In a programme note Lloyd Webber called Eva Perón 'easily the most unpleasant character about whom I have written, except perhaps Perón himself'.

THE PLOT

A student, Che, who is in a Buenos Aires cinema when the film is stopped to announce the death of Argentina's first lady, Eva Perón, is unimpressed at the vast expense lavished on her funeral. 'Oh, what a circus,' he storms, '. . . she did nothing for years.'

With Che as narrator, the musical tells Eva's story from her early days in her native town of Junín, where she seduces a cabaret singer and persuades him to take her to the capital city. Once in Buenos Aires, Evita (as she is eventually nicknamed by the public) spies the fast-rising colonel and politician Juan Perón. She persuades him that 'I'd be good for you' and her political path is set.

Perón's ascendancy to the presidency of Argentina sees Evita's dreams fulfilled. She finds, however, that having power is only the beginning. She now must face the regime's critics and eventually a new foe arises that dwarfs all she has previously faced – a serious illness.

NUMBERS TO LISTEN OUT FOR

'Oh, What a Circus'
'On This Night of a Thousand Stars'
'Buenos Aires'
'I'd Be Surprisingly Good for You'
'Another Suitcase in Another Hall'
'A New Argentina'
'Don't Cry for Me Argentina'
'High Flying Adored'

'Rainbow High'
'You Must Love Me' (written for the 1996 film)

RECOMMENDED RECORDINGS

First of all, sad to report, the Alan Parker film is a dead loss. Handsome and sometimes magnificent to look at, a gripping first half is thrown away by the funereal pace of the second. Part of the problem is Madonna's performance, which is charismatic and very accomplished to a point – but she doesn't have the depth to sustain interest when the second half rests more or less squarely on her shoulders. Antonio Banderas, on the other hand, is a fabulous narrator, eaten up with fury and bitter in his humour. The soundtrack fares better as an audio-only experience, with Madonna's and Parker's shortcomings far less in evidence.

With so many (and there are dozens) of recordings, it comes as a bit of a surprise to discover that the concept album still has the edge. Covington is a brilliant actress, and really sounds ready to fight for what she sees as a better life – for this Eva, her journey is all about crawling as far out of the gutter as possible and helping others to do the same. It's just that the last bit is far less important to her than the first. Wilkinson gives as good as Argentina gets as the narrator, that remarkable voice all but howling with outrage (I do wish he would record Lloyd Webber's Judas, a role he played on stage). Purely vocally speaking, nobody really comes close to Elaine Paige on the London cast album, and she is almost as good an actress as Covington. But to my taste David Essex as Che makes far less of an impression, unbalancing the piece. So Covington on MCA it is.

Fiddler on the Roof

Music by Jerry Bock
Lyrics by Sheldon Harnick
Book by Joseph Stein
Premiere: 22 September 1964, at the Imperial Theatre, New York

Mark the date well. The musical-theatre historian Mark Steyn is among those who have pinpointed the end of the glory days of the Broadway musical to the opening, or rather the closing (after a record-breaking 3,242 performances), of *Fiddler on the Roof*. It was simply, he has suggested, the last of the best. After *Fiddler*, a Jewish folk musical based on the stories of Shalom Aleichem, nothing could improve on what had gone before.

While it's not quite that simple, there is truth in the statement. Musical theatre as envisaged by Hammerstein had been realised. The big successes to follow *Fiddler* would look to new areas for inspiration – mainly rock music and opera, at the hands of Stephen Schwarz and Andrew Lloyd Webber. And those movements, Schwarz notwithstanding, mainly emanated from Europe. The reason it's not that simple, by the way, is the reason that musical theatre got a lot more complicated – Stephen Sondheim, who has somehow managed to keep a stylistic foot in the Hammerstein household where he studied at the feet of the master, even as he has forged ahead to test the boundaries of what the genre could do.

And yet, even as the milkman Tevye and his family and his community set out to seek a new life in America at *Fiddler*'s close, there was the sense that the American musical, largely created by Jewish immigrants and their families, had reached some kind of closure – at least as far as its first chapters were concerned.

What had *Fiddler* got so right? Much of its success is due to a total sympathy and understanding between score and lyrics and between the book and the songs, between Joseph Stein and Jerry Bock and Sheldon Harnick. The three Jewish boys knew what it would mean to write a klezmer musical; they understood this Jewish music form. Just as every Jewish festival or happy event includes almost as a point of principle moments in which the suffering of others is remembered, klezmer music – the folk music Jews played at weddings and the like in Eastern Europe – catches a sense of joy and affliction simultaneously. In its wrenching shifts from major to minor keys and back again, there is always the sense of the unpredictability of life, of the two faces of fate.

As these shifting moods suffuse the music, so they direct the lyrics and the book. It's all there in a couplet such as: 'God has told us to be joyful even when our hearts lie beating on the floor/How much more can we be joyful when there's really something to be joyful for?' It's funny and sad with a hint of anger but held together by a strong bond of faith – the more so when belted out in a rousing drinking song ('L'chaim' – the Jewish toast, which itself means 'to life'; here there are no illusions as to what life has in store). Similarly, Stein's book allows characters to feel two things at once – as in Tevye's dilemmas, argued over with his now funny, now deadly serious 'on the other hand' device.

The show took a risk of sorts with its leading man. Zero Mostel was one of the biggest box-office draws on Broadway and yet one of its least predictable leading men. With a strong director and the right mood, he could be electric, a force of nature. Surrounded by yes men or simply on a whim, he could indulge his own dramatic tics to the point of destroying a play. Stein and Mostel clashed once or twice over his habit of ad-libbing, sometimes in Yiddish, but generally this show caught Zero at his best. For those of us too young to have seen him on stage, the Broadway cast recording happily enshrines one of the Great White Way's classic performances.

When it came to casting the movie, the director Norman Jewison passed over Mostel in favour of Chaim Topol, the Israeli actor who had opened the show in London and who Jewison felt was less stagy. Mostel's fans were outraged as, reportedly, was Zero himself. The truth is, Jewison was probably right; Topol was more realistic than Mostel would have been. The difference is, when a Zero Mostel is on song, realism becomes a relative term. Schmaltzy? A little. Larger than life? Certainly. But Mostel writ large an emotional realism that goes straight to the heart, and cuts the *kreplach*.

TRIVIA

The original Broadway cast included Julia Migenes, who would later find fame as a leading opera singer (starring in Francesco Rosi's 1984 big-screen film of *Carmen* opposite Placido Domingo), as Hodel.

Norman Jewison was worried that he had been asked to direct the film version because the producers had wrongly thought he was Jewish. He was right, they had, but he kept his job!

The now celebrated (and much imitated) opening number, 'Tradition', was a late addition. The original plan was to start with Tevye and his family, until it was realised that the show was really about continuity and community and that these things needed to be shown at the outset.

During the 1980s, the time of my childhood, no Jewish bar mitzvah was complete without a very badly played *Fiddler on the Roof* medley. If few musicals are as good as *Fiddler* done well, very few so make you want to drown yourself in a shallow bowl of chicken soup when done badly. Granted, it's not really trivia, but I had to get it off my chest.

THE PLOT

Amidst Cossack pogroms and anti-Semitism in the tiny Russian town of Anatevka, the milkman Tevye tries to eke out a living and bring up his five daughters according to Jewish tradition. As the level of violence in the town takes a sudden turn for the worse and life starts to become unbearable for the Jewish community, Tevye's daughters question the tradition of arranged marriages. They want to arrange their own matches. But some are less suitable than others.

NUMBERS TO LISTEN OUT FOR

'Tradition'
'Matchmaker'
'If I Were a Rich Man'
'Sabbath Prayer'

'To Life'
'Sunrise, Sunset'
'Do You Love Me?'
'Far from the Home I Love'
'Anatevka'

RECOMMENDED RECORDINGS

There are several excellent versions, and few to stay away from. A fine new entry comes from a 2007 London production that started life at the Sheffield Crucible and which features a wonderfully charismatic Tevye from Henry Goodman (the British actor who had been prematurely ousted from *The Producers* in New York some years previously) alongside the doughty Golda of Beverly Klein. However, as you'll have surmised from the above, nobody really comes within touching distance of Zero Mostel in this role. Just as the music, lyrics and book are at one with each other, he is at one with them all. He inhabits the show's twisting moods and generous spirit as though born to it all which, in many ways, he was. Just listen to his wordless mini-chant at the climax of 'Sabbath Prayer' and you will hear all you need to know. Topol is excellent on the original London cast and film soundtrack (and the film, despite feeling a bit overlong and overworthy, is required viewing); Goodman is terrific. Mostel, to coin a cliché, simply *is* Tevye.

Follies

Music and lyrics by Stephen Sondheim
Book by James Goldman
Premiere: 4 April 1971 at the Winter Garden Theatre, New York

There's a school of thought that Sondheim's collaborators have not always matched up to the composer's genius. There's some truth to that perhaps in *Follies*, a show whose book is not on the same level of a score that finds Sondheim in full formidable command of his powers – the sharpness of his lyrics, his ability to encapsulate complex relationships in a verse or two, or for that matter to anatomise a mind (in the self-knowing 'Buddy's Blues', or the breakdown-on-stage that is 'Live, Laugh, Love'), is simply awesome. As, for that matter, is the way he turns his characters' acidity or ebullience on a die to show the hurt beneath the anger, or the longing behind the banter.

Still, James Goldman is no slouch. If a subject that cried out for the deftness of an (American) Alan Ayckbourn never gets close, it does at least convey powerfully the ghosts of the past, haunting the present.

Despite its theatrical setting, and some numbers that have since become widely hummed classics ('Broadway Baby', 'Losing My Mind'), *Follies* surprised Broadway-watchers by not becoming a big hit when it opened. It was no *Merrily We Roll Along*-style disaster, but 522 performances marked a respectable flop. Little comfort to Sondheim then, but the show's fate was only appropriate to its subject matter – the decay of a theatre echoing the erosion of the values and dreams of its one-time stars. For all the romantic trappings of a showbiz reunion and warbling about 'beautiful girls', *Follies* is a tragedy. It is, perhaps, many tragedies.

And a major piece of work, one that is often revived. Both Sondheim and Goldman made revisions for various revivals. It seems likely that *Follies* will never be a perfect show, but one that cannot be ignored. Oh, and if there was a prize for a single musical number with the most accomplished lyrics, the bloody-minded 'I'm Still Here' would be one heck of a strong contender.

TRIVIA

The book writer on *Follies*, James Goldman, won an Oscar for his film script for the 1969 movie *The Lion in Winter*. He was also the brother of another Oscar-winning screenwriter, William Goldman (who collected his little gold men for *All the President's Men* and *Butch Cassidy and the Sundance Kid*).

THE PLOT

As their old, beloved theatre faces demolition, members of the now defunct Weisman Follies return for a reunion. But as Ben and his wife Phyllis encounter once again their old colleagues Buddy and Sally, emotions once thought buried resurface – while new problems can no longer be ignored.

NUMBERS TO LISTEN OUT FOR

'Beautiful Girls'
'Waiting for the Girls Upstairs'
'Broadway Baby'
'In Buddy's Eyes'
'I'm Still Here'
'One More Kiss'
'Could I Leave You?'
'Buddy's Blues'
'Losing My Mind'
'The Story of Lucy and Jessie'
'Live, Laugh, Love'

RECOMMENDED RECORDINGS

The wonderful surprise about the 1985 concert performances of *Follies* at New York's Avery Fisher Hall is that for a cast list fairly bulging with stars, the live recording is the most emotionally truthful on disc. The sense of ensemble catches you unawares. The individual brilliance on display – with a line-up that includes Barbara Cook, Carol Burnett, Elaine Stritch, Mandy Patinkin, George Hearn, Lee Remick, Betty Comden, Adolph Green, Liliane Montevecchi and even the great, aged diva Licia Albanese – is only to be expected.

Neither Barbara Cook, filling 'Losing My Mind' with agonised yearning, nor Elaine Stritch – all gin-soaked deadpan humour turning to gutsy bravado in 'Broadway Baby' – has ever done anything better (which is saying something) and they deliver definitive renditions of those songs. Burnett's timing is spot on (in a way that her pitch isn't always, but who cares?) in 'I'm Still Here'. Happily, if you can find it, there's a 'making of' film of the fraught circumstances in which this once-in-a-lifetime cast came together – no wonder they bonded.

Otherwise the 1987 London cast is worth hearing. Julia McKenzie's moving Sally isn't entirely eclipsed by Cook, while Diana Rigg is a trenchant Phyllis (and she gets a new number written for her by Sondheim, 'Ah, But Underneath').

Funny Girl

Music by Jule Styne
Lyrics by Bob Merrill
Book by Isobel Lennart
Premiere: 26 March 1964 at the Winter Garden Theatre, New York

The words 'Funny Girl' are inseparable from the name Barbra Streisand. She it was whom this show, and her bravura turn in it, confirmed as a megastar, no longer in the making, but made. In fact, the musical is an approximate retelling of the career and marriage of a previous era's star entertainer, Fanny Brice. Yet Streisand's success was only enhanced by the connection: 'Miss Streisand imagining herself in a radiant future . . . is not only Fanny Brice but all young performers believing in their destinies,' enthused the New York Times review. 'Fanny and Barbra make the evening. Who says the past cannot be recaptured?'

The extent of Streisand's identification with the part in the public's mind perhaps explains the surprising scarcity of Funny Girl productions over the years. And if she doesn't perform it on stage any more, well, there's always the 1968 film. It is, nevertheless, a shame, because Styne's score is terrific and this is a show for much more than its time.

TRIVIA

Streisand's stint in the London production was cut short because she became pregnant.

THE PLOT

Fanny Brice is one of the most successful entertainers of her age, yet her marriage has been put under enormous strain with her husband Nick Arnstein's continual brushes with the police. As she waits for him to return from prison, she looks back over her life and their relationship.

NUMBERS TO LISTEN OUT FOR

'I'm the Greatest Star'
'I Want to Be Seen with You Tonight'
'People'
'You Are Woman'
'Don't Rain on My Parade'
'Sadie, Sadie'
'The Music that Makes Me Dance'

RECOMMENDED RECORDING

Streisand gives one of the great individual recorded performances on the Broadway cast album, mesmerising in its variety, its vulnerability and its sheer guts. The rest of the cast also shine, but this is Streisand's parade, and nobody would dare to try and rain on it.

Gentlemen Prefer Blondes

Music by Jule Styne
Lyrics by Leo Robin
Book by Joseph Fields and Anita Loos
Premiere: 8 December 1949, at the Ziegfeld Theatre, New York

This is one of those shows that would become deeply associated with more than one performer. Carol Channing was iconic in the lead role of Lorelei Lee. And yet no less so was Marilyn Monroe in the 1953 film version. It is surely no accident that both of these performers had very idiosyncratic singing styles – one would be unlikely to get the two versions of 'Diamonds Are a Girl's Best Friend' mixed up. It is a role that rewards individuality. Less famous, but still marvellous (as far as one can tell from the recording), was Dora Bryan in the London cast.

The musical was drawn from Anita Loos's hugely popular 1925 novella. And, although Jule Styne's collaborations with writers were not always happy (English playwright Jack Rosenthal was so traumatised by his experience of working with the boisterous Styne on the musical *Barmitzvah Boy* that he wrote a bitter comedy about it, called *Smash!*), this resulted in a fizzing show that has stood the test of time. And, in 'Diamonds Are a Girl's Best Friend', yielded one of the very finest and most recorded of show tunes.

TRIVIA

Anita Loos wrote a sequel, entitled *But Gentlemen Marry Brunettes*.

THE PLOT

Lorelei Lee is determined to make the most of the Roaring Twenties. Consequently she becomes attached to a string of wealthy bachelors – the button king, the zipper king and others. Predictably, all does not turn out quite as she expects.

NUMBERS TO LISTEN OUT FOR

'Bye Bye Baby'
'I'm Just a Little Girl from Little Rock'
'It's Delightful Down in Chile'
'Diamond's Are a Girl's Best Friend'
'Gentlemen Prefer Blondes'
'Homesick'

RECOMMENDED RECORDING

The London cast album has its admirers, but you really must hear Channing, positively electric in her star-making role. For that reason, it has to be the 1949 original Broadway cast recording.

Gigi

Music by Frederick Loewe
Book and lyrics by Alan Jay Lerner
Premiere: 13 November 1973, at the Uris Theatre, New York

More popular in its movie incarnation than in the stage version that followed it, *Gigi* still has the power to charm and fascinate. That fascination centres chiefly on the girl who has suddenly blossomed into a mature and captivating woman – but also on the change it provokes in her friend-turned-admirer Gaston, and the sage reflections it inspires in her Aunt Alicia and her old flame Honoré.

If all of Lerner and Loewe's shows tend to pale next to *My Fair Lady*, this stands the test better than most. Its great virtue, when all is said and done, is a magnificent catalogue of songs whose blends of melody and lyrics aspire to poetic heights.

TRIVIA

For Lerner, the most difficult part of getting *Gigi* right was the casting of Gaston – finding an actor who could play a man who was bored but would not be boring. It is a point on which productions of the stage show have often fallen down.

THE PLOT

The eminent, eligible and much gossiped-about bachelor Gaston Lachaille lives at the centre of Paris's social whirl. Everybody is interested in his romantic adventures, but his eye is caught, to his own surprise, by the young, inexperienced Gigi – as she grows into a lady in her own right. Her grandmother and aunt are delighted, as they have been training her to be a rich man's mistress. Gigi, however, has her own ideas of romance. As, for that matter, has her irrepressible uncle, Honoré.

NUMBERS TO LISTEN OUT FOR

'Thank Heaven for Little Girls'
'It's a Bore'
'The Night They Invented Champagne'

'She's Not Thinking of Me'
'I Remember It Well'
'Gigi'

RECOMMENDED RECORDING

The original Broadway cast features Karin Wolfe, Daniel Massey, Maria Karnilova and Alfred Drake as a charismatic Honoré. The collectors' buying point may well be that Agnes Moorhead's Aunt Alicia was her final stage outing. The production was not well received but it's the best we have, for now.

The Gilbert and Sullivan Shows

The Gondoliers
HMS Pinafore
The Mikado
The Pirates of Penzance
Ruddigore
Trial by Jury
The Yeomen of the Guard

Granted, it's cheating to put seven shows into one small entry (even though I've only included my *favourite* seven), but firstly space is short, and secondly these comedic masterpieces have one foot in the world of opera and have rarely been properly taken up by the musical-theatre world (with the notable exception of Joe Papp's hugely successful, much travelled and excruciatingly overdone production of *The Pirates of Penzance*). Yet the operetta format and the comedy genre G&S used were highly influential on musicals and in many ways qualify these works as much as musicals as opera. They might have come to hate things about each other, but by goodness they could write great shows!

TRIVIA

The ghost story *Ruddigore*, originally spelled *Ruddygore*, was deemed to be highly offensive to Victorian audiences and the show was a flop, despite being one of G&S's very best shows.

RECOMMENDED RECORDINGS

Of course, space is too limited to discuss each individually. But there are various complete series of recordings. The best are the D'Oyly Carte company series on EMI. Most cast members had played their roles on stage with Gilbert and Sullivan's own company, and series conductor Isidore Godfrey conducts with a real feel for the theatre. The rival sets, mainly conducted by Sir Malcolm Sargent, are more carefully considered and cast with many great voices, but sometimes feel a little staid.

Girl Crazy (and *Crazy for You*)

Music by George Gershwin
Lyrics by Ira Gershwin
Book by Guy Bolton and Jack McGowan
Premiere: 14 October 1930, at the Alvin Theatre, New York

The Gershwins' reputation as a hit factory was confirmed with 1930's *Girl Crazy*. The pair contributed such songs as 'Embraceable You' and 'I Got Rhythm' to popular culture. And the production made the reputations of both of its leading ladies, Ethel Merman (one can just imagine the impact she must have had, fizzing along at high volume in 'I Got Rhythm') and Ginger Rogers.

TRIVIA

The show played only 227 performances, its success curtailed when Ethel Merman and co-star Willie Howard left.

The band for that production included Benny Goodman, Gene Krupa and Glenn Miller.

In 1992 *Girl Crazy* mutated into the very successful *Crazy for You* with a new plot and extra songs.

THE PLOT

A father pays a taxi driver to take his son away from temptation, to the town of Custerville, where women never venture.

The son quickly changes that situation, opening a gambling den complete with female dancers. Both he and the driver find love.

NUMBERS TO LISTEN OUT FOR

'Bidin' My Time'
'The Lonesome Cowboy'
'Could You Use Me?'
'Embraceable You'
'Sam and Delilah'
'I Got Rhythm'
'But Not For Me'
'Treat Me Rough'
'Boy! What Love Has Done to Me!'

RECOMMENDED RECORDINGS

The original Columbia recording with Mary Martin is OK (or Oh! Kay to coin another Gershwin title), as is the 1990 album with Lorna Luft and Judy Blazer. But to be honest I'd forget about *Girl Crazy* and pick up the fabulous Broadway cast recording of *Crazy for You* – the best Gershwin musical that he never wrote.

Guys and Dolls

Music and lyrics by Frank Loesser
Book by Abe Burrows and Jo Swerling
Premiere: 24 November 1950, at the 46th Street Theatre, New York

The powerful British theatre critic (turned first dramaturge of the National Theatre) Kenneth Tynan called *Guys and Dolls* 'the second best American play'. In first place, he said, was Arthur Miller's harrowing *Death of a Salesman*. For a product of a genre still frequently (ridiculously) accused of a lack of intellectual weight and seriousness, that's not bad company to keep. Laurence Olivier himself wanted to play the pivotal role of Nathan Detroit and only illness prevented him. Years later

Richard Eyre, one of Olivier's successors at the helm of the NT and director of a dazzling UK production of the show, wrote in a newspaper that an Act of Parliament should guarantee that there would at all times be at least one production of *Guys and Dolls* playing in his country.

Why is it so loved? Why considered so important? It contains no cultural crusades, as do *Show Boat* and *South Pacific*, no sense of the ideology of an age like *Camelot* – not even the stamp of an age-old classic writer like *My Fair Lady* or *Les Misérables*. No, but it takes the stories of an American writer whose characters were as vivid and idiomatic of their locale as anything in Dickens and fleshes out the caricatures with songs of seemingly boundless wit and, above all, heart. Or, to put it another way, *Guys and Dolls* is, in its way, a perfect musical.

Frank Loesser was exactly the right composer for the project – instinctively gifted, he wrote and composed from the heart. Once the idea was mentioned to him by the producers Ernest Martin and Cy Feuer, he swiftly delivered a batch of uncommissioned songs as though he had, simply, been unable not to write them (this caused the original book-writer, Jo Swerling, to be replaced by Abe Burrows who would better follow Loesser's lead). Passion was Loesser's watchword, and it wasn't always pretty. During one rehearsal he actually hit Isabel Bigley (who played Sarah Brown) when she didn't deliver as well as he thought she could (he later atoned with a diamond bracelet).

The sense of a brilliant play where songs are an integrated part of the whole was doubtless helped no end by the engagement of the master of the theatrical comedy, George Kaufman, to direct. Indeed, so set was Kaufman on seeing the show as a play with the songs distinctly secondary that he would often leave for a cigarette during the music numbers. During one rehearsal he was, Eyre has written, once overheard to say, as he hurriedly stomped up the aisle, 'Good God, do we have to do every number this son-of-a-bitch ever wrote?'

The show was always going to be a smash, its reputation building fast on the road. When it arrived in New York, it duly delivered and has seldom been revived without success. Land-mark productions include Jerry Zaks's 1992 Broadway retread with Nathan Lane and Peter Gallagher, but better still was Eyre's own 1982 NT production (which I caught on Eyre's 1997 revival, with a treasurable cast including Henry Good-man, Imelda Staunton, Clarke Peters and Joanna Riding). The most recent London production, from the Donmar Ware-house, became fashionable for film stars to inhabit – among them Ewan McGregor, Patrick Swayze and Don Johnson. As for Eyre's plea for an Act of Parliament, I'd vote for it.

TRIVIA

So furious was Frank Sinatra to discover, having signed up for the leading role of Nathan in the film version, that his co-star Marlon Brando had all the best songs, that he insisted on a specially written number, 'Adelaide'. He also made a point of taking 'Luck Be a Lady' into his stage act, in part to show that he could sing it better than Brando.

THE PLOT

Nathan Detroit, a small-time crap-game fixer on a Broadway populated by colourful gamblers and hoods, hears that a wealthy gangster, the Greek, is in town and looking for a game. Nathan must raise $1,000 to hire a venue or his reputation will be shot. He bets the inveterate gambler Sky Masterson exactly that sum that Sky cannot romance a girl of Nathan's choosing and entice her to go to Havana with him. Sky accepts, but to his horror Nathan selects a missionary, Miss Sarah Brown.

When Sky, posing as a sinner desiring salvation, hears that Sarah's mission is in danger of closing down due to poor attendance, he promises to deliver 'one dozen genuine sinners' – in return for her agreeing to have dinner with him. She reluctantly agrees, and is surprised when the dinner is in Cuba! She accidentally gets drunk in Havana, and falls in love with Sky. On their return she realises that the match can't work.

At the big crap game, which is held in a sewer, Sky wins and instead of money demands that the attendant reprobates go to Sarah's prayer meeting. Meanwhile, Miss Adelaide, Nathan's fiancée of fourteen years, is furious when their wedding is postponed yet again. When Nathan protests that he is obliged to attend a mission she accuses him of lying. After Sky saves Sarah's mission she and Adelaide lament the bad characters of the men they love. Adelaide has a brainwave – that they should marry their men today, and change their ways tomorrow. Both couples are wed, and Sky joins the mission.

NUMBERS TO LISTEN OUT FOR

'Fugue for Tinhorns'
'Follow the Fold'
'The Oldest Established Crap Game in New York'
'I'll Know'
'A Bushel and a Peck'
'Adelaide's Lament'
'Guys and Dolls'
'If I Were a Bell'
'I've Never Been in Love Before'
'Luck Be a Lady'
'Sue Me'
'Sit Down, You're Rockin' the Boat'
'Marry the Man Today'

RECOMMENDED RECORDINGS

Although the original cast album boasts Stubby Kaye's classic Nicely-Nicely Johnson, two modern versions vie for first choice. Most characterful is the 1992 Broadway cast, with Nathan Lane, Faith Prince (a really touching Adelaide), Peter Gallagher and Josie de Guzman. But TER's 1997 recording is far more complete, and though less starry (Kim Criswell's Adelaide notwithstanding) it has a fabulous sense of ensemble. The stand-out is Emily Loesser, daughter of Frank, as the most adorable Miss Sarah on disc.

Gypsy

Music by Jule Styne
Lyrics by Stephen Sondheim
Book by Arthur Laurents
Premiere: 21 May 1959, at the Broadway Theatre, New York

In fact, by the time it opened on Broadway in 1959, *Gypsy* had been around the block. A period of try-outs normally occurs out of town for big musicals – it's a chance for expensive shows to be tested in front of an audience and fine-tuned before braving the New York critics – but *Gypsy* was forced to wait and wait, to play and play before taking Manhattan. The reason? Its infamous producer, David Merrick, a rather tyrannical figure who had for some reason taken against this show. According to Howard Kissel's wonderfully entertaining biography of Merrick (*The Abominable Showman*), *Gypsy*'s hugely popular star Ethel Merman was visited backstage by fellow Broadway royalty Carol Channing, while the musical was moored in Philadelphia. 'When is it coming in?' asked a nonplussed Channing. 'When that son of a bitch gives the OK,' replied Merman grimly.

All of which is odd, given that *Gypsy* not only went on to be recognised as one of the very greatest of musicals, it was Merrick's own idea in the first place. He it was who read the autobiography of the famous stripper Gypsy Rose Lee, he who immediately thought of Merman as Lee's pushy mother, and he who brought in the director Jerome Robbins.

The omens could hardly be better. Yes, Merman needed to bounce back from her first ever flop, *Happy Hunting*, but that failure was unique in her career to date. And in Robbins, writer Arthur Laurents and librettist Stephen Sondheim, Merrick reunited the golden team that had delivered *West Side Story*. Substituting that show's composer Leonard Bernstein for Jule Styne, the man behind *Gentlemen Prefer Blondes* and *Bells Are Ringing*, was hardly a step down (indeed, Styne, never a man to sell his talent short, would probably have said it was a step up). So why the hostility from Merrick, to the extent that co-producer Leland Hayward had to insist that Merrick stay away from rehearsals, since his 'negative' attitude was disturbing the cast?

It could just be down to Merrick's contrary nature. Or it might be due to the fact that, though the producer found the source material, it was Laurents who really worked out how to put it on stage. What started out as a love letter to old-time American vaudeville became, in Laurents's hands, something much darker, hard-hitting and painful. Suddenly the character of Rose, the stage mum, became a psychologically complex, at times bitter study in regret and vicariously displaced ambition. Her big number, 'Rose's Turn', veers dangerously close to a mental breakdown as she confronts her real motivations.

What emerged was, as in other great stage-set shows from *Pagliacci* to *A Chorus Line*, a revelation of the true power of theatre – as a mirror for human nature. Rose gazes at her favourite daughter's fate and sees her own frailties and failures. But then there is the allure of the stage too, and with it always comes renewed hope, however illusory that might be. Everything may be coming up roses indeed, but look closely and they may yet be made out of plastic.

TRIVIA

Before commissioning Jule Styne, David Merrick asked Irving Berlin, Cole Porter and Cy Coleman (who even wrote four songs, which were rejected – though one went on to become the Tony Martin hit song 'Firefly').

The show was subtitled 'A Musical Fable' at the insistence of Gypsy Rose Lee's sister, the actress June Havoc, who felt that the depiction of herself, in particular, distorted the fact that she was very talented and had been working steadily since a very young age.

THE PLOT

Mama Rose is determined that her two daughters will be stars. She concentrates her efforts on Baby June, touting her cutesy kid act around America. When June eventually can take her mother's pushiness no more and runs away with a boy in the show, Rose turns her full attentions to the shy Louise. But vaudeville is dying, increasingly the only venues who want to book Mama Rose are bawdy burlesque houses. This tests the relationship between mother and daughter to the limit, as her mother must decide just how far she is prepared for Louise to go.

NUMBERS TO LISTEN OUT FOR

'Some People'
'Small World'
'If Momma was Married'
'Everything's Coming up Roses'
'Let Me Entertain You'
'Rose's Turn'

RECOMMENDED RECORDINGS

When it comes down to it, it doesn't matter how good everyone else is, you just have to hear Ethel Merman in the role that was written for her. That trumpet voice (rising, at full blast, to sound like the entire brass section of an orchestra) and vocal mannerisms that today can sound dated perfectly suit the smothering character of Rose. One can readily understand how claustrophobic the daughters' lives truly are. Nobody can stand up to the force of this Rose's personality, while when she falls apart, the fall-out is almost frightening. Happily, the original cast recording is strong all round, making it a clear favourite. For a more modern sound and a different take on Rose (younger-sounding, a woman who would be considered past her prime only in the unforgiving world of theatre) it's well worth hearing the 2003 Broadway cast album, starring Bernadette Peters.

Hair

Music by Galt MacDermot
Lyrics and book by James Rado and Gerome Ragni
Premiere: 29 April 1968, at the Biltmore Theatre, New York

The first thing to say is, if you're looking for a cogent story-line, tight structure and songs that teach you about character or move the plot forward (the usual rules for a good musical), *Hair* is not for you. The script is messy, the songs are chaotic and arrive with the rapidity and often the aggression of machine-gun fire, and for much of the time it can be hard to tell exactly what's going on, or to care very much about any of the principals. And yet, when it works – and the circumstances have to be absolutely right (usually meaning there has to be something happening in the world to protest about) – there are few musical theatre experiences that can match its brand of intensity.

Hair is an out-and-out assault on the senses. It is determined to make audiences care, really care about society. In this, like the drop-out hippies it depicts, it often goes to strange-seeming lengths – songs attack censorship by listing drug names, sexual reticence by detailing sex acts, the fashion police by eulogising long hair (hence the title). At one point, famously, the entire cast strips naked.

Its main target is war – *Hair* was born out of the anti-Vietnam sentiment coursing through many US citizens in the 1960s. The actors James Rado and Gerome Ragni brought together the improvisatory techniques of, respectively, Lee Strasberg's Actors' Studio and New York's Open Theatre Group. Which might account for the all-over-the-place structure.

When it opened, debuting off-Broadway at Joe Papp's new Public Theatre, it created a sensation. Audiences loved it, and unsurprisingly there was corresponding outrage in some quarters. There were threats of violence against the cast, and two actions trying to stop the show failed at the Supreme Court. It is ironic that the show was in some ways a victim of its own success – people happily whistle its tunes without realising for one minute the principles they were created to draw attention to. 'Good Morning, Starshine' popped up in an episode of *The Simpsons*, 'Aquarius' accompanies a UK television advert for water. Gradually, the show's potency was diluted (a 1993 London revival notoriously drew a reviewer's observation that, 'This show is as topical as *The Pirates of Penzance*').

When the London Fringe's Gate Theatre (echoing the show's off-Broadway origins) updated the musical for a 2005 production targeting the war in Iraq, some felt that it had once again found a moment where it worked. (Not all, though: Michael Billington's review in the *Guardian* called it 'as much a period piece as *No, No, Nanette*'.) I loved it, finding that *Hair* in fact works best when one all but ignores the story, gives up searching for structure and just allows oneself to be blown away by its rage, joy, desperation and hope, all at their most raw.

TRIVIA

The original cast included writers Rado and Ragni. Other early line-ups in the US and UK featured, variously, Diane Keaton, Keith Carradine, Meat Loaf, Elaine Paige and Tim Curry.

THE PLOT

Depends which version of the show you see, as it has varied rather a lot, with the 1979 film version wildly different again. Broadly, though, it focuses on a hippie group calling themselves The Tribe, and the relationship between the charismatic Berger and the curious Claude. And, for all their love of the free life (and free love), there is a threat on the horizon – draft orders for Vietnam.

NUMBERS TO LISTEN OUT FOR

'Aquarius'
'Hashish'
'Sodomy'

'Manchester England'
'I Got Life'
'Hair'
'Where Do I Go?'
'Black Boys'
'White Boys'
'What a Piece of Work Is Man'
'Good Morning, Starshine'
'Let the Sunshine in'

RECOMMENDED RECORDINGS

This show is all about the time in which it was written (for all that the 2005 London revival found new resonance with Iraq). The original off-Broadway cast album is raw, unpolished, full of energy, exuberance, arrogance, charm – exactly the qualities that gave *Hair* such impact. The Broadway cast recording is already more accomplished, and just a touch poorer for it. The film is good fun, with John Saxon in particular providing a likeable hick as the out-of-towner Claude. The new ending doesn't really work, though.

Hairspray

Music by Marc Shaiman
Lyrics by Scott Wittman and Marc Shaiman
Book by Mark O'Donnell and Thomas Meehan
Premiere: 15 August 2002, at the Neil Simon Theatre, New York

'They've watched me crawl on glass, climb the walls: I've paid my dues for twenty-five years,' a delighted Margo Lion told the *New York Times* in October 2002. The independent producer's new show, *Hairspray*, had just opened with a box-office advance of $20 million. After more than two decades of struggle, with her own apartment on the line and at a time when Broadway was dominated by big corporations and producing conglomerates, this old-style producer finally had a smash hit.

It could easily have gone either way. True enough, Lion opened her show at a time when, following *The Producers*, screen titles were being fitted with songs, shaped up for the stage and shipped out to the West End or Broadway faster than you could say *The Lion King*. But there would always be the danger that sooner or later, bringing multiplex fare to the stage, a place that has traditionally thrived on originality, would provoke nothing more than a 'been there before' yawn from audiences. That the title had been optioned once before for a musical, which never transpired, did not bode well.

Yet, in the event, this remake of the 1988 John Waters film had too much going for it to fail; an underdog-against-the-world story, anti-racism themes, big hair, fabulous costumes and Harvey Fierstein in drag. And then there are the show's magic ingredients. A warm, knowing sense of humour, a big heart and musical numbers that that make the most buttoned-up of spectators want to start Mexican waving in the stalls. What's not to love?

Affection permeates every bar of this show: for its subject, for its setting (like Waters, Margo Lion had lived in Baltimore) and in one sense most of all for its archetypal characters. 'The real reason I'm praying that *Hairspray*, the Broadway musical based on my 1988 movie, succeeds', Waters wrote shortly before its New York opening, 'is that if it's a hit, there will be high-school productions, and finally the fat girl and the drag queen will get the starring parts.'

TRIVIA

On the set of the original movie, star Rikki Lake found the work caused her to lose weight so fast she had to keep eating to maintain the obesity that was crucial to the plot. A similar problem has beset the various Tracys in productions of the stage show – with its fast-moving choreography – with London lead Leanne Jones admitting on radio at one point that having to wear a fat suit was becoming a real possibility.

The Corny Collins Show was based on Baltimore's *The Buddy Deane Show* (Deane had a cameo in the 1988 film).

Michael Ball, playing Tracy's mother Edna in London, found the biggest single demand of the role wearing heavy fake breasts.

THE PLOT

In 1960s Baltimore, the cheerful teenager Tracy Turnblad sees her obesity as no bar to winning a spot on her favourite TV dance extravaganza, *The Corny Collins Show*. Along the way she inspires other viewers, her friends and even her own mother. She finds, however, that achieving her dream leads only to a larger, more noble ambition – getting blacks and whites to dance together on television.

NUMBERS TO LISTEN OUT FOR

'Good Morning Baltimore'
'The Nicest Kids in Town'
'Mama, I'm a Big Girl Now'
'I Can Hear the Bells'
'It Takes Two'
'Run and Tell That!'
'Big, Blonde and Beautiful'
'Without Love'
'I Know Where I've Been'
'(It's) Hairspray'
'Cooties'
'You Can't Stop the Beat'

RECOMMENDED RECORDING

The 2007 film of the musical is a great watch, boasting three delicious turns by Hollywood royalty – Michelle Pfeiffer as the devious Velma Von Tussle, Christopher Walken as Tracy's clutzy father Wilbur and especially John Travolta as a sweet but silly Edna Turnblad. Yet, soundtrack-wise, even this doesn't stand up against the non-stop, infectious energy of the original Broadway cast album, rightly dominated by Marissa Jaret Winokur's appealing, relentlessly optimistic Tracy. Other stand-outs include Corey Reynolds's strongly sung Seaweed – Tracy's friend from the other side of the colour divide. For all his stage success in the role, I just cannot get used to Harvey Fierstein's cheese-grater voice and uncertain (that's putting it mildly) pitch as Edna, but as he/she hasn't got much to sing on the album it's not a reason for this album not to be on every show-lover's shelves.

Half a Sixpence

Music and lyrics by David Heneker
Book by Beverly Cross
Premiere: 21 March 1963, at the Cambridge Theatre, London

Already an established pop star by the time he ventured onto the musical theatre stage, mention the name Tommy Steele to most Brits (of a certain generation) today and they will most likely shoot back, with a fond grin, '*Half a Sixpence*'. The show, based on an H. G. Wells novel, was a precise fit for Steele's talents and it helped to turn him into an enormous star. With success on Broadway as well as in London and the film version that followed, it has become part of Steele's identity as a showman.

TRIVIA

Marti Webb, who starred in the London stage production and would later find wider fame in Andrew Lloyd Webber's *Tell Me on a Sunday*, lost out for the movie to Julia Foster – at least in terms of screen time. When Foster opens her mouth to sing, it is actually Webb's voice that comes out!

THE PLOT

Young orphan and apprentice to a drapery, Arthur Kipps comes into money through an inheritance. Letting it go to his head, he throws aside his faithful girlfriend Ann and his modest lifestyle, preferring instead to seek a woman and way of living more in keeping with his bank balance. When he loses all the money, he comes to his senses. But renewed temptation is on its way.

NUMBERS TO LISTEN OUT FOR

'All in the Cause of Economy'
'Half a Sixpence'
'Money to Burn'
'She's Too Far Above Me'
'If the Rain's Got to Fall'
'Flash, Bang, Wallop!'

RECOMMENDED RECORDING

Since nearly all the numbers feature the main character, and since it was such a successful Tommy Steele vehicle, the 1963 London cast recording really gives fans of the show all they might need. There is also lovely work from Marti Webb as the put-upon Ann.

Hello, Dolly!

Music and lyrics by Jerry Herman
Book by Michael Stewart
Premiere: 22 September 1928, at the St James Theatre, New York

Jerry Herman's first big success and arguably most famous show was originally to have been called *Dolly, a Damned Exasperating Woman*. Exasperating was just what, on occasion, this great lady of a show could be. Producer David Merrick wanted Bob Merrill to compose, but Merrill refused to work with Merrick's choice of director, Gower Champion – so Jerry Herman was brought on board. The out-of-town try-outs were a convoluted and difficult process. Herman had written the songs with Ethel Merman in mind for the title role, but she turned him down (although she did play the role on a later occasion). The most notorious failure attached to this musical, though, was the 1969 film version – one of the most expensive flops to date and widely 'credited' with (temporarily) killing off the movie-musical genre.

Despite all of which, the film is rather good (Herman

reportedly loves it). Merman's place was more than ably taken by Carol Channing. And the stage show was a great hit, wining rave reviews, a (then) record number of Tony Awards and notching up 2,844 performances on Broadway – more than any other show before it.

It all nearly didn't happen. The road to Broadway was paved with bad reviews (one quipped, 'Goodbye, Dolly!') and Merrick stormed and threatened to close the show before it reached New York. At which point his director threatened to buy him out and Merrick, eventually, relented. The new and catchy title came when Louis Armstrong had a chart hit with the song 'Hello, Dolly!'

The show, a musicalisation of the Thornton Wilder play *The Matchmaker*, duly became a smash. Whenever momentum threatened to sag (not often) its ever resourceful producer came up with one of his trademark strokes of brilliance to keep it fresh, and in the news. So, Dolly was sent to say hello to American GIs serving in Vietnam. The Democrats welcomed Johnson's presidency by singing, 'Hello, Lyndon!' – and a Channing record of those lyrics swiftly followed. At one point, Merrick mounted *Dolly* with an all-black cast, starring the very popular Pearl Bailey.

It remains one of Herman's best-loved scores. Channing was followed in the part by Mary Martin and many others, but history has judged it to be hers.

TRIVIA

The 1975 all-black cast included the pre-screen-fame Morgan Freeman. To persuade Pearl Bailey not to take too many performances off (she was famous for not showing up), Merrick personally bought her jewellery. She announced the fact in a curtain speech.

THE PLOT

The matchmaker Dolly Levi misses her late husband Ephram, but decides to move on with her life and marry the wealthy Horace Vandergelder. He, however, becomes convinced that her aim is to have him marry someone else. With various other love affairs blossoming around her, Dolly determines not to let Horace get away.

NUMBERS TO LISTEN OUT FOR

'I Put My Hand in'
'It Takes a Woman'
'Put on Your Sunday Clothes'
'Ribbons Down My Back'
'Dancing'
'Before the Parade Passes by'
'Elegance'
'Hello, Dolly!'
'So Long, Dearie'

RECOMMENDED RECORDINGS

Never having quite 'got' the idiosyncratic attractions of Carol Channing, I would opt for the film soundtrack on Philips. Barbra Streisand is marvellously engaging, playing well off Walter Matthau's not-easily-wooed Horace, and there is a fine turn too from Michael Crawford. Above all, there is Louis Armstrong singing *that* song. However, if you are one of Channing's legion of fans or simply want to investigate what all the fuss was about, there is much to recommend the 1964 Broadway cast recording on RCA. Also for that label, there's a well-worth-hearing recording of the all-black cast, with Bailey and Cab Calloway resplendent in their roles.

Into the Woods

Music and lyrics by Stephen Sondheim
Book by James Lapine
Premiere: 5 November 1987, at the Martin Beck Theatre, New York

The nursery-rhyme-like cadences of the title song to this labyrinthine musical are deliciously deceptive. What starts as a simple and gently funny retelling of some old fairy stories, complete with narrator, turns into something much darker, much more complex – finally an existential riff on who we are and should be, where we want to go, the whole thing. Musically, too, those lilting tunes soon twist into songs of loneliness and despair (and I love the hints of things to come, as when the witch tells her story with a slightly discomforting rap number). More than any other of Sondheim's shows, in *Into the Woods* can be felt his famous love of puzzles. And when the narrator gets killed, it's like somebody threw away the rule book.

For all its crack cast (Bernadette Peters in the best of her Sondheim turns to date, the marvellous Chip Zien – like Mandy Patinkin without the sugar rush, and the hilariously deadpan Joanna Gleason) and general brilliance, *Into the Woods* has never been a true smash. How could it be? Sondheim doesn't do smashes. But it ran nearly two years on Broadway, a little under six months in London and has been fairly often revived ever since. I suppose if you do want a cast-iron money-maker, it's all very well to include beloved characters like Red Riding Hood, Cinderella and Prince Charming (two of them, indeed); but don't kill your narrator.

TRIVIA

Persistent rumours of a film version have never come to fruition. Reportedly, Danny De Vito had been lined up to play the giant (honestly).

THE PLOT

Various fairy-tale stalwarts are wishing hard for their hearts' desires. Jack wishes that his cow would yield milk, Cinderella wishes to go to the king's festival, a baker and his wife want a child. The 'witch from next door' pops around to see the baker, and reveals that the spell she put on them to make his wife infertile can be reversed, but the couple need to collect four unlikely items: 'a cow as white as milk, a cape as red as blood, hair as yellow as corn and a slipper as pure as gold'. They have three days. She also tells the couple of her own daughter, Rapunzel, whom she has locked in a tower for her own good.

At the same time, Cinderella decides to defy her family and steal away to the festival, while Jack's mother sends him to sell the cow – which he sells to the baker's wife for what she pretends are magic beans. Little Red Riding Hood trots off to her grandmother's house in the woods. Indeed, they all eventually head into the woods, where vain Prince Charmings chase their dream women and hungry wolves lurk for their next meal. And when a giant beanstalk grows to the heavens, the trouble really starts.

NUMBERS TO LISTEN OUT FOR

'Into the Woods'
'Hello, Little Girl'
'I Know Things Now'
'First Midnight'
'Giants in the Sky'
'Agony'
'Last Midnight'
'No One Is Alone'
'Children Will Listen'

RECOMMENDED RECORDINGS

The original Broadway cast recording is a deeply satisfying affair. Almost every major character undergoes a real emotional journey, especially Chip Zien's baker – gradually maturing from stooge to a loving and responsible protector – and Julia McKenzie's witch (what starts out as flip stereotype becomes a mass of insecurities). It is, however, well worth buying the DVD featuring this cast. All are just as good as on the disc, with the added advantage of James Lapine's witty, multi-hued production.

Jerry Springer – The Opera

Music by Richard Thomas
Book and lyrics by Richard Thomas and Stewart Lee
Premiere: 29 April 2003, at the National Theatre, London

In what you might call a high-art-meets-pop-culture experiment – with plenty of swearing and sexual fetishes thrown in – Thomas's and Lee's operatic take on the *Jerry Springer* TV show attempted to show the heartbreak behind Springer's trailer-trash guests. 'When someone is screaming, "I hate you, I wish you were dead", sometimes they really want to say, "I miss you, I love you" – and the operatic form can help to show that,' Thomas said shortly before the show's premiere, sounding unintentionally (or perhaps not) like Springer himself in one of his famous 'final moments'.

Thomas was right, there is plenty of heart to the show. First and foremost, however, it is scabrously, outrageously funny. There aren't many musicals that feature a foul-mouthed transsexual, a man who gets his kicks from wearing diapers and gives audience members badges bearing such legends as 'Three-nipple cousin-f*cker'. This one has them all. Not to forget the surreal parade of dozens of identical dancing Jerrys at the curtain.

Despite winning a clutch of awards (six Oliviers, as well as Best Musical prizes in both the *Evening Standard* and the Critics Circle awards) and a West End transfer, *Jerry Springer – The Opera* was decidedly unpopular with some radical Christian groups such as Christian Voice. The second half, in which the guests turn into biblical characters (including the diaper fetishist as Jesus), provoked furious denunciations and death threats from groups. Those threats were extended to staff at the BBC, who were placed under police protection when it screened a filmed version. Previous to the broadcast, the BBC had received around a record-breaking 47,000 complaints. Theatres for the planned UK tour (which did eventually happen) started dropping out under pressure, and lyricist Lee later told me in an interview that the Christian Voice affair had deterred him from writing similar material in the future. To date, the show has not had a New York production though it has made it to Chicago for its US bow. Further regional productions are planned. As for the real Jerry Springer, he loved it, telling reporters, 'I only wish I had thought of it first!'

TRIVIA

This show has more swear words than any other musical – with the total being reckoned at somewhere between four hundred and many thousands (the high end tends to count each chorus member separately).

THE PLOT

At a routine taping of the *Jerry Springer Show* the crowd seems restless, eager both to scream at the 'freaks' who will be Jerry's guests and to worship their hero, Jerry. Their excitement is stoked to near hysteria by the irresponsible warm-up guy, with security guards (including Jerry's faithful security chief, Steve) frequently having to control them.

Jerry enters (he and Steve having the only speaking roles while all others sing); the show begins. Among his guests are a husband cheating on his wife with a transsexual lover, a diaper fetishist and a woman who cherishes an ambition as a pole-dancer and is married to a member of the Ku Klux Klan (whose fellow Klan members interrupt proceedings with a tap dance). During a commercial break, Jerry has fired his insubordinate warm-up guy – and in a moment of revenge the ex-employee gives a Springer guest a gun. Jerry is shot dead.

In Act II, Jerry and Steve find themselves in purgatory where they are confronted by the warm-up guy, who reveals himself as the Devil. He demands Jerry's help with a family argument. Jerry must now stage a special edition of the TV show from hell, featuring the Devil, Jesus and God. If he refuses, the penalty will be deeply unpleasant, involving sex and barbed wire.

'Jerry Eleison'
'Chick with a Dick'
'I Just Wanna Dance'
'This Is My Jerry Springer Moment'

RECOMMENDED RECORDINGS

There are at present only two, the original London cast album and the BBC film. Both are live (one from the National, the other from the Cambridge Theatre), Most of the cast are identical, but the clincher is Michael Brandon – doing an uncanny Springer impersonation on the CD (hilariously catching exactly the politician-turned-presenter's air of wily self-interest). He beats David Soul's more hapless Springer on the DVD hands down. Both versions feature David Bedella's spitefully Satanic Devil, Alison Jiear's honey-voiced would-be pole-dancer and Benjamin Lake – who nearly steals the show with his sovereign-voiced God's bluesy 'It So Ain't Easy Being Me'.

Jesus Christ Superstar

Music by Andrew Lloyd Webber
Lyrics by Tim Rice
Premiere: 17 October 1971, at the new Mark Hellinger Theatre,
   New York

'This play is blasphemous!' read one picketer's sign outside an early production of *Jesus Christ Superstar*. 'Burn Andrew Lloyd Webber,' someone shouted. All par for the course in this musical's first weeks and months.

And yet, *Superstar* was hardly irreverent (though I suppose it depends whom you ask as to what comprises irreverence). It never went as far as equating Jesus with a diaper fetishist, as did the later *Jerry Springer – The Opera* (death threats ensued for that one), nor showed him fantasising about cavorting with Mary Magdalene (as in the Martin Scorsese film *The Last Temptation of Christ*). OK, so the life of Jesus was turned into a rock opera; the Bible had taken this treatment before (Stephen Schwarz's *Godspell* a notable example). What was so special about this?

Well, the fact that it was indeed a rock opera probably didn't help. Ideas about 'the devil's music' were probably not completely dead in some areas when the 1970s dawned. And this was rock music, in a way, before it was theatre. The fledgling show-writers Andrew Lloyd Webber and Tim Rice had struggled to get their show backed, so released it first as a concept album. Starring Murray Head, Yvonne Elliman and Ian Gillan, the album did phenomenally well, topping the US charts three times. Robert Stigwood came in as producer, and a theatre was found.

But this was a time, with the Vietnam War raging in East Asia, when the younger generation was questioning everything. And questions abound in *Jesus Christ Superstar*. The priests worry about how exactly to deal with Jesus and his followers. Mary Magdalene's big torch song 'I Don't Know How to Love Him' examines the precise nature of her feeling for Jesus. Jesus's own 'Gethsemane' meditation questions God, in Rice's searing lyrics, with something approaching fury: 'Why should I die? Can you show me now that I would not be killed in vain? Show me just a little of your omnipresent brain.'

Most controversial of all, the musical is told mainly through the eyes of Judas, who dares to ask the biggest question of all: is Jesus really the Messiah, or has he just started believing his own publicity? Lines such as 'I remember when this whole thing began. No talk of God then, we called you a man' were hardly calculated to placate Christian extremists (for that matter, many Jews weren't thrilled that Jewish characters such as Caiaphas were so obviously villainous).

Despite the protests, audiences braved the protesters at the Mark Hellinger Theatre every night to make the show a hit. But that was only the beginning. Robert Stigwood, a far more important producer than is often realised, knew that he had a story to which anyone in the world who had heard of Jesus could relate. The album had blazed a trail, now he resolved to walk it with his stage show. For the first time, the original production was replicated and licensed to many countries worldwide.

This was a seismic moment in musical-theatre history. Because now that one production could essentially be exported, a winning formula could be kept intact and a successful show's earning power could be vastly multiplied. This, in 1971, was the start of the era of the mega-hits – when *Cats*, *Les Misérables*, *Miss Saigon*, more recently *Mamma Mia!* and the rest, could have identical productions running almost wherever they were required, raking in money and enjoying long runs wherever there was an appetite.

Unlike some other rock shows of the period (*Godspell*, *Hair*), *Superstar* has neither dated nor turned into a period piece. So tight is the structure, so finely paced the drama and so strong its characters, that it remains a deeply compelling experience at each viewing. To my mind, this is Lloyd Webber's great masterpiece.

The show ran on Broadway for a year and a half. When its Judas, Ben Vereen, was taken ill, Carl Anderson stepped into the breach. Throwing everything into the role, his tortured, howling performance became almost definitive – and is captured for posterity in the 1973 Norman Jewison film.

In London, it had even greater success. With Paul Nicholas as Jesus, *Superstar* ran for eight years at the Palace Theatre. The film version, starring Anderson and Ted Neeley, was a similar success, one of the most viewed movies of 1973.

TRIVIA

In the title song, Judas sings, 'Israel in 4 BC had no mass communication.' Some have attributed this to a mistake, or artistic licence, as Jesus is commonly held to have been born at the beginning of AD 1. However, there is an ongoing debate about the precise year of Jesus's birth. The New Testament says that he was born while Herod the Great was alive and if true that would mean Jesus must have been born in or before 4 BC the year Herod died.

Carl Anderson returned to the role of Judas in 1992, and then again shortly before he died, in 2004, in a touring production for which he was widely praised. He left the tour when he was diagnosed with leukaemia.

THE PLOT

For a fuller synopsis, consult your Bible. Just kidding. The story is told principally through the eyes of Judas, who is dismayed at the boisterousness of Jesus's followers and worried about attracting the authorities. Jesus, he reasons, is likely to be destroyed but there may also be repercussions for the entire Jewish race in Judaea if they further antagonise the Romans. He is also unimpressed at the way Mary Magdalene pampers Jesus, spending charitable donations on soothing ointments and, given that she is a former prostitute, risking Jesus's good name. Jesus tries unsuccessfully to placate Judas.

Meanwhile, the priests Caiaphas and Annas are also worried about the 'Jesus mania', concerned about the reactions of the Romans as well as their own positions. They decide he must be killed. Judas, unable to bear the situation any longer, turns on his old friend – just as Jesus has predicted.

NUMBERS TO LISTEN OUT FOR

'Heaven on Their Minds'
'What's the Buzz?'
'Everything's All Right'
'This Jesus Must Die'
'Hosanna'
'Simon Zealotes'
'Pilate's Dream'
'I Don't Know How to Love Him'
'The Last Supper'
'Gethsemane'
'King Herod's Song'
'Could We Start Again Please?'
'Superstar'

RECOMMENDED RECORDINGS

The concept album is the original, but not in this case the best. Murray Head, a very English-sounding Judas, is committed but without an exceptional voice. The rest of the cast are similarly decent without being outstanding. From stage productions the pick of the bunch is probably the twentieth-anniversary recording (made to accompany a tour) with London's first Jesus, Paul Nicholas, resuming his role to fine effect. Keith Burns is a scorching Judas, and Claire Moore a sympathetic Mary. There's an enjoyably eccentric Herod from Victor Spinetti.

I'd go though for the soundtrack of the Jewison film. André Previn conducts the London Symphony Orchestra in a deeply felt, yet driving reading that propels the drama with inexorable force. Ted Neeley is a bit of a hippie Jesus, by which I mean that he sounds rather passive – but when he opens up his tonsils in 'Gethsemane' he wails those high notes like no other Jesus I've heard. Above all, Carl Anderson is a riveting Judas, a man audibly unravelling with every scene, and he and Neeley are electric in their antagonistic duets. The film itself is marvellous, Jewison mixing a sense of the historical (it was filmed on desert locations) and the modern (miners' helmets for the guards, scaffolding and tanks). It is presented as a group of travelling actors putting on a mystery play, except that their Jesus is mysteriously absent when they leave.

There is also a fine studio film from Lloyd Webber's Really Useful Group. If Jewison's was an interpretation for the era of flower power, this is defiantly for a more radicalised society. Jesus's followers cannot wait, it seems, to commence guerrilla (even terrorist?) operations against the Romans. Only their leader is holding them back. The weak spot is Jerome Pradon's Judas, a dead ringer for Quentin Tarantino, who tends to overact.

Joseph and His Amazing Technicolor Dreamcoat

Music by Andrew Lloyd Webber
Lyrics by Tim Rice
Premiere: 17 September 1973, at the Albery Theatre, London

The Albery opening is the date generally given for *Joseph*'s premiere, but in fact its start was far more convoluted than that suggests. Friends and aspiring songwriters Andrew Lloyd Webber and Tim Rice met at college, and shortly thereafter embarked on a phenomenally successful partnership – the greatest surprise of which is that it yielded only three shows, albeit each hugely successful. *Joseph* was the first they wrote together, though it took the smash hit *Jesus Christ Superstar* to get its biblical stablemate to the West End. *Joseph* had been written for Colet Court, St Paul's Junior School where Lloyd Webber's younger brother Julian was a student and, before reaching Theatreland, had been making its way through a variety of venues, gradually adding to its initial fifteen-minute running time and being made ready for the big time. The school performance had been seen by a *Sunday Times* critic, who wrote a positive review – and Decca subsequently recorded an album. Lloyd Webber and Rice were signed to the impresario David Land and their income guaranteed.

That *Joseph* has proved so popular with children and adults alike is testament to the standards the writers clearly set themselves. A school show for children it might (originally) be, but Lloyd Webber and Rice filled it to bursting with invention, with imagination, with humour and even with genuine pathos. Rice's lyrics are at their cleverest and most tongue-in-cheek – 'It's all there in chapter thirty-nine of Genesis' indeed – and Lloyd Webber turns in a dazzling array of melodies. The solemnity of 'Close Every Door' is leavened by the fresh optimism of 'Any Dream Will Do', and adults will enjoy the parody of many a French chanteuse in 'Those Canaan Days'.

Gary Bond was the West End's first Joseph, and since then the dreamcoat has been seen in hundreds of towns and cities around the world. Indeed, there must be very few times when it is not playing somewhere. Subsequent Josephs have included pop singers Donny Osmond and Jason Donovan, and British TV presenter Philip Schofield. The show has even embraced a reality-TV series (not entirely originally called *Any Dream Will Do!*).

TRIVIA

The brief from the school was for a 'pop cantata' and Rice and Lloyd Webber first considered a spy story before settling on the biblical tale of Joseph.

THE PLOT

Joseph, his father's favourite, is gifted a coat of many colours, much to the envy of his brothers – whom he further enrages by telling them about his dreams in which they were subservient to him. The brothers sell him into slavery, telling Isaac that his son has been killed. Joseph is taken to Egypt where his gift for interpreting dreams comes in very handy and will make his fortune.

NUMBERS TO LISTEN OUT FOR

'Any Dream Will Do'
'Jacob and Sons'
'Joseph's Coat'
'Poor, Poor Joseph'
'Potiphar'
'Close Every Door'
'Go, Go, Go Joseph'
'Those Canaan Days'

RECOMMENDED RECORDINGS

After the mixed bag that was their *Cats* film, Lloyd Webber's Really Useful Group hit gold with their *Joseph*. The opening sets the tone – as a stuffy, monochrome school is visited by Maria Friedman's clumsy but likeable guest speaker (i.e. Narrator). Gathering confidence and strength, she begins the story, then strides through the school hall to throw open the doors to Joseph. Donny Osmond walks in through a cloud of dry ice and he and Friedman mount the stage, which suddenly houses sets in blazing colour. The children cluster around excitedly, and the show has started. It really catches a sense of chasing one's dreams, and a top-drawer cast (also including Joan Collins and Richard Attenborough) is splendidly entertaining.

As an audio-only alternative, there's a fine 1991 London cast recording. Jason Donovan, Australian soap actor-turned-pop singer, scored a major hit in the title role and sounds appropriately clean-cut and charismatic. Only that extra degree of depth is missing in the voice to give weight to 'Close Every Door' (something Philip Schofield managed rather better in the same production). The rest of the cast are excellent, particularly Linzi Hateley's spirited narrator – the decision to cast a female voice in that role had been taken on tour, and it lends the score balance. If, by the way, you can get hold of the original twenty-minute album, it's well worth hearing as a curiosity. Tim Rice sings Pharaoh and Lloyd Webber's composer father is on the organ. Aaaah.

The King and I

Music by Richard Rodgers
Book and lyrics by Oscar Hammerstein II
Premiere: 29 March 1951, at the St James Theatre, New York

By this stage of their careers, just after the enormous success of *South Pacific* (and before their last great hit *The Sound of Music*), Rodgers and Hammerstein had a system. They searched for source material they liked, bought the rights, wrote the thing, put it together, usually produced and when possible enjoyed the fruits of their labours. *The King and I* was different. They were approached by a star, Gertrude Lawrence, who had a feeling that Margaret Landon's book, *Anna and the King of Siam*, would make a fine musical and, more important, a splendid vehicle for her talents.

Composer and lyricist were sceptical. Lawrence was indeed a great star of the time but, in Rodgers's opinion, she had a tendency to sing flat. Besides which, with the actress effectively pulling the strings, would she expect the writers to bow to her demands?

The King and I, as the project was to become, did run into star trouble on several fronts, and one of those was Lawrence. She also had insecurities about her singing, and tended to take these out on Rodgers. Then there was the question of who would play the King, for which a leading man was needed with the charisma to play opposite the English actress. Rex Harrison had the authority, and the ego, to do it and he was keen, but discussions foundered over contracts. Then there was Alfred Drake, who had become Broadway's most bankable male star after *Oklahoma!* He too expressed an interest, but on his terms – no more than a six-month run and a guarantee that Rodgers and Hammerstein would produce him in a play of his choice afterwards. They declined.

After their lunch with Drake, a depressed Rodgers and Hammerstein went to the Majestic Theatre where auditions were being held (more in hope than expectation) for the role. Which is where they caught their first glimpse of a man recommended to them by Mary Martin, the then little-known Yul Brynner. Not only was the Russian-born actor exactly what they were looking for, he was a linchpin of the company – not least in helping to keep Lawrence's moods in check.

The show's final casting problem was a tragic one. More than a year after beginning her run in the part, Lawrence developed a very rapid cancer, which killed her within days of diagnosis. The company had to deal with its grief and help a replacement find her feet simultaneously, and quickly. In the short term, Lawrence's understudy Constance Carpenter went on. That she had been a friend of Lawrence must have made it all the harder.

The musical, however, was a great success. The songs were deliberately structured so that Anna's would not stretch Lawrence beyond her comfort zone, while the more ambitious melodies were given to secondary characters.

Rodgers always maintained that his and Hammerstein's version of Siamese customs and indeed music would never be anything more than an American idea of what these might be like. Despite a few critical barbs for his score, though, there was no great outcry. At least not at home. Thailand was rather less forgiving of what it insisted were historical inaccuracies that were insulting to its royal family. To this day, the 1956 film version of the musical is banned in that country.

TRIVIA

The melody of one of the score's most popular numbers, 'Getting to Know You', was a *South Pacific* reject – replaced for that show by 'Younger than Springtime'. When Gertrude Lawrence suggested that the show's first half felt a mite heavy and a song was perhaps needed for Anna and the children, Rodgers remembered his old tune, and Hammerstein came up with new lyrics.

THE PLOT

A British teacher, Anna Leonowens, brings her son to live with her in the kingdom of Siam, where she has agreed to teach the children of the King. He is a paradoxical character, eager to learn the ways of the West himself but stubbornly clinging to ancient traditions and beliefs. His children, however, for the most part quickly take to Anna and she builds up a fine rapport with them – and eventually with their father.

Their burgeoning friendship is put to the test when a slave of the King wishes to elope with the man she loves. The King captures her, and proposes a harsh punishment.

NUMBERS TO LISTEN OUT FOR

'I Whistle a Happy Tune'
'Hello, Young Lovers'
'The March of the Siamese Children'
'A Puzzlement'

'Getting to Know You'
'We Kiss in a Shadow'
'Something Wonderful'
'The Small House of Uncle Thomas'
'Shall We Dance?'

RECOMMENDED RECORDINGS

Several excellent recordings to choose from, with no clear front runner. My personal favourite is the original cast recording. Yes, Gertrude Lawrence has a peculiar way with the notes, but she really seems to live the role and, important in this part, her diction is superb. Brynner is wellnigh definitive as the King (though arguably even more authoritative on the film soundtrack). Anyone who wants better sound, or to steer clear of Lawrence, could go for the Philips version with a properly mature and charismatic Julie Andrews with Ben Kingsley as her King. Conductor John Mauceri uses the movie orchestrations. And the film itself, let it not be forgotten, is richly rewarding.

Kiss Me, Kate

Music and lyrics by Cole Porter
Book by Bella Spewack
Premiere: 30 December 1948, at the New Century Theatre,
    New York

This is the sort of show that has one reaching for the superlatives – you know: 'Never before or since has there been a greater play-within-a-play show.' So, never before or since has there been a greater play-within-a-play show. Nor, I'd go further and say, has there been a greater musical adaptation of Shakespeare since Verdi's *Otello* and *Falstaff*.

The main device of *Kiss Me, Kate* – like all great ideas – seems in retrospect fairly obvious. A theatre troupe is performing *The Taming of the Shrew* and their real-life situations loosely mirror those of the play. The brilliance of this though is that the two lead actors are can't-live-with-can't-live-without, estranged lovers – so their cruelty to one another has a history and a reason (it is said that the characters were based on the famous American showbiz couple Alfred Lunt and Lynn Fontanne, who reportedly argued incessantly while performing *Shrew*). Which renders it all deeply funny and deeply touching.

True, Shakespeare managed very nicely without gangsters wandering around and disturbing the proceedings, but what's a Cole Porter musical without comedy hoods? The scene in which the stone-faced enforcers find themselves trapped, incongruously on the wrong side of the stage curtain, to tell the audience what a knowledge of the Bard is really good for – impressing women ('Brush Up Your Shakespeare') – is a classic. But every scene is tightly scripted and propelled by a score in which almost every single song, from confessional romantic ballads such as 'Were Thine That Special Face' to a steaming dance number such as 'Too Darn Hot', finds one of Broadway's greatest song-and-dance men at the very top of his game.

TRIVIA

One of the gangsters in the first London production (1951) was played by *Carry On* comedian (as he later became) Sid James.

The 1953 big-screen version was first screened in 3D.

THE PLOT

Fred Graham and his ex-wife Lilli Vanessi are preparing for their out-of-town opening in *The Taming of the Shrew*. It seems for a moment that their love will be rekindled, until Lilli opens a love letter from Fred mistakenly thinking it intended for her – at which point their mutual ire is rekindled as never before (not least because they now realise that they still love each other).

Two gangsters arrive backstage to demand money from Fred which they think he owes – although in fact his name was signed on a debt by another company member, Bill Calhoun. Bill, who plays Lucentio, is in love with the Bianca, Lois Lane. She must deal with his gambling problem; he must deal with her flirtatiousness. Fred must deal with Lilli and her military-man fiancé – and he thinks he can use the gangsters to help him. It all gets rather chaotic.

NUMBERS TO LISTEN OUT FOR

'Another Op'nin', Another Show'
'Why Can't You Behave?'
'Wunderbar'
'So in Love'
'We Open in Venice'
'Tom, Dick or Harry'
'I Hate Men'
'Were Thine That Special Face'
'Kiss Me, Kate'
'Too Darn Hot'
'Where Is the Life That Late I Led?'
'Always True to You in My Fashion'
'Bianca'
'Brush Up Your Shakespeare'

RECOMMENDED RECORDINGS

Nothing wrong with the original-cast version, starring Alfred Drake and Patricia Morison, but to today's ears it sounds just a trifle dated (heresy, I know). For a recording that finds the ideal contrast between the more 'classical' songs, which nod respectfully towards Shakespeare, and the jazz-flecked 'modern' numbers – and then mixes them up gleefully – I'd recommend above all a DVD film of the 2001 West End revival. The marvellously paced Michael Blakemore production, which had already been a huge hit on the other side of the Atlantic, houses spot-on, fizzing performances from Brent Barrett (a brilliant leading man whose subsequent career has yet to live up to this promise) and Marin Mazzie. Once you've watched this, you will want to keep it handy on a nearby shelf for frequent viewing. For an audio-only version, I'd – no, no, once you've seen this DVD nothing else will do. OK, the 1990 EMI album with Josephine Barstow, Thomas Hampson and Kim Criswell if you must.

Lady in the Dark

Music by Kurt Weill
Lyrics by Ira Gershwin
Book by Moss Hart
Premiere: 23 January 1941, at the Alvin Theatre, New York

To my mind, *Lady in the Dark* is one of those musicals that, while not a great show, is still hugely important for what it achieved. In what was originally to be a straight play by Moss Hart, this musical dared to go beyond traditional plot formulas to delve into the psychology of its main character. And, in so doing, it paved the way for the likes of Sondheim's *Assassins* and *Sunday in the Park with George* and arguably even the hyper-stylisation of Kander and Ebb's *Cabaret* and later *Kiss of the Spider Woman* (the latter just missed out on this list, but is a fascinating psychological exploration of the states of mind of two prisoners).

The show did not want for cast quality, with Gertrude Lawrence headlining alongside Victor Mature (not yet the movies' leading man he would soon become) and a star-making turn from Danny Kaye. It was Lawrence and Kaye who were given the songs to shine in the two most celebrated numbers – the fiendish, nearly unsingable (just try 'There's Glinka, Winkler, Bortniansky, Rebikoff, Ilyinsky/There's Medtner, Balakireff, Zolotareff and Kvoschinsky') composers patter-song 'Tschaikowsky' for Kaye, and the jazzy 'The Saga of Jenny' for Lawrence. She also had one of Weill's most haunting songs, 'My Ship', which, beautiful as it is, typically for this composer secretes hints of menace in its shadows. The show was a hit, spawning a film version starring Ginger Rogers.

TRIVIA

In 'Tschaikowsky', Ira Gershwin mentions the names of forty-nine composers, some of whom he knew. Rumshinsky was a Yiddish theatre composer, who was friendly with Gershwin's father. And Godowsky's son was Ira Gershwin's brother-in-law.

THE PLOT

Liza Elliott is the powerful editor of an influential magazine. For all her success, however, she is troubled by strange dreams and feels depressed. She turns to a psychiatrist for help. He helps her to understand where her insecurities lie. And, in turn, she is finally able to choose between the men in her life.

NUMBERS TO LISTEN OUT FOR

'Girl of the Moment'
'The Princess of Pure Delight'
'Tschaikowsky'
'The Saga of Jenny'
'My Ship'

RECOMMENDED RECORDINGS

There's an excellent 1963 recording with Rise Stevens, an opera singer totally at home in the musical and entirely on top of the role. It is not much of a loss doing without Danny Kaye, as Adolph Green is superb, but in any case you don't have to as the Sony release includes extra tracks including Kaye in the role. The sound is very good for its period, but if you really want a modern version, there's nothing at all wrong with the National Theatre production, starring Maria Friedman (who has real dramatic weight in the lead), and James Dreyfuss copes well with the demands of 'Tschaikowsky' (though he's not in the Kaye/Green league).

The Lion King

Music by Elton John
Lyrics by Tim Rice
Book by Roger Allers and Irene Mecchi
Premiere: 13 November 1997, at the New Amsterdam Theatre,
    New York

When Disney looked to extend the mouse's kingdom from
films to musical theatre, there were plenty of critics (myself
included) who feared the end was nigh. And their first effort,
Beauty and the Beast, seemed to confirm fears that this was
simply a commercially driven enterprise, all about throwing
(albeit with high production values) proven movie brands onto
the stage. Then came *The Lion King*, and the company proved
it could be as inventive in the theatre as it had so often been
in the cinema.

The brilliance of this show was the way that producer
Thomas Schumacher (who had also worked on the animated
film) turned the story into something utterly, and purely,
theatrical. He brought in Julie Taymor, a fairly experimental
director who created the animal kingdom through exotic
puppetry – the people operating the beasts could be clearly
seen at the same time as their puppet alter egos – and
enhanced the show's stylised story-telling with Oriental Nō-
theatre techniques (the lionesses pull streamers from their eyes
to symbolise tears when their king is killed). Added to all this,
the South African composer Lebo M was invited to expand
the Zulu music influences that were only touched on in the film.

I can't speak for New York, but the London first night was
one of the most exciting in my experience. For all the red
carpets and banks of paparazzi, stars and reviewers alike
entered the Lyceum Theatre with fairly low expectations. This
was, we thought, going to be a children's show at best, as Eric
Idle was to write of his *Monty Python* tribute *Spamalot* years
later, 'lovingly ripped off from the original'. Then, as the lights
went down and the jungle came to life around us – with rhinos
and elephants lumbering through the stalls, giraffe cantering

on the stage and birds flying high near drummers pounding away in the theatre boxes – the audience as one was transported back to their first vivid experiences of what theatre could do. There were tears and a wild ovation after that first number, and this from one of the toughest, seen-it-all audiences in the world. Disney's theatrical street cred went sky high, and the musical – as a visual experience in the theatre – joined the ranks of the greats.

TRIVIA

As if she didn't have enough on her plate, director Julie Taymor was rushed into hospital to have emergency gallbladder surgery just prior to the start of rehearsals in Minneapolis.

Taymor couldn't work out how to change the set in time for the wildebeest stampede, so that in early previews there was a gaping pause before the scene. A new scene was eventually written to give the crew time to make the change.

THE PLOT

Not many Disney stories have been compared to Shakespeare plays, but *The Lion King* is commonly held to be a version of the Bard's *Hamlet* (presumably minus the contemplated suicide and various secondary deaths). Mufasa, lion king of the jungle, is murdered by his brother Scar, whereupon Scar persuades Mufasa's cub, Simba, that the king's death was his, Simba's, fault. Simba flees the kingdom to find nomadic happiness of a kind with Pumbaa the warthog and Timon the Meerkat. Years later, Simba returns, to discover the truth.

Other discrepancies with *Hamlet* should also be pointed out. Most significantly, Scar does not have sex with his murdered brother's wife. Nor have any psychologists deduced that Simba subconsciously lusts after his mother. These Shakespeare comparisons can be taken too literally.

NUMBERS TO LISTEN OUT FOR

'Circle of Life'
'The Morning Report'

'I Just Can't Wait to Be King'
'They Live in You'
'Hakuna Matata'
'Shadowland'
'Can You Feel the Love Tonight?'

RECOMMENDED RECORDING

Not much choice here, but then the original cast recording touches all bases very effectively. It is enthusiastic and occasionally majestic. The Zulu harmonies come across most powerfully, offsetting the fun Disney hits like 'Hakuna Matata'. There will never be any real substitute for seeing Taymor's amazing production, but as a souvenir this will do nicely.

A Little Night Music

Music and lyrics by Stephen Sondheim
Book by Hugh Wheeler
Premiere: 25 February 1973, at the Shubert Theatre, New York

In what must have come as a surprise to his fans, Sondheim followed the 'concept' style of *Company* and the sometimes savage tragedy of *Follies* with a graceful, well-made waltz musical. There was even a traditional story, a comedy of sexual manners adapted from the Ingmar Bergman film *Smiles of a Summer Night*. It is, also, a quite perfect piece of work. Perfect in terms of construction (as the plot moves along each character's viewpoint is represented), perfect in terms of the characters' arcs, as elegant as a ceramic statue. Which is not to say that there is not emotional complexity, the odd attempted suicide and some decidedly free-spirited morals – but without some unexpected twists, Sondheim wouldn't be Sondheim.

Musically, the show is as clever as one had come to expect from this source. But it also gave Sondheim his one really solid-gold hit – the mocking, regretful and unutterably haunting 'Send in the Clowns'.

TRIVIA

Woody Allen's film *A Midsummer Night's Sex Comedy* was motivated by the same Bergman film that inspired Sondheim to write *A Little Night Music*.

THE PLOT

The lawyer Fredrik Egerman is frustrated at his new teenage wife Anne's continuing reluctance to make love to him. He suggests that they go to see the famous actress Desirée Armfeldt in a play. Anne is thrilled, unaware that Desirée is an old flame of Fredrik's. When, at the theatre, Desirée glances longingly in Fredrik's direction, the shocked Anne demands to be taken home.

If Anne has trouble with Desirée, the actress herself has trouble with a current lover, the pompous and possessive (even though he is married) Count Carl-Magnus Malcolm. Carl-Magnus's wife Charlotte has learned to cope with his infidelities largely through her defence method, sarcasm.

When the Egermans are invited *en masse* to the Armfeldt estate (on Desirée's initiative – her mother disapproves of any romantic affair not suitably glamorous), Count Carl-Magnus, whose suspicions of Fredrik grow daily, insists that he and Charlotte gatecrash. There will be dramas before the weekend away is over.

NUMBERS TO LISTEN OUT FOR

'Night Waltz'
'Now'
'Later'
'Soon'
'The Glamorous Life'
'Remember?'
'You Must Meet My Wife'
'Liaisons'
'Every Day a Little Death'
'Weekend in the Country'

'Send in the Clowns'
'The Miller's Son'

RECOMMENDED RECORDINGS

For a long time the original London cast album held pride of place for this work, with the wistful Jean Simmons edging out Broadway's feisty but rather more slight Glynis Johns, and Joss Ackland presenting a more sophisticated Fredrik than Len Cariou. Both sets have as the jewel in their crowns the never-surpassed, knowing and haughtily naughty Madame Armfeldt of the great Hermione Gingold.

But the National Theatre production of 1995 trumped them all with the lovable and poignant Desirée of Judi Dench. Here, more than anywhere, the actress makes her limited singing prowess irrelevant as she gives Desirée a positively Shakespearean depth. Her Fredrik is the resonant Laurence Guittard (Count Carl-Magnus Malcolm in the original Broadway cast), and the marvellous cast also features Joanna Riding's amusingly prissy Anne and Patricia Hodge's beyond-sardonic Charlotte.

Mack and Mabel

Music and lyrics by Jerry Herman
Book by Michael Stewart
Premiere: 6 October 1974, at the Majestic Theatre, New York

It is often said that *Mack and Mabel* is a fantastic set of songs looking for a decent book. The initial production toured before reaching Broadway, as is common in the US, and strains were evident from early on. The main problem was that this was a musical comedy (and a musically rather old-fashioned comedy at that) with the darkest of endings – the heroine dies, her dreams in tatters, of tuberculosis. It is ironic for a show that features a character, Mack, who is a self-proclaimed expert at structuring entertainments. Had Michael Stewart taken a leaf out of Mack's book – 'Heartbreak and passion may both be in fashion, but I want to make the world laugh' – he and Jerry Herman might have had a hit on their hands. As it was, fixes made in the run-up to Broadway only served to make things worse and the show flopped.

Despite some successful revivals, especially in London, the show has never really caught on. I once asked a very eminent producer whether there was any hope of getting *Mack and Mabel* to work some day. 'No!' he chuckled back, with a mixture of sorrow and mirth. So why does it qualify as a great musical? Because of that marvellous song list. More specifically, because of an original cast album that ranks among the very finest. When you have Bernadette Peters and Robert Preston at their best in songs like 'I Won't Send Roses', 'Look What Happened to Mabel' and 'I Promise You a Happy Ending' you cannot go far wrong. In the album there is no sense of the incongruously dark ending. You can pretty much make up your own story if you like, and just sit back and enjoy a classic. Just don't go and see it.

TRIVIA

In the most recent London revival, director John Doyle had his entire cast playing musical instruments as well as singing, except David Soul who played Mack.

THE PLOT

Ace silent-film director Mack Sennett has returned to the studio where he shot so many of his triumphs; only now talkies are all the rage. He remembers meeting and making the career of deli-girl turned actress Mabel Normand. As the world falls in love with her, she falls for Sennett. Not only, though, are movies changing around them, but Mack remains frustratingly the same. Sometimes a custard pie in the face is not, despite Mack's best intentions, enough.

NUMBERS TO LISTEN OUT FOR

'Movies Were Movies'
'Look What Happened to Mabel'

'I Won't Send Roses'
'I Wanna Make the World Laugh'
'Hundreds of Girls'
'Time Heals Everything'
'I Promise You a Happy Ending'

RECOMMENDED RECORDING

As suggested above, the Peters–Preston version is a classic, required listening for every lover of musical theatre. But it's also worth hearing a 1988 recording from a charity benefit at London's Theatre Royal, Drury Lane. Various guest stars, including Denis Quilley, Tommy Tune, Stubby Kaye and Georgia Brown, sing their numbers interspersed with narration from Jerry Herman. Touching.

Mame

Music and lyrics by Jerry Herman
Book by Jerome Lawrence and Robert Edwin Lee
Premiere: 24 May 1966, at the Winter Garden Theatre, New York

Considering that he was considered a risk when, as a young man, he was picked to provide the score for *Hello, Dolly!*, Jerry Herman more than made good. A truly remarkable string of hits saw him become one of the most popular of all Broadway tunesmiths. In 1966 *Mame* followed *Dolly* and duly took its place in a parade of great shows that would march on with *Mack and Mabel* (well, a great score) and *La Cage aux Folles*. Even his flops (*Mack and Mabel*, *Dear World*, *The Grand Tour*) are widely thought to be more than interesting.

Then, after *La Cage*, next to nothing. Herman seemed to shut up shop. In 2003 what could have been a comeback to musical theatre, a show called *Miss Spectacular* written for Las Vegas, fizzled out and became nothing more than a concept album. Whether he was dispirited at the paucity of traditional musical comedies through the 1980s and 1990s, bereft of inspiration or silenced by some other reason (and in the dying years of the century he almost succumbed to grave illness), his fans have had to cling to the classics he has given us. At the time of writing he is in his late seventies, and it could be that we must resign ourselves to expect nothing else.

Mame is not quite a classic, but it is very good and full of funny lines and – as always with Jerry Herman – instantly hummable tunes. He has a great gift for memorable female characters (Dolly, Mabel) and dear Auntie Mame is yet another. It is a shame that the 1974 movie version cast the vocally underpowered Lucille Ball rather than the stage production's Angela Lansbury – who replaced Rosalind Russell in the lead – (though not surprising given that Lansbury was not as famous as she would later become through her TV series *Murder, She Wrote*). The London production went for a more famous film name, Ginger Rogers, unfortunately not preserved on record.

TRIVIA

Lucille Ball poured her own money into the film, but stipulated that she should play the title role and that her singing would not be dubbed.

THE PLOT

Mame Dennis is determined that having to look after her dead brother's young son Patrick will not disturb her bohemian lifestyle. She teaches him her view of the world, enduring even when the Wall Street Crash hits. She marries a wealthy southerner, which necessitates placing Patrick in boarding school. But when she pauses for long enough to inspect his progress for herself, she is not at all pleased with what she finds.

NUMBERS TO LISTEN OUT FOR

'It's Today'
'Open a New Window'
'The Man in the Moon'
'My Best Girl'
'We Need a Little Christmas'

'Bosom Buddies'
'If He Walked into My Life'

RECOMMENDED RECORDING

In the absence of an original London cast album, there aren't many to choose from. Since Lucille Ball can't sing, we're left with the Broadway cast – which, thanks to Lansbury's nimble turn in the title role, is treasurable. Her give-as-good-as-I-get duet with Bea Arthur, 'Bosom Buddies', is a hoot (I love Lansbury's approximation of Arthur's age – 'Oh, somewhere between forty and dead').

Mary Poppins

Music and lyrics by Robert B. and Richard M. Sherman, with
    additional songs, scoring and new orchestration by George Stiles
    and additional lyrics by Anthony Drewe
Book by Julian Fellowes
Premiere: 15 December 2004, at the Prince Edward Theatre, London

Even in this age of co-productions (with musicals so expensive to stage – at a time when a £4 million price tag is considered reasonable – there is often little choice), getting two of the big beasts of the theatre world to collaborate can be difficult. Both Disney and Cameron Mackintosh wanted for years to bring *Mary Poppins* to the stage. But they each faced an impasse. Mackintosh owned the rights to the original stories by Pamela Travers, but Disney had the Sherman Brothers songs which, thanks to the 1964 film, were as closely associated with the magical nanny as her bottomless bag and gravity-defying umbrella. Neither party wanted to work together, as they both insisted they had a very definite vision of what *Poppins* on stage should be.

It took a secret, informally arranged meeting between Mackintosh and Disney's Thomas Schumacher for them to realise that, in fact, they shared the same vision. Mary on film was a spoonful of sugar. In the books she was not only much more strict, but actually pretty frightening (in one memorable description, Travers writes that Mary's apron is 'crackling with anger'). For the stage, something else was needed. Not as anti-heroic as the books, perhaps, but for a stage musical longer on running time and shorter on special effects, less unvaryingly saccharine than Julie Andrews.

So an entirely new Mary was created, in some ways a mid-point between the two. With a new book by the Oscar-winning (for *Gosford Park*) writer Julian Fellowes, the children became wilder, more unruly – and they needed a Mary who could make them toe the line. New songs from Mackintosh favourites George Stiles and Anthony Drewe added flesh; notably the number 'Temper, temper' in which the toys in the nursery come to life and put Jane and Michael on trial for their bad behaviour. In fact, some of the action was considered too scary for toddlers, who were banned from attending (and under-sevens were cautioned as to the content).

Elsewhere, Mrs Banks became a far more active figure. Mary teaches her, and her husband, as much as she teaches the children, and when Mary leaves their mother is far more able to look after them. In short, this *Mary* became less about magic and more about a dysfunctional family put right.

As if the rights battle hadn't been enough to cope with, the producers now found themselves in competition with Andrew Lloyd Webber for the services of their would-be leading lady, Laura Michelle Kelly. One of Theatreland's fast-rising young talents, she was wanted by Lloyd Webber for his forthcoming revival of *The Sound of Music* (eventually, turned down by Kelly and, reportedly, Scarlet Johansson, Lloyd Webber opened the matter to a public vote via the TV talent series *How Do You Solve a Problem Like Maria?*). Kelly opted for *Poppins* and enjoyed great success.

The show ran for three and a half years in London. Both that staging and the Broadway transfer won prizes and one night the show was graced with a visit from Julie Andrews herself!

TRIVIA

The show was warmed up in Bristol, where at the Hippo-drome there were technical problems with Mary's flight over the audience at the show's close. So there was quite some consternation on the press night – but happily Mary Poppins took to the air in some style.

THE PLOT

The mischievous children Jane and Michael Banks manage to cause every nanny to walk out. A mysterious new nanny, however, arrives and declares that she meets both the children's and their parents' ideas of what a nanny should be – indeed, she is 'practically perfect'.

The children turn their noses up when they meet Mary's friend Bert, so she teaches them not to judge people by their appearance – and promptly brings to life the statues in the park. Among other outings, Mary takes the children to see their father at the bank where he works. Initially impatient with the children, he is inspired by Mary to see things differently – and he rejects the investment proposal of a wealthy client in favour of a more modest proposal which will create new jobs, from the middle-class Mr Northbrook.

The children visit Mrs Cory in her words-selling shop. There they encounter the strangest word they have ever heard, supercalifragilisticexpialidocious. On returning home though, they find their father in a rage as he has been suspended for turning down his wealthy client's proposal. The children return their father's anger, whereupon Mary leaves them to the judgment of the toys in the nursery. Frightened, they emerge to find that she has left the house.

Mr Banks frequently talks about the great example set by his own former nanny, Miss Andrew. Mrs Banks sends for her to replace Mary Poppins – but when she tells her husband he is terrified and flees. Miss Andrew does indeed arrive and is frighteningly harsh, until Mary Poppins returns to drive her away and rescue everybody. When Mrs Banks finds her husband cowering in the park, she realises where his character flaws come from and that he needs some rescuing himself.

Bert and his chimney-sweep friends arrive to sing and dance their way through the house and across the rooftop. As they do so, Mr Banks is reminded of the optimistic child he once was. As he sets off to learn his fate from the bank, his wife and – secretly – Mary and the children go with him to show support. As it turns out, though, the scheme he did back has made the bank a vast amount of money. He is reunited with his job, apologises to his now well-adjusted family, and Mary realises that she is no longer needed. She kisses Bert goodbye, and takes off into the sky.

NUMBERS TO LISTEN OUT FOR

'Chim Chim Cheree'
'Practically Perfect'
'Jolly Holiday'
'A Spoonful of Sugar'
'Feed the Birds'
'Supercalifragilisticexpialidocious'
'Fly a Kite'
'Being Mrs Banks'
'Step in Time'
'Anything Can Happen'

RECOMMENDED RECORDING

The London cast recording is excellent, and contains the excellent new songs from Stiles and Drewe (particularly good are 'Practically Perfect' and especially 'Anything Can Happen'). Laura Michelle Kelly is a practically perfect fit for the title role – a real case of the right actress in the right part, at the right time. Gavin Lee is an enthusiastic sidekick as Bert. But the real stand-out is David Haig's vulnerable, little-boy-gone-wrong Mr Banks – there can be found this show's great heart.

Me and My Girl

Music by Noel Gay
Lyrics and book by Douglas Furber and L. Arthur Rose
Premiere: 16 December 1937, at the Victoria Palace, London

It hasn't often happened, at any rate with British musicals, that a show pre-dating the Second World War has come back into vogue and proved more popular than ever. But there's something visceral about the way *Me and My Girl* keys into Britain's perception of itself – a certain sunny determination to sing come what may (of course, most Brits generally don't tend to go warbling around the markets or the pub piano these days but we like to think we do, or at least would if we were in the Blitz).

In any case, a show that was a big hit in 1937 (running for several years) returned to become a smash in 1984, enjoying eight years in London and success in New York too. So popular was it that star Robert Lindsay even beat Colm Wilkinson – widely presumed a shoe-in for his remarkable performance as Jean Valjean in *Les Misérables* – to an Olivier Award. But with such a tuneful score and a secret weapon in the shape of the irrepressible 'Lambeth Walk' (a number that simply cannot fail to have an entire audience shouting out in ecstasy 'oy!') it seems almost that rarest of things, a spectator-proof musical.

TRIVIA

That 1980s revival co-starred Emma Thompson, in the days before she became one of cinema's leading ladies.

Noel Gay also wrote 'The Sun Has Got His Hat On' (which the Lindsay production appropriated).

Me And My Girl was billed as a sequel to the popular musical *Twenty to One*, and it featured that show's lead actor, Lupino Lane, as the same character, Bill Snibson.

For any show to run so long was very rare in the 1930s, but *Me and My Girl* benefited from a happy accident, when a BBC radio team found itself unable to report the story it had planned to cover, so filled in the time by broadcasting *Me and My Girl* – bringing the musical to a delighted nation.

THE PLOT

Working-class Lambeth resident Bill Snibson is amazed to discover that he is the illegitimate son – and heir – of the recently deceased Lord Hareford. He is brought to the family seat at Hareford Hall and taken under the wing of the Duchess of Dene, who declares that she will turn him into a gentleman. This involves him leaving his girlfriend Sally, a solution that also pleases Lady Jacqueline Carstone, who has her eye on marrying into his money. Sally, however, is not to be underestimated and is determined to keep her man.

NUMBERS TO LISTEN OUT FOR

'Me and My Girl'
'The Family Solicitor'
'The Lambeth Walk'
'Take It on the Chin'

RECOMMENDED RECORDINGS

If you can ever get hold of it, there is a simply fabulous record of Lupino Lane and Teddie St Denis from the original production storming their way through 'The Lambeth Walk' – with the audience joyfully joining in with each and every 'oy!' There is all you need to know about the joyful, cockney spirit of this show. Apart from that, choices get more complicated. None of the complete recordings is completely satisfactory. On balance EMI's 1985 London cast – Robert Lindsay fine but not at his most characterful, Emma Thompson not the world's best singer – is the most consistent, but Lindsay is better for Broadway the following year (the rest of the cast aren't as good, though).

Merrily We Roll Along

Music and lyrics by Stephen Sondheim
Book by George Furth
Premiere: 16 November 1981, at the Alvin Theatre, New York

When once I tentatively put it to Sondheim that *Merrily We Roll Along* 'did not do quite as well as might have been hoped for' he roared with laughter, exclaiming, 'That's the understatement of the century!' At least he can laugh about it now.

It has long been a source of frustration for Sondheim-lovers that his shows have rarely been commercial hits on their first outings (some, of course, didn't deserve to be – for all its good intentions, 2003's *Bounce* stayed resolutely earthbound and didn't even make it to Broadway). But none failed quite so spectacularly, while deserving exactly the opposite reaction, as *Merrily*.

While newish kid on the block Andrew Lloyd Webber romped home the big hit of that 1981 Broadway season, *Joseph and his Amazing Technicolor Dreamcoat*, Sondheim's follow-up to *Sweeney Todd* ran for precisely (count 'em) 16 performances. The Lloyd Webber work is marvellous, imaginative fun but there is no question as to which is the great work of art of the two.

Like Harold Pinter's play *Betrayal*, *Merrily* begins at the end and works backwards in time (as did Sondheim's source, a play of the same name by George S. Kaufman and Moss Hart). Yet the effect is very different. The Pinter savagely charts a relationship gone wrong by tracing the problems back to their seeds. In the Sondheim, a three-way friendship torn apart by, variously, contorted ambition, the decadence of success and communication problems is gradually put back together. The final image we have of its anti-heroes is as decidedly heroic students – ready to take the town, determined to do it together come what may. We know what is coming, sure, but there's always a hope that next time they – or we – will get it right. And in that *Merrily* cunningly bypasses the tragedy of *Follies* to become a hopeful, cautionary tale.

If it is dramatically smart, it is also musically sophisticated. A seemingly simple, hummable score is in fact made up of layers upon layers of motifs, brilliant linking themes, and tunes that change their trappings according to the situation.

The musical refused to die with its Broadway demise. Regional productions kept the flame alive until a new audience was found via director Michael Grandage's acclaimed 2000 production at London's prestigious Donmar Warehouse. A large-scale revival in the West End or New York has yet to materialise, but *Merrily* is now, at least, a cult favourite. And the wheel turned full circle, incidentally. In that 2000 season Lloyd Webber's latest, *The Beautiful Game*, was beaten to the UK's Olivier Award by none other than that first London production of *Merrily We Roll Along*. This, too, brought a grunt of ironic appreciation from Sondheim.

TRIVIA

Such was the success of Grandage's *Merrily We Roll Along* production at the Donmar Warehouse that, soon afterwards, he was selected to succeed Sam Mendes to the artistic directorship of the venue.

The Charlie in that production, Daniel Evans, went on to another high-profile London Sondheim revival in 2005, when he took the title role in *Sunday in the Park with George*. This was so admired that the composer made the journey from New York to see it.

THE PLOT

Successful composer Franklin Shepard attends his old school to lecture the students on how to get ahead. But, contrary to their expectations, his speech focuses on the need to compromise beliefs and to go for the possible, not necessarily the best. The students are scornful, and ask him to tell them his story, and explain how he became so disillusioned.

Once firm friends Shepard, his former librettist Charlie Kringas and the boozy writer Mary Flynn are then seen, coincidentally at the same party. Mary tries to mediate between Shepard and Kringas, who have not spoken to one another in years. She is unsuccessful.

Gradually, the unravelling of the trio's relationship – but especially that of Charlie and Frank – is shown. Frank is seduced by money and distracted from composing, Charlie cannot handle his friend's frittering away of his gifts. Finally the show ends as the friends stand together as students, ready to do or die, and always together.

NUMBERS TO LISTEN OUT FOR

'The Hills of Tomorrow'
'Not a Day Goes by'
'Good Thing Going'
'Franklin Shepard Inc.'
'Merrily We Roll Along'

RECOMMENDED RECORDING

The original cast recording is first-rate, characterful and atmospheric. It also bristles with a sense of the theatre – just listen to Charlie's televised breakdown, absolutely coruscating in the hands of Lonny Price.

Les Misérables

Music by Claude-Michel Schönberg and Alain Boublil
Book and lyrics by Alain Boublil and Herbert Kretzmer
Premiere: 8 October 1985, at the Barbican Theatre, London

Here's what isn't true about *Les Mis* (as it is popularly and affectionately known). It is not, as theatre mythology would have it, the musical that beat the critics. Although it did not get especially enthusiastic notices from some of the British daily newspapers, notably the powerful Jack Tinker at the *Daily Mail*, it made up for it with its share of raves from the Sunday papers as well as *Time* and *Newsweek* magazines.

Here's what is true. The French have long been the butt of jokes among West Enders and the denizens of Broadway for not being able to appreciate or produce decent musicals. Almost invariably, when a show works in France, it flops else-where. *Notre Dame de Paris*, for instance, was a smash in Paris, selling out sports stadiums months in advance. When it came to London's Dominion Theatre it was (barely) kept ticking over by package tours of French tourists crossing the Channel to see a double-bill of *Notre Dame* and much loved French crooner Sacha Distel down the road in *Chicago*. *Les Misérables* is one of the count-'em-on-one-hand French musicals to have made an impression in London and New York. And one of the count-'em-on-one-hand few places it was not a success was Paris. *Allez*, figure, as they say.

Britain's Royal Shakespeare Company was criticised by some when in 1985 it climbed into bed with a commercial producer, Cameron Mackintosh, to produce a sung-through version of Victor Hugo's classic and weighty novel. Large portions were trimmed when it quickly transferred to the West End's Palace Theatre in December of the same year. It has been running – first there, then at the nearby Queen's – ever since. Doubts about the ethics of the RSC producing a commercial-minded work have since turned into doubts that the company could have remained solvent without the much needed box-office receipts that its Gallic cash cow has generated.

From concert versions in Scandinavia to an officially pro-duced performing text for schools, *Les Misérables* has been seen the world over. To date, it has played more than 220 cities to more than 51 million people. It has won in excess of 50 inter-national awards.

It is very clear why *Les Mis* has endured. To be sure, Trevor Nunn's powerhouse production conveying a sense of the epic with a nearly bare stage aside from the huge barricades that slide on and off in the second half. And the original cast was a classic – Colm Wilkinson as Jean Valjean providing unforget-table howls of moral outrage at its centre, Roger Allam as the implacable Javert, Patti LuPone as the unfortunate Fantine, the young Michael Ball making an early impression as the gallant Marius and Alun Armstrong seedy and funny as Monsieur Thenadier. But it is the combination of Kretzmer's strong, dramatic yet sophisticated lyrics and a broad canvas across which are painted an array of deeply felt, long-breathed songs that give this musical such a feeling of integrity, of universal scope. It has the breadth to encompass the same themes that Hugo targeted in his novel – justice, humanity, love. If *Les Mis* feels, perhaps more than any other, like a literary musical, it does so in the sense that, as with a great novel, you emerge feeling the richer for it.

TRIVIA

The many casts of *Les Mis* have included then-unknowns such as Ricky Martin.

Among the die-hard *Les Mis* fans is a lady who knits each new London Valjean a jumper bearing the face of little Cosette.

Israeli Valjean Dudu Fisher (see below) once recorded an unusual version of the *Kol nidrei*, one of the very holiest of Jewish prayers. He starts with a traditional melody, then it gradually morphs into the tune of 'One Day More'.

THE PLOT

In the turbulent decades before the French Revolution, Jean Valjean is driven to steal a loaf of bread to feed his starving family. Having served nineteen years for the offence and for various attempts to escape, he is finally allowed out on parole. The ravages of prison life and the injustice he encounters upon release have turned him to a life of crime. Only when a priest shows him kindness and mercy does he repent, promising his life to the service of God and to his fellow man. He resolves to start again, tears up his parole papers and by the time eight years have passed, under an assumed name, he becomes Mayor of Montreuil-sur-Mer.

He cannot, however, escape his past for ever. A policeman, Javert, is hunting for him. Javert does not recognise the Mayor's true identity when they meet, but remarks to him that he has finally arrested his quarry, the notorious Jean Valjean. Valjean realises of course that Javert has the wrong man and, remembering his vow to God, he confesses to the court his real name. Javert is dispatched to bring him back to prison, but in the meantime Valjean has pledged to a dying woman, Fantine, to take care of her daughter, little Cosette. With the little girl, he goes on the run again. Javert's chase for Valjean will span many years, during which they both will get caught up inexorably in the whirlwind of the coming Revolution.

NUMBERS TO LISTEN OUT FOR

'I Dreamed a Dream'
'Master of the House'
'Castle on a Cloud'
'Do You Hear the People Sing?'
'One Day More'
'On My Own'
'Empty Chairs at Empty Tables'

RECOMMENDED RECORDINGS

There is plenty of choice – more than thirty albums, from the rather small-scale French-language version to the Israeli cast recording in Hebrew featuring the great cantor Dudu Fisher (he reprised the role on Broadway, but refused to work on Saturdays – the Jewish sabbath). Completists will not want to be without the 'symphonic recording' and that has its strengths – not least the unbeatable Javert of Philip Quast and a fully mature Michael Ball. But beware, country singer Gary Morris is disastrous casting in the lead, with his vocal mannerisms (strange vowel-stretching, odd scoops up to high notes) ruling the set out of court. A DVD version is sadly only of a fairly static concert celebrating the show's tenth anniversary at the Royal Albert Hall, but is worth seeing for Colm Wilkinson's Valjean and Quast. Still the best, though, is the original London cast recording. Wilkinson, LuPone *et al.* are on top form, and not forgetting a knockout Eponine from Frances Ruffelle.

Miss Saigon

Music by Claude-Michel Schönberg and Alain Boublil
Book and lyrics by Alain Boublil and Richard Maltby Jr
Premiere: 20 September 1989, at the Theatre Royal, Drury Lane,
    London

After the success of *Les Misérables*, Schönberg and Boublil were
the toast of London and New York (at least among those who
didn't mistakenly think that *Les Mis* was written by Andrew
Lloyd Webber – with the fact that all three men shared the same
producer in Cameron Mackintosh only contributing to the confusion). Their brilliant follow-up seemed to confirm their promise and a new golden era seemed imminent. There were now
three sources of great musical theatre – Sondheim in America,
Lloyd Webber and now Schönberg and Boublil in London.

That the golden age didn't last as long as had been hoped
is due partly to changing tastes, somewhat to the mature
Sondheim's strange inability to write commercial hits and
greatly to the fact that after *Miss Saigon* and then its good but
not overwhelming follow-up *Martin Guerre* the French duo
have seemed – to date – all but creatively spent, or perhaps
nervous of their own reputations.

Any nerves they might have had in the wake of *Les Mis* were
perhaps allayed by the phenomenal amount of care they took
over the crafting of *Saigon*. Inspired both by Puccini's opera
Madama Butterfly and by a photograph of a Vietnamese mother
sending her child to live with her American father, the casting
of the marathon title role was crucial (though in fact, the character of Kim is Miss Saigon only by implication, in that she
represents a common plight of Vietnamese women during the
war – the actual Miss Saigon beauty-contest winner is a minor
character). Both the writers and the director Nicholas Hytner
felt that Kim had to be played by an Asian actress. Since Asia
has a much smaller musical theatre culture than the West, the
search was exhausting and exhaustive.

The creative team, including Boublil, Schönberg, Mackintosh and Hytner, toured Asian countries holding open auditions

to find their ideal. The young actress Lea Salonga landed the role in the Philippines. If they thought that audiences would never accept a European actress as Kim, they had no such qualms over the casting of the manipulative pimp (and scene-stealer) the Engineer. Jonathan Pryce seized the part with glee, confirming his own arrival as one of the world's most bankable musical-theatre stars (like Michael Crawford in *Phantom*, Pryce was not previously known for musicals – but he followed this success with later stints in *Oliver!* and *My Fair Lady*, both also for Mackintosh).

If some critics had been reticent about applauding *Les Mis*, there were no such reservations about *Miss Saigon*. The reviews were ecstatic, and the show played London for ten years. (Every big musical of the period seemed obliged to include a show-stopping 'effect' and *Saigon* achieved perhaps the most famous, with a spectacular helicopter landing on stage.) Controversy before the New York opening – Mackintosh butted heads with American Equity over the importing of Pryce and Salonga over US actors until, insisting that they were irreplaceable, he threatened not to transfer the show – did not harm its prospects there. Its box-office advance of around $24 million set a new Broadway record and it remained at the Broadway Theatre for a decade.

TRIVIA

This was producer Cameron Mackintosh's heyday, a time when the British – and although Schönberg and Boublil are French their shows were British-produced – were dominating the genre. With so much money flying about there was plenty of extravagance, and Mackintosh's flamboyant after-show parties were looked forward to almost as much as the shows themselves. Privileged attendees of the London *Saigon* opening were sailed down the Thames in Vietnamese barges.

THE PLOT

Towards the end of the Vietnam War, a Saigon nightclub owner and pimp known as the Engineer is anxiously getting his girls ready to perform in his club's beauty contest – the girl named 'Miss Saigon' for the night will be won by one of his American GI customers. It is the virginal Kim's first night working there.

A Marine, John, tries to cheer up his friend Chris by buying him a girl for the night – Chris refuses until he sees Kim. During the course of a night, they fall in love. After Kim tells Chris how her village was burned and her parents died, he asks her to live with him in America. She arranges a wedding ceremony (somewhat to his surprise) – which is interrupted by Kim's arranged fiancé Thuy. As the two men face off, Kim tells Thuy to leave.

Three years later we meet Thuy once more, now an official for the new Vietnamese government. He has tracked down the Engineer, who in turn finds Kim for him. Kim, abandoned by Chris, reveals to Thuy the son she keeps hidden. Shocked, he orders her to kill the boy, but Kim shoots Thuy dead. She begs the Engineer to take her and the baby to America to find Chris – and the pimp, realising that a half-American child is as good as a passport to his beloved US, agrees. The trio board a ship and leave Vietnam.

Meanwhile, John now works for an organisation devoted to helping the children of American soldiers and Vietnamese women (Bui-Doi). He tells Chris – now married to an American woman named Ellen – that he has discovered Kim's whereabouts, working for the Engineer in Bangkok, and that she has a son. Chris's son. Ellen, Chris and John head for Bangkok.

Once there John tries to tell Kim that Chris is married but is unable to go through with it. He promises that Chris will visit her soon. As she prepares, alone, the spectre of Thuy appears to remind her of the time Chris left her alone. Cue a flashback of the night Saigon fell, as Chris is trapped in the Embassy, fails to reach her on the phone and is airlifted out against his will.

Unable to bear the wait any longer Kim goes to find Chris. She encounters Ellen instead and realises the full truth. She returns home to tell her son that his father will give him a better life and, as Chris arrives, she shoots herself, dying in his arms. Ellen embraces the child.

NUMBERS TO LISTEN OUT FOR

'The Heat Is on in Saigon'
'The Movie in My Mind'
'Last Night of the World'
'If You Want to Die in Bed'
'Bui-Doi'
'The American Dream'
'Now That I've Seen Her'
'I'll Give My Life for You'

RECOMMENDED RECORDINGS

As with *Les Misérables*, Mackintosh followed up the original London cast album with an every-note-included Complete Recording. Unlike in its *Les Mis* predecessor, the hand-picked cast here is extremely fine, without a weak link. And it does run the London cast close – with a strong-voiced Kim from Joanna Ampil (her interpretation occasionally marred by showy effects), a jolly good Chris from Peter Cousens and Ruthie Henshall's Ellen arguably having the edge over the rival set's Claire Moore. Finally though, it misses Lea Salonga's Kim (who has you believing that her life depends on this performance – as, in a way, it did, as her once-in-a-lifetime break) and even more Pryce's cynical Engineer. There is also more strength in depth on the first recording, with Peter Polycarpou's deeply felt John and Keith Burns's savage Thuy. Simon Bowman's Chris is fine but no Michael Ball in the vocal stakes. So the London cast is essential, but it'd be nice to have both.

The Most Happy Fella

Music, lyrics and book by Frank Loesser
Premiere: 3 May 1956, at the Imperial Theatre, New York

For *Guys and Dolls* fans who were expecting more of the same from its follow-up, there would be some confusion. Frank Loesser created something totally different with *The Most Happy Fella* – effectively a kind of folk opera (to borrow Gershwin's phrase), with the emphasis on 'folk'. Because this is an old-fashioned tale of love and dreams, and it is given an old-fashioned feel. But beyond this, there is an emotional complexity – themes of betrayal and redemption – that start to move into traditional operatic territory dramatically as well as musically.

Indeed, the main role of Tony was taken originally by a fully fledged opera singer, Robert Weede (and later by other opera stars such as Giorgio Tozzi and Louis Quilico). Although various popular singers recorded some of the numbers, among them Dean Martin and Sammy Davis Jr, in 1956 it must have all seemed a very far cry from that season's more traditional Broadway hit, *My Fair Lady*. Still, it ran for more than a year and a half in New York and had another very decent run in London.

The Most Happy Fella has always been liked by musicals fans. It is affecting and, somehow, the emotion feels honest. It is generally regarded as an important show, for its ambition, and the original Broadway cast was honoured by being given a deluxe three-album soundtrack.

TRIVIA

Frank Loesser was unhappily married when he started work on the show. He later married its leading lady, Jo Sullivan.

Although opera singers have often sung Tony, in an unlikely piece of casting New York City Opera turned to an actor when they mounted the show – Paul Sorvino, so often one of Hollywood's 'go-to gangsters' for mobster films.

The writer Samuel Taylor had been approached by Loesser to write the book, but was put off by Loesser's habits of partying all night and working odd hours. So, the composer had to go it alone.

THE PLOT

Tony, who owns a vineyard in the Napa Valley, feels lonely and increasingly old. He dreams of a waitress, Rosabella, whom he has spotted in a San Francisco eatery. He writes her a love letter but, convinced that his age and looks will count against him, passes off a photograph of his foreman, Joey, as himself. Rosabella is charmed by both note and photo and arrives in the valley, where she discovers the truth. She samples the charms of both men, but marries Tony. When she finds that she is pregnant with Joey's baby, Rosabella and Tony find their love tested to the limit.

NUMBERS TO LISTEN OUT FOR

'Ooh! My Feet!'
'Somebody, Somewhere'
'The Most Happy Fella'
'Standing on the Corner'
'Joey, Joey'
'Rosabella'
'Abbondanza'
'Sposalizio'
'Big D'
'How Beautiful the Days'
'Warm All Over'
'I Like Everybody'
'My Heart Is Full of You'
'Mamma, Mamma'
'Song of a Summer Night'

RECOMMENDED RECORDINGS

The pretty complete Broadway cast version on Sony is excellent and, in its length, musically satisfying. Robert Weede and Jo Swerling are a touching pair. Also highly recommended, and even more complete, is a TER recording with Louis

Quilico who, though no longer in the first flush of vocal youth, plays the Italian immigrant vintner to the life. And his lovable Rosabella is Swerling's and Loesser's daughter Emily Loesser – Swerling herself makes a cameo appearance. TER as so often has the enormous benefit of John Owen Edwards conducting.

The Music Man

Music, book and lyrics by Meredith Wilson
Premiere: 19 December 1957, at the Majestic Theatre, New York

To call *The Music Man*'s development troubled is an understatement. Meredith Wilson had no track record in composing a musical, let alone writing the lyrics and book as well. He spent more than six years on dozens of drafts – in fact, so difficult was the process that Wilson later wrote a book about it. To make matters harder on himself, he entrusted the pivotal title role (and as important as the heroine Marian the librarian is, without a great music man there's no show) to the film star Robert Preston. Who had also never done a musical before. Not many people even knew whether he could sing.

Easy to say in retrospect, but perhaps people should have trusted Wilson. A flautist originally, he had certainly put in his time and knew the music world backwards – on his résumé were stints playing for John Philip Sousa (and the march king's influence is certainly felt in *The Music Man*) and Arturo Toscanini, composing credits for Charlie Chaplin (he was Oscar-nominated for his score to *The Great Dictator*) and presenting as well as undertaking musical-director duties for big radio programmes. He nearly always did only what he felt he was capable of, and when he said he could write a big Broadway show, they should have believed him.

In the event, *The Music Man* was a triumph. Small-town Americana was caught to the life in music that pulsated to the country's marching beat. Preston gave a magnificent performance that has gone down in Broadway annals and was happily preserved in the movie version. Opposite him, Barbara Cook was similarly acclaimed but lost out for the film to Shirley Jones.

TRIVIA

Other actors considered for the Robert Preston role included Gene Kelly, Jason Robards and Danny Kaye.

The Music Man is often revived at both the professional and amateur levels, and has a reputation for being a die-hard favourite. However, its first New York revival in 1980, a starry affair with a cast that included Dick Van Dyke and the young Christian Slater, was a disaster.

THE PLOT

Harold Hill, masquerading as a professor, is a serial con-artist whose scam of choice is to persuade a town that they need a youth band – and give him the money to buy instruments. At which point he moves on to the next town. He plans to work the same racket in River City, Ohio. All is going well until he falls in love with the very moral local librarian, Marian. She feels the same way about him even though he is unable to fool her as to his real character. To earn her love, Hill decides to do some good, starting with helping her shy brother. And then there's the question of that boys' band.

NUMBERS TO LISTEN OUT FOR

'Trouble'
'Seventy-six Trombones'
'Sincere'
'Pick a Little, Talk a Little'
'Marian the Librarian'
'Shipoopi'
'Till There Was You'

RECOMMENDED RECORDINGS

As with his *Mack and Mabel*, Robert Preston helped to deliver one of the great Broadway cast recordings with *The Music*

Man. The whole thing is bursting with those great tunes, and feels fresh and alive. Barbara Cook is adorable as Marian, but it's Preston's show. The film soundtrack is also extremely good, and there's nothing remotely wrong with Shirley Jones, but you do miss Cook.

The film itself, despite rather unimaginative direction from Morton DaCosta, is fine, and of course has the enormous benefit of Preston re-creating his stage role and still bursting with charisma. A 2003 made-for-TV film with Matthew Broderick just underlines what a deceptively difficult role Harold Hill is – and Broderick simply hasn't got the measure of it.

My Fair Lady

Music by Frederick Loewe
Book and lyrics by Alan Jay Lerner
Premiere: 15 March 1956, at the Mark Hellinger Theatre, New York

If it is true, as the musical-theatre commentator Mark Steyn has suggested, that Lerner and Loewe spent much of their lives rehashing the same basic plot – involving a Svengali-like older man and an unsophisticated younger girl who suddenly blossoms into an object of desire – then this story has never been better told, by this or any other writing team, than in *My Fair Lady*. It is generally accepted that, with music adding heart to the intellectual wit of George Bernard Shaw's satire *Pygmalion*, the show even improves upon the original.

Not that its creation was by any means plain sailing. The great Broadway diva Mary Martin, upon hearing the initial batch of songs written for it, reportedly let it be known to lyricist and composer that she thought they had 'lost their talent'. Persuading the famously difficult English star Rex Harrison to accept the lead role of Higgins was made no easier when he too declared that he hated the songs (Lerner and Loewe simply agreed to replace most of them with better ones, which they duly did).

Neither could Harrison sing a note. Fine, reasoned the writers, he could speak the musical numbers in rhythm. Having secured Harrison's signature, they cast the other key role, Eliza Doolittle, with the inexperienced but impressive teenager Julie Andrews. That too had its perils, as her failure to grasp the role in rehearsal led to tension with Harrison (eventually, master director Moss Hart drummed Eliza in a private, weekend-long cramming session). To round off their troubles, Harrison announced on the first night (of the out-of-town warm-up run) that he wasn't ready and would not go on. Only when the furious theatre manager replied that he would tell any audience members who showed up exactly why the show was cancelled did Harrison change his mind. Unfortunately by that time the rest of the cast had been given the night off, and the town's cinemas and health clubs had to be frantically searched to bring back errant company members in time for curtain up.

Despite all this, *My Fair Lady* was a smash. It became one of the longest-running shows in Broadway history, turned Julie Andrews into Julie Andrews and sold more than a million cast albums for the show's backers, CBS. My favourite story, cited in Gene Lees's biography of Lerner and Loewe, is of a night when the composer decided to check out that evening's performance. He caught a taxi and asked for the Mark Hellinger Theatre, whereupon the driver roundly told him off for daring to be late for one of the great shows of the era. Loewe meekly accepted the castigation, and at the journey's end gave the driver an enormous tip.

TRIVIA

For the film version, Julie Andrews was famously passed over in favour of Audrey Hepburn, whose singing was judged to be so inadequate that Marni Nixon dubbed her musical numbers. When Andrews won an Oscar for *Mary Poppins*, she acidly introduced herself by saying, 'I'm Marni Nixon.'

Alan Jay Lerner thought of the song for Higgins, 'Why Can't a Woman Be More Like a Man', after a conversation with Harrison – both men having been married multiple times – during which the actor suggested that life would be far easier if they both were gay.

Lerner married the Eliza, Liz Robertson, from a 1979 London production.

An early Mexican production of *My Fair Lady* featured the young Placido Domingo in a tiny role.

THE PLOT

Self-absorbed and chauvinistic linguistics expert Professor Henry Higgins is fascinated by the dreadful tones of a flower-seller in Covent Garden, Eliza Dolittle. He accepts the challenge of a colleague, Colonel Pickering, to teach Eliza to speak like a lady and pass her off as such at a royal ball. Eliza moves in with Higgins for her lessons, and he succeeds. After the ball, however, Higgins forgets to thank Eliza and she, humiliated and worried about her future, walks out on him. When the professor tracks her down to his mother's house, and she refuses to return, he realises to his irritation that he has developed feelings for her. She does come back to him, upon which he demands his slippers.

NUMBERS TO LISTEN OUT FOR

'Wouldn't It Be Loverly'
'Why Can't the English'
'With a Little Bit of Luck'
'Why Can't a Woman Be More Like a Man'
'I Could Have Danced All Night'
'On the Street Where You Live'
'I'm an Ordinary Man'
'I'm Getting Married in the Morning'
'A Hymn to Him'
'I've Grown Accustomed to Her Face'

RECOMMENDED RECORDINGS

There are many splendid versions, though I'm not a fan of the stiff-sounding Tinuke Olafmihan's Eliza in the widely praised

TER recording. A favourite must always include the definitive trio of Rex Harrison, Julie Andrews and Stanley Holloway (as Eliza's father) and they are all sharper in the original Broadway cast compared to the (still-fine) London counterpart. For novelty, there's also a studio version on Decca with Jeremy Irons as a wonderful Higgins, Warren Mitchell as Dolittle and John Gielgud popping up as a lovely Pickering – the snag is Kiri Te Kanawa's unidiomatic Eliza.

As for the film, there is much that is wonderful about it, Harrison and Holloway above all. Audrey Hepburn just about passes muster as the commoner of the first half but comes into her glamorous own in the second, and the dubbing is well done. The main flaw is the stuffy studio sets – why on earth didn't they film the Covent Garden scenes on site? – which rob the film of that all-important atmosphere of a London firmly divided by its class structure.

Oklahoma!

Music by Richard Rodgers
Book and lyrics by Oscar Hammerstein II
Premiere: 31 March 1943, at the St James Theatre, New York

There are two shows commonly held to be the real turning points in the evolution of musical theatre as an art form. Both were written by Oscar Hammerstein II, although sixteen years after he penned *Show Boat* with Jerome Kern he was a senior figure on Broadway, no longer a guaranteed hit-maker and seen by some as yesterday's man. Composer Richard Rodgers, on the other hand, was in his pomp – but, having just extricated himself from his long-time working relationship with the unreliable and alcoholic (if brilliant) Lorenz Hart, nobody was at all sure if he could match earlier successes with a new lyricist. That his choice of collaborator was Hammerstein reassured no one.

The two men were brought together by their love of the Lyn Riggs play *Green Grow the Lilacs*. And the genre of the play remained vital to their vision. Before *Oklahoma!*, musicals still retained elements of their stop-and-entertain-and-to-hell-with-the-story beginnings (even *Show Boat* has such moments). Hammerstein and his new collaborator set out to create a musical play – in which every song would serve a dramatic purpose and be an essential part of the story.

The two men retreated to their respective farms and began to work. They didn't write especially fast, that was part of the point – Hammerstein would agonise over almost every line before lyrics were delivered to Rodgers to set to music, who in turn would throw out the conventions of the genre. Musicals should start with a chorus? Rodgers and Hammerstein brought in a lone figure, Curly, singing reflectively about the beautiful morning. Cowboys should be figures of fun? Curly would become a fighter for an ideal as much as an ardent lover, Jud the dark side of frontier life. Musicals themselves should not depict violence? The show built swiftly to an onstage killing. Characters in musicals should be largely decent, well-balanced folk? What would audiences make of Jud, the unhinged social misfit whose turbulent emotional state leads to his own death?

Not very much, was the forecast. Out-of-town try-outs drew gloomy, or downright dismissive notices. In one of the most fabulously wrong headed of critical predictions, the columnist Walter Winchell wrote, 'No gags, no girls, no chance.'

Of course, two vital ingredients were missing for most of its life on the road. The title, and the title song. Rodgers and Hammerstein originally named the show *Away We Go*, not nearly so inspiring as the punchy (with exclamation mark!) *Oklahoma!* And the song of that name was given a pivotal role. Now the show had an instantly memorable title, and an instantly recognisable song that could be turned into a marketable hit. It worked dramatically, too, as the song's optimism threw into sharp relief the difficulties and deprivations of frontier life.

Much to the relief of its cash-strapped producer, the Theatre Guild, *Oklahoma!* was a smash. The course of musical theatre was changed as audiences, having tasted a new kind of musical theatre, hungered for more. And Rodgers and Hammerstein were established as kings of Broadway, a title they would retain through many more successful shows (and the odd notable flop).

TRIVIA

Having struck gold twice, Richard Rodgers was not to be so lucky in his choice of lyricist for a third time. After Hammerstein's death in 1960, he unsuccessfully sought a successor. Among those he wooed were England's Lionel Bart, but the Londoner wanted to compose as well as write lyrics. Collaborations with others, including Hammerstein's protégé Stephen Sondheim, never quite caught fire.

The original cast album for *Oklahoma!* is the first of its kind to include all the major songs, establishing a trend that continues today.

The Oscar-winning film of the musical was shot in Noquales in Arizona. The Governor of Oklahoma declared Noquales to be an honorary part of his state for the duration of the filming.

Hugh Jackman was asked to screen-test for big-screen blockbuster *The X-Men* after the producer spotted the then little-known actor in the National Theatre's 1990s *Oklahoma!* staging.

THE PLOT

As farmers and cowboys argue over borders and land rights in the days before Oklahoma was officially named an American state, amiable cowboy Curly can't seem to find the right way to confess his affection for the beautiful Laurey. Frustrated that he won't ask her to the box social dance, she agrees to go with her somewhat slow and sinister farmhand, Jud. Curly is distraught and pays a visit to Jud in which, in a vaguely threatening manner, he plays mind games and indulges in 'friendly' gunplay with the farmhand.

At the box social, Curly bids for Laurey's basket against strong competition from Jud who, it is now clear, is very determined to have Laurey for himself. Selling nearly everything he owns, Curly wins. Later, though, Jud reveals to Laurey the depths of his obsession with her. Curly comes to her rescue, and proposes to Laurey. Their union has eventually lethal results, however. In a fight on their wedding day, Jud falls on his knife and is killed. Curly must stand trial for his murder.

NUMBERS TO LISTEN OUT FOR

'Oh What a Beautiful Mornin''
'The Surrey with the Fringe on Top'
'I Cain't Say No'
'People Will Say We're in Love'
'Poor Jud is Daid'
'The Farmer and the Cowman'
'Oklahoma'

RECOMMENDED RECORDINGS

The 1940s original cast recording is an important historical document, as the first of its kind (see TRIVIA, above). It's also darn good. There's a wholesomeness and solidity about Alfred Drake's Curly that is most appealing, matched by Joan Roberts's sunny Laurey. And Celeste Holm is the most characterful Ado Annie on record. For all that, though, they don't quite realise all that there is to be found in this many-layered show. It took the English director Trevor Nunn in his 1990s National Theatre production to really release that all-important sense of pioneers a long way from where many of them grew up – battling loneliness and very real hardships to establish a new community, a new home. Maureen Lipman's Aunt Eller, tough first, warm and loving when there's time and it's practical, typifies this approach. It sheds new light on many of the characters, crucially Jud. In Shuler Hensley's hands, Jud becomes a tortured outsider, teased and tormented. You can't help but wonder just how long he has been there, and whether he was quite so unbalanced when he arrived. Hugh Jackman, not yet the movie star he would later become, is a fine Curly, striking sparks with Josefina Gabrielle's feisty Laurey.

It is a shame that the filmed version of this production was rather ham-fisted – it was (very obviously) shot in a studio with, strangely, shots of a live National Theatre audience edited in. The result misses the frisson of the live event while seeming to be embarrassed at being studio-bound. It's all very odd, if still worth seeing.

The 1955 movie is straightforward, apart from Rod Steiger's louring Jud. If you never quite feel sorry for him as you do for Hensley, Steiger suggests a disturbed, complex villain.

Oliver!

Music, book and lyrics by Lionel Bart
Premiere: 30 June 1960, at the New Theatre, London

Selling the rights to his greatest show was one of the worst financial decisions its writer Lionel Bart ever took and one, as he watched his fortune melt away in later years until he ended up living above a shop in London's fairly down-at-heel Acton district, that he must have reflected on ruefully and often. But there will have been pride there, too, because *Oliver!* brought out everything that was wonderful about Bart. The buoyant spirit, the brilliant ear for a catchy rhyme to match a catchy tune, the love of music-hall and of course the cockney speech rhythms with which he had grown up. (Once, on my first meeting with Bart, he kindly wished me success in my career – 'I don't know, somehow, I think you'll do well,' he said cheerfully as his parting farewell, instantly reminding me of Fagin's song, 'I don't know, somehow, I'll miss you.') It was all there in this tale of a poor boy trying to make his way in the big city.

This was also a time when British musicals were tapping into a social-awareness movement gaining force in mainstream English theatre. Bart had direct experience of this from his work with Joan Littlewood's social-theatre projects in East London (not to mention his own World War II-set musical, *Blitz*). And Dickens's seedy London underworld, with its preyed-upon orphans, offered plenty of opportunities for gentle social commentary.

The premiere was dominated by two characterisations – the unforgettable Fagin of Ron Moody, and the strong, ballsy Nancy of Georgia Brown. Also in the cast, as a tipsy undertaker, was the comedian Barry Humphries, who would step up to play Fagin in Sam Mendes's London 1994 revival.

The show was a great hit in London, and won Bart a Tony on its move to New York. It remains one of the world's most popular and most frequently performed musicals. And there was a happy footnote to Bart's *Oliver!* dealings – when Cameron Mackintosh produced that Mendes staging, he brought Bart back as a consultant and, in return, gave the composer back a percentage of his show. It gave him a little more financial security in his last days.

TRIVIA

The pop star Phil Collins played the Artful Dodger in London in 1964.

THE PLOT

Born into a harsh orphanage, young Oliver Twist escapes to London where he meets a thief of similar age, known to all as the Artful Dodger. He is introduced to Dodger's patron, Fagin, who runs a stable of child pickpockets. Fagin takes Oliver in, but his new charge is soon arrested unjustly, for stealing a gentleman's purse. The gentleman, Mr Brownlow, believes Oliver's protestations and offers to take him under his own protection. Oliver seems to have at last found happiness. However Bill Sykes, a sinister burglar who sells his wares to Fagin, doesn't trust Oliver not to reveal their whereabouts and enlists the help of his lover, Nancy. She reluctantly assists Bill in abducting Oliver and bringing him back to Fagin. But Nancy cannot live with what she has done and risks everything to help Oliver escape Bill and Fagin.

NUMBERS TO LISTEN OUT FOR

'Food, Glorious Food'
'Oliver'
'Where Is Love?'
'Consider Yourself'
'Oom-Pah-Pah'
'I'd Do Anything'
'Be Back Soon'
'Who Will Buy?'
'As Long as He Needs Me'
'Reviewing the Situation'

RECOMMENDED RECORDINGS

In an extremely crowded field, it's hard to point to an out-and-out winner. The original London cast bristles with energy, and has the enormous advantage of Georgia Brown's matchless Nancy, but Moody's Fagin today seems caricatured, vivid though it is. He is much better, indeed definitive, in Carol Reed's film – but that cuts a few of the songs and the pace occasionally sags. There are wonderful, almost *Les Mis*-esque orchestrations in the 1994 London cast album, and Jonathan Pryce offers a splendidly shifty Fagin and Sally Dexter a wounded Nancy. And a personal favourite is the TER studio recording, mixing musical-theatre singers with weightier operatic voices. It shouldn't work, but it does. Richard Van Allan is the scariest Bill Sykes on record, while soprano Josephine Barstow (not singing, it must be said, in full opera mode) is a gutsy Nancy. And Julian Forsyth, less starry than his rivals, offers a deliciously nuanced Fagin. I think you need two versions, the TER and the original London cast. If you have to make a decision, I suppose the original cast shades it.

On the Town

Music by Leonard Bernstein
Book and lyrics by Betty Comden and Adolph Green
Premiere: 28 December 1944, at the Adelphi Theatre, New York

It was Rodgers and Hammerstein in 1943 who popularised the idea of having lengthy ballet sequences in musicals. The following year, Leonard Bernstein would produce a musical that actually had its origins as a ballet.

Jerome Robbins, one of that handful of choreographers who have had a profound impact on the development of musicals, approached Bernstein with the idea of a ballet about three sailors who have twenty-four hours to spend in New York before having to report back to their ship. As a dance work, *Fancy Free*, their series of adventures worked well. As a musical, with all the extra space and dimensions that can give, Bernstein was able to fine-tune the wit as well as the emotional resonance. So what seems like a simplistic idea for a story was turned into a very sophisticated musical (even with its slapstick moments). The composer turned to two favourite comedians, Betty Comden and Adolph Green, for lyrics and book, and they delivered words of the same range of styles and moods as his music.

And so *On the Town* spins on a coin, one minute all cartoonish wordplay ('Come up to My Place'), the next full-blown opera parody ('Carried Away'), with room for moments of quiet soulfulness ('Lonely Town', or – with its lovely nods to Richard Strauss – the quartet 'Some Other Time'). Although it would never quite match the popularity of Bernstein's other great hit, *West Side Story*, *On the Town* runs it a respectable second among his works. The Broadway production was a great success (though its first London outing was far less so) and there was a fun – though thoroughly bastardised – film version in 1949 starring Gene Kelly and Frank Sinatra.

TRIVIA

Once the screen rights to the stage show had been purchased, studio chief Louis B. Mayer went to see it and did not approve. Comden and Green were set to deliver substantial rewrites and most of Bernstein's score was thrown out by the film.

THE PLOT

Gabey, one of three sailors on twenty-four-hour shore leave in New York is determined to find the object of his fantasies, 'Miss Turnstiles', whose picture he holds dear. As they explore New York trying to find her, his friends Chip and Ozzie encounter their own romantic dilemmas. And all the time the clock is ticking . . .

NUMBERS TO LISTEN OUT FOR

'New York, New York'
'Gabey's Comin''
'Come up to My Place'
'Carried Away'
'Lonely Town'
'Lucky to Be Me'
'I Can Cook, Too'
'Some Other Time'

RECOMMENDED RECORDINGS

Plenty of good options and, of course, the film soundtrack gives you the talents of Sinatra, Kelly *et al.* – just not very much Bernstein. The original Broadway cast is full of exuberance but the TER recording is not only the most complete, it feels the most of a piece, with a real ensemble feel. A smashing cast includes Kim Criswell, Judy Kaye, Gregg Edelman and Tim Flavin – and a most enjoyable cameo from the opera star Valerie Masterson. John Owen Edwards as always proves one of the most sympathetic of all musical-theatre conductors. Still, my first choice just beats it with an extra dash of charisma and some fifteen-carat voices – the DG recording of a 1993 London Symphony Orchestra concert performance from the

Barbican (and it's even better on DVD). It boasts one of those once-in-a-lifetime casts, with Cleo Laine, Tyne Daly, Frederica von Stade, Thomas Hampson (whose gorgeous 'Lonely Town' has to be heard), Samuel Ramey and Comden and Green themselves. The conductor is Bernstein protégé Michael Tilson Thomas.

On Your Toes

Music by Richard Rodgers
Lyrics by Larry Hart
Book by Richard Rodgers, Larry Hart and George Abbott
Premiere: 11 April 1936, at the Imperial Theatre, New York

There are some lovely twists in the tale of how *On Your Toes* got up on its feet. First, Rodgers and Hart designed the story as a vehicle for Fred Astaire, on the grounds that it would give him a chance to get away from his ubiquitous image of top hat and tails. Astaire turned them down, feeling that his audience would accept him only in top hat and tails. Then, the song-writing team pitched the show to the big producer Lee Shubert. They had an inkling that he was not as interested as he pretended to be when he fell asleep during the pitch. Shubert kept making encouraging noises but never actually started producing the musical, so Rodgers and Hart had to do another show while waiting for his option to lapse.

As soon as it did *On Your Toes* was picked up by the very enthusiastic Dwight Deere Winman, and Ray Bolger was brought in to replace Astaire. When they encountered book problems the team went to the comedy master George Abbott to co-write and to direct. He agreed, did his bit of the writing and then, just as rehearsals were about to start, went unannounced on holiday. It took frantic missives from the *On Your Toes* camp to prick his conscience enough to get him back.

Despite all this, Rodgers and Hart had another success. Notable revivals have starred Elaine Stritch, and the great Russian ballerina Natalia Makarova.

TRIVIA

The big ballet sequence – 'Slaughter on Tenth Avenue' – introduced the great choreographer George Balanchine, newly settled in the US, to musicals.

THE PLOT

Vaudeville performer-turned-music teacher Junior Dolan is drawn into the Russian Ballet's show *Slaughter on Tenth Avenue*, and into the arms of its star Vera Barnova. Not everybody is happy about the arrangement, however. And neither does the ballet, with Dolan's participation, go exactly according to plan.

NUMBERS TO LISTEN OUT FOR

'It's Got to Be Love'
'There's a Small Hotel'
'Princesse Zenobia'
'Glad to be Unhappy'
'On Your Toes'
'Slaughter on Tenth Avenue'

RECOMMENDED RECORDING

John Mauceri conducts a fine 1983 performance that places the spirit of dance front and centre. Natalia Makarova and Christine Andreas head an excellent cast on TER.

One Touch of Venus

Music by Kurt Weill
Lyrics by Ogden Nash
Book by Nash and S. J. Perelman
Premiere: 7 October 1943, at the Imperial Theatre, New York

This was one of Kurt Weill's more by-the-book musical-theatre outings, and saw its leading lady Mary Martin emerge as one of Broadway's first ladies. That it has not seen as many revivals over the years as might have been expected probably owes something to the fact that audiences now tend to expect the more complex Weill of, say, *Lady in the Dark* or *Street Scene* (a show that has now been claimed by the opera world as one of its own, and perhaps rightly). But there remains a 1948 film with Ava Gardner.

TRIVIA

Mary Martin was all set to reprise her stage turn in the movie version, but when she became pregnant the producer Mary Pickford had to turn elsewhere.

THE PLOT

A New York museum is displaying a statue of Venus that is around three thousand years old. However, when a barber puts his fiancée's ring on the statue's finger, it comes to life. The barber must now choose between his fiancée and the statue, while the statue must choose between her former life and present-day New York.

NUMBERS TO LISTEN OUT FOR

'One Touch of Venus'
'How Much I Love You'
'I'm a Stranger Here Myself'
'Foolish Heart'
'Speak Low'
'That's Him'

RECOMMENDED RECORDING

We have yet to have a good complete recording of this musical, but there is a Mary Martin and Kenny Baker (who was also in the original cast) recital of favourite songs. It's rather lovely, and only makes one lament more that they didn't record the whole thing.

Pacific Overtures

Music and lyrics by Stephen Sondheim
Book by John Weidman
Premiere: 11 January 1976, at the Winter Garden, New York

The first of Sondheim's collaborations with John Weidman was also his first overtly political musical (the second being 1991's *Assassins*). Never one to be accused of a lack of creative ambition, he decided to chart the enforced opening up of secluded, old-fashioned Japan in 1853 – the Western states' overtures ostensibly peaceful, but delivered by ambassadors sailing on warships – through to the country's contemporary Westernisation. As Japan's native culture is subsumed by Western commercial forces, so a score that begins by using the Japanese pentatonic scale gradually becomes much more American in flavour.

Producing what amounted to (or at any rate was nick-named) a 'kabuki musical' on Broadway was a huge risk. Accepted wisdom has it that the Great White Way's traditional audiences do not like anything too experimental and if you are going to go that route, you'd better have a ready-made alternative audience standing by (so, for instance, *Hair* became a cult hit among a younger generation that shared its peace-and-love messages). Needless to say, a fairly uncompromising Japanese-themed show (no pretty *faux*-Japanese water gardens, no sweet humming songs *à la Madama Butterfly*, not even any familiar stars among the all-Asian cast) stood little chance of running for decades.

It passed the five-month mark before coming off, but was nominated for ten Tonys, winning two. And the fairly frequent revivals since have usually been well received. If Weidman's book can be heavy-handed, this is still one of the most original, challenging and rewarding of musicals.

TRIVIA

The actor Mako, who created the role of the Shogun in *Pacific Overtures*, was living in Japan at the time of the attack on Pearl

Harbor. His parents were studying in the US and they were unable to meet again until after the war.

THE PLOT

A quartet of warships from Western powers moors off the Japanese coast. Their ambassadors seek to open trade links. This is the first time in a millennium that the country has received official visitations from outsiders. The population is divided in their opinions; the Shogun vacillates, much to the concern of his advisers (who are eyeing the big guns on the warships), and he is assassinated by his mother (in one of the score's most brilliant and strangely moving numbers, she poisons his chrysanthemum tea). Japan is opened up for trade and centuries later the country has evolved to a point where its ancient traditions have been pushed aside by the besuited servants of commercialism.

NUMBERS TO LISTEN OUT FOR

'The Advantages of Floating in the Middle of the Sea'
'Four Black Dragons'
'Chrysanthemum Tea'
'Lion Dance'
'Please Hello'
'A Bowler Hat'
'Pretty Lady'
'Next'

RECOMMENDED RECORDINGS

In one of the early ventures by an opera house into the Sondheim catalogue, English National Opera staged and recorded *Pacific Overtures* in 1987 – a worthy project that did not, finally, work. The opera voices, some good actors among them, come across as lugubrious in a text and score that needs pointed simplicity, and elegance laced with irony as surely as the Shogun's last drink is laced with its lethal dose. A far better bet is the original Broadway cast (just beating that of the 2004 Broadway revival for its freshness), which catches exactly the required spirit. I have to admit, though, that this is one of those shows better seen than heard.

The Pajama Game

Music by Richard Adler and Jerry Ross
Lyrics by Richard Adler and Jerry Ross
Book by George Abbott and Richard Bissell
Premiere: 13 May 1954, at the St James Theatre, New York

The story of Jerry Ross, with Richard Adler writer and composer of *The Pajama Game*, is a sad one. A graduate of New York's Yiddish theatre, he and Adler were taken under the wing of the great show-writer Frank Loesser. They didn't take long to taste major success. Ross was still only twenty-eight years old when *The Pajama Game* opened to huge acclaim. He and Adler followed it a year later with an equal smash, *Damn Yankees*. Months after that, Ross was dead, at twenty-nine, from a lung ailment.

Remarkably, in such a short span, he sealed a place in popular American culture. *The Pajama Game*, adapted from the Richard Bissell novel *7½ Cents*, a tale of love amidst an industrial dispute, has almost the sense of a folk musical about it. These characters are working class, they are affected by everyday problems – not only love, but pay, and they understand that it can be impractical to talk about passion and sonnets while struggling to pay the bills. Americans took *The Pajama Game* to their hearts. With John Raitt in the lead, it ran for two and a half years on Broadway and has often been revived since, not least by schools and local drama societies across the US.

The 'musical for the people' idea is also reinforced by the easy-going, jazz-hued score. Whether it be the driving beat of 'Steam Heat', the irresistible foot-tapper that is 'Fernando's Hideaway' (during which number, when Harry Connick Jr starred in a 2006 revival, he would take to a piano and improvise his own jazz variations) or the folksy 'There Once Was a Man' – these were songs people wanted to hear.

It's also worth pointing out a real stroke of ingenuity on the part of Ross and Adler in the song 'Hey There', in which the leading man, frustrated with himself, records a message to himself on a dictaphone, giving himself romantic advice. He plays the message back, argues with the message, then effectively duets with himself to close out the song. It's a brilliant piece of stagecraft and vocal writing, absolutely in keeping with the youthful invention that shoots through this entertaining show.

London also took to *The Pajama Game*, if not with the same abandon as New York. The successful 1955 West End production starred the popular Max Wall. A Simon Callow-directed revival in 1999 was not, however, quite the rediscovery of this show for a new UK generation that its director had hoped. It came off after four months.

TRIVIA

Shirley MacLaine had her big break in the original Broadway production of *The Pajama Game*. When cast regular Carol Haney had a break of a different kind (to her ankle), MacLaine, the understudy, took over some performances – which is when she was spotted and signed up to Paramount Pictures.

This was also Haney's breakthrough show. A favourite of the choreographer Bob Fosse, she had been cast in a smaller role but so impressed in her first rehearsals that she was bumped up to the second female lead, as the secretary, Gladys.

And this was Fosse's own big opportunity. Previously a dancer, this was the first high-profile stage musical he choreographed. A string of hits followed, among them *Damn Yankees*, *Sweet Charity* and *Chicago*. He is now generally regarded as one of the iconic American choreographers.

THE PLOT

Sid Sorokin is the superintendent of the Sleep-Tite pajama factory. He faces an imminent industrial strike over the management's refusal to award workers an extra seven and a half cents per hour. However, this strike comes with a special problem. Sid has fallen in love with Babe Williams, one of the principal unionists. He must work out how, if it is even possible, he can win Babe while resisting the pay dispute. Meanwhile Gladys Hotchkiss, the boss's secretary, may prove an excellent, if unwitting, accomplice.

NUMBERS TO LISTEN OUT FOR

'Racing with the Clock'
'I'm Not at All in Love'
'Hey There'
'There Once Was a Man'
'Steam Heat'
'Hernando's Hideaway'

RECOMMENDED RECORDINGS

The 1957 film is a magnificent achievement, with Doris Day running rings around her stage predecessor in the lead role of Babe Williams, the spirited but less polished Janis Paige. The other leads were held over from the Broadway cast, and their stage experience pays off. That said, in terms of recordings, I'd still go for that first Broadway album. It's the old thing about the freshness and excitement of discovering a smashing new work, and in this show, filled as it is with youthful exuberance and sheer fun, that counts for much.

Pal Joey

Music by Richard Rodgers
Lyrics by Larry Hart
Premiere: 25 December 1940, at the Ethel Barrymore Theatre, New York

Broadway audiences received one heck of a Christmas present in 1940 with a show that is nowadays generally reckoned to be the Rodgers-and-Hart masterpiece. It is also their bravest work. Out went any idea of stock romantic figures, out went any easy resolution or characters walking off together into the sunset, out went a typically picturesque setting. What came in, relative to its time, was realism, realism, realism.

Based on a series of *New Yorker* magazine articles by John O'Hara, *Pal Joey* dwelled in the shady world of seedy nightclubs. Its characters, one way or another, were losers, weak but colourful and in their way compelling. Larry Hart knew the territory well; he spent quite a bit of time in just these kinds of clubs. Rodgers delighted in alternating a jazzy score with some overtly sentimental numbers that contrast bitingly with Hart's acerbic lyrics. And George Abbott, though he sometimes seemed less than certain about the show's prospects, agreed to produce and direct.

With the young Gene Kelly a galvanising presence in the lead, the main question was whether the press and audiences would be too shocked by the setting to enjoy it. In the event, the *New York Times* asked whether one could 'draw sweet water from a foul well', although the critic later recanted (after the revival that followed the original production a couple of years later, to much more widespread acclaim). Fortunately, the show was simply too good for anything to sink its long-term prospects. The roll-call of great songs is long and distinguished, from 'Bewitched, Bothered and Bewildered' to 'The Lady Is a Tramp'. And – despite its many changes from the stage show – there is a particularly good film version starring Frank Sinatra.

If in the end, you don't find yourself loving – or perhaps even liking – any of the main characters, it doesn't diminish the achievement. *Pal Joey* offers a vivid and irresistible journey into a world of which many of us would rather steer clear (there's none of the affection that, say, Frank Loesser found for his gamblers in *Guys and Dolls*). It doesn't offer sympathy; it does find some understanding. And finally, it is fabulous, yes, and enjoyable, but deeply, deeply sad.

TRIVIA

Having suggested the show in the first place, John O'Hara proved terribly difficult to pin down during the creative process. At one point a frustrated Rodgers even sent him a telegram, which read 'SPEAK TO ME JOHN SPEAK TO ME.'

THE PLOT

The singer and dancer Joey Evans has a dream – to open his own nightclub. But he needs finance, and to this end strikes up with the rich Vera Simpson. All does not go smoothly, with Joey even resorting to blackmail. And the long-suffering Linda English has her own ideas.

NUMBERS TO LISTEN OUT FOR

'You Mustn't Kick It Around'
'I Could Write a Book'
'That Terrific Rainbow'
'What Is a Man?'
'Bewitched, Bothered and Bewildered'
'Pal Joey'
'The Flower Garden of My Heart'
'Zip'
'Do It the Hard Way'
'Our Little Den of Iniquity'
'Take Him'

RECOMMENDED RECORDINGS

There is no straightforward choice as every album has its flaws, and sadly nobody bothered to record the first cast with Gene Kelly. The best we have is a 1995 American cast album with Peter Gallagher and Patti LuPone – there are some flaws, but nothing seriously wrong with it. It's just that we're still waiting for a truly great recording of a truly great musical. The film, as mentioned above, is great – but the score is so distorted, with new numbers, moved numbers, axed numbers, it's something rather different.

Phantom of the Opera

Music by Andrew Lloyd Webber
Lyrics by Charles Hart
Premiere: 9 October 1986, at Her Majesty's Theatre, London

'Actually, *Phantom* is really about rock'n'roll,' Andrew Lloyd Webber once told me during an interview. For the grandest, most romantic of modern musicals with its opera-house setting that might at first hearing sound ridiculous. But, in fact, the idea stands up. At its heart *Phantom* is about three people – the conventionally heroic and slightly dull Raoul, the dark and mysterious Phantom and the young girl who must choose between them. On one level, and especially given the crashing orchestration of his 'theme tune', the Phantom could be seen to represent what used to be called the devil's music. He lives outside the law, he forges his own path. Yes, he kills the odd person, but these artists are sensitive creatures. He might almost be the spirit of the 1960s that so frightened the parents of 1950s babies.

Next to wholesome, vanilla Raoul, the Phantom also perhaps represents lust where his rival offers love and security. As Christine reaches the end of adolescence, she must choose her path.

Such are the broad brushstrokes of a show that, with its lush melodies and lyrics that occasionally sound like love sonnets, has become the world's highest-grossing entertainment. At the time of writing, *Phantom* productions worldwide have been seen by around 80 million people and taken around £900 million. It is the longest-running musical ever on Broadway, second to that title in the West End (behind *Les Misérables*) and has played in hundreds of cities in more than twenty countries.

Some of this success is thanks to Hal Prince's superb production, some to fortuitous (or very clever) casting. Prince's staging, all smoke and mirrors, brilliantly uses illusions to create a mysterious, labyrinthine world. The big effects (most famously when a chandelier descends headlong towards the stalls, threatening to crash onto the audience) are as memorable as the sleight-of-hand moments – as when Christine suddenly steps through a mirror, or the Phantom disappears into a chair.

The casting of the title role was a surprise. Michael Crawford was best known for his buffoonish comedy role in the UK television series *Some Mothers Do 'Ave 'Em*. Though he had appeared in musicals before with success, notably in John Barry and Don Black's *Billy* and Cy Coleman and Michael Stewart's *Barnum*, heavyweight dramatic territory was not thought to be his strong point. Alongside him, Sarah Brightman (Lloyd Webber's then wife) had solid musical-theatre and dance credentials, having appeared in *Cats* and played the lead in *Song and Dance*. But this was the first time she had opened as the star of one of her husband's shows.

In the event, the pairing not only worked, it went down in theatre history as one of the great pieces of casting. Crawford, always a more versatile actor than he is (still) given credit for, oozed charisma, while Brightman's Christine, voice as delicate and beautiful as an ornament, was virginal and vulnerable. There may be those (OK, hands up, I'm one of them) for whom subsequent Phantoms have been finer singers (Colm Wilkinson, and especially Dave Willetts, a much overlooked actor whose voice has sadly lost its former power in recent years) but Crawford and Brightman set the standards by which all others are measured. More, they became a must-see combination that established *Phantom* as an essential theatre date.

And it's all too easy amid all of this to lose sight of what is still one of Lloyd Webber's most beautiful scores, and his own favourite of his musicals. *Jesus Christ Superstar* might be more tautly constructed and pacier, *Sunset Boulevard* more haunting, but much of the composer's writing for *Phantom* is irresistible. The dark musical caress of 'Music of the Night', the plaintive torch song that is 'All I Ask of You', the Puccinian sweep of the 'Prima Donna' ensemble are rich and tuneful. Charles Hart's heart-on-sleeve lyrics (Richard Stilgoe's initial contributions having not been thought emotional enough) are swept up in the rush of melodic invention, and serve the big, dramatic moments well.

With such a success, it is strange that Hart, aside from a collaborative effort on Lloyd Webber's *Aspects of Love*, never followed up with any other major projects. Perhaps he made too much money from this to bother, or perhaps his particular voice was really suited only to a rare, flamboyant subject such as this. Then again, Sarah Brightman quit musical theatre shortly after *Phantom* (a stint in *Aspects* and then nothing). Was this because she divorced Lloyd Webber, or was her heart simply more in solo pop-singing (an area in which she has triumphed)? Strangest of all, Crawford, the toast of the West End and Broadway, retreated to a high-paying Las Vegas special effects cabaret show and did not venture back to the musical theatre stage until 2002's Broadway disaster *Dance of the Vampires* (he since returned for Lloyd Webber's *The Woman in White*, not a good show but he was well reviewed in it).

Lloyd Webber himself reached the peak of his composing career, at least in terms of box office, with *Phantom*. His subsequent struggle to match the magnitude of this hit, though, has less to do with declining powers than with the end of the 1980s' West End theatre boom and his own admirable insistence on trying out new styles, new sound-worlds with each show. So *Phantom* was followed by the intimate *Aspects of Love*. Having said he usually tries new things, rumours of a sequel to *Phantom* persist (the composer has now confirmed it), and the writer Frederick Forsyth has penned a novel – *The Phantom of Manhattan*. Sounds made for Broadway.

TRIVIA

Crawford and Brightman were set to reprise their *Phantom* roles for the film version in 1990, but the plans fell apart. The director Joel Schumacher kept faith with the project though, finally realising it – with different leads – fourteen years later.

The chandelier used in the London stage production includes 6,000 beads and weighs one tonne. The version created for the film weighed 2.2 tonnes, held 20,000 crystals and was valued at considerably more than half a million pounds.

THE PLOT

Paris, 1911. As the furnishings of the old Opéra Populaire in Paris are auctioned off, an aged Raoul finds his memories awakened once more by a music box on which sits the figure of a monkey and, more chillingly, by the old chandelier – once said to have been dropped on an audience by the mysterious Phantom of the Opera – which is lit and raised to the theatre's ceiling as the overture plays.

The story morphs back to the same location in 1881. The opera *Hannibal* needs a new lead when the reigning diva, Carlotta, is frightened by a piece of scenery that falls threateningly near by and she quits. Young ingénue Christine Daaé is asked to step in by the opera house's new managers – she agrees and enjoys a great success.

The opera house's sponsor, Raoul, Vicomte de Chagny, recognises his childhood friend Christine. He visits her in her dressing-room after the show and asks her to join him for dinner. She declines nervously, saying that her teacher, 'the Angel of Music' would not approve. As Raoul leaves, resolving to find out more about this so-called angel, Christine's teacher appears in her mirror. Masked, wearing a black cloak, it is the much feared Phantom of the Opera. He takes Christine to the subterranean depths where he lives. She is to learn his terrible secret and face an agonising decision. Meanwhile, Raoul's love for Christine will set him on a collision course with the most formidable of enemies.

NUMBERS TO LISTEN OUT FOR

'Think of Me'
'The Phantom of the Opera'
'The Music of the Night'
'Prima Donna'
'All I Ask of You'
'Masquerade'

'Wishing You Were Somehow Here Again'
'The Point of No Return'

RECOMMENDED RECORDINGS

Unfortunately, the film and its soundtrack are hampered by a rather thin-voiced Emmy Rossum as Christine and, more crucially, the vocally inadequate Phantom of Gerard Butler. This music calls for extremes of emotion, for voices that can leap or (in the Phantom's case) smother. The best he manages is an occasional jump and a bit of gentle stroking. A shame because visually the film works well and Schumacher's kinetic camera has a restlessness and an inclination to spectacle (the overture, where a tidal wave of colour puffs the dust from the previously black-and-white, dilapidated opera house, is immensely exhilarating) that is perfect for this show. But even visually Butler is pretty stiff. The best things about the soundtrack are the very good Raoul of Patrick Wilson and a terrific supporting cast including the ever delightful Simon Callow.

And so the original London cast album is really the essential buy. I must say that on record Michael Crawford's Phantom tends to croon rather than sing, but his is a properly creepy, malevolently seductive interpretation. Brightman sings prettily, while Steve Barton makes much of comparatively little as Raoul.

Porgy and Bess

Music by George Gershwin
Lyrics by Ira Gershwin and DuBose Heyward
Book by DuBose Heyward
Premiere: 30 September 1935, at the Colonial Theatre, Boston

Is it an opera? Is it a musical? Probably a bit of both and at the same time, something entirely new. Certainly George Gershwin felt this passionately. In response to opera critics hostile to an operatic work from a mere Broadway tunesmith, he wrote in the *New York Times* of 10 October 1935, 'Because *Porgy and*

Bess deals with Negro life in America it brings to the operatic form elements that have never before appeared in opera . . . I have created a new form which combines opera with theatre.' He called it his 'folk opera'.

The composer had integrated jazz rhythms and classical structures before, not least in his *Rhapsody in Blue* of more than a decade earlier – but here he was to try the same trick on a far larger, more ambitious scale. A three-hour, through-sung show would need to learn lessons about pacing from opera, as clearly just a string of memorable tunes would not by themselves sustain the running time. And not only would Gershwin call on his love of black music – jazz, blues and spirituals – but he would go a step further and set the vernacular of African-American culture. Lines like 'Bess, you gots your man' may sound patronising in the twenty-first century, but in the 1930s, they were an honest attempt to penetrate a culture still victimised and kept at arm's length.

Fascinatingly, *Porgy*'s running time works to its advantage. It gives Gershwin the time he needs to build the great climaxes – the lament of Robbins's wake, for instance, becomes a soul-swaying spiritual so that when Crown, his murderer, bursts in the shock is seismic. It also allows for numerous detours so that secondary characters can have telling moments of reflection, the most beautiful of these being Clara's show opening, 'Summertime'.

Thanks to the show's poor showing in New York, closing after only 24 performances, a drastically cut version was shown there in 1942. It was far shorter, used speech rather than recitative, and was a hit. This version has resurfaced from time to time, not least for a big West End production in 2007, but it rips the guts out of the show. Paradoxically, with its structure and pacing so tampered with, the shorter *Porgy* feels a far longer show than the original. Which is never a good sign.

With *Porgy*, Gershwin mined new emotional depths. His music added real dramatic weight to his natural and unsurpassed melodic gifts. Audiences might come out of this show humming 'Summertime', but should also be reeling from a tale of humanity shown at, variously, its most brutally ego-tistical (in the character of Crown), its most loving (Porgy) and its most vulnerable (Bess). The great tragedy is that the world never discovered where Gershwin could go from here. Two years later, aged only thirty-eight, he was killed by a brain tumour.

TRIVIA

Porgy and Bess is one of the favourite works of Stephen Sondheim.

THE PLOT

It is an achingly hot evening on Catfish Row, an African-American district in Charleston. During a bad-tempered crap game, the bully Crown is defeated by Robbins and, infuriated by heat and booze, kills him. He flees, leaving his woman, Bess, to look after herself. As the police draw near, nobody will open their door to Bess, except for the cripple, Porgy.

Both outcasts in their own ways, Porgy and Bess confess their love to each other and both find a new lease of life. He is no longer bad-tempered and impatient; she finds respecta-bility and a community to belong to. But Crown is on his way back. Bess knows she must resist her attraction to him and Porgy is determined that, come what may, Crown will never take her away. And then there is the wise-cracking drug-dealer Sportin' Life and his 'happy dust' . . .

NUMBERS TO LISTEN OUT FOR

  'Summertime'
  'A Woman Is a Sometime Thing'
  'My Man's Gone Now'
  'It Take a Long Pull to Get There'
  'I Got Plenty O'Nuttin''
  'Bess, You Is My Woman Now'
  'It Ain't Necessarily So'
  'I Loves You, Porgy'
  'There's a Boat Dat's Leavin' Soon for New York'
  'O Lawd, I'm on My Way'

RECOMMENDED RECORDINGS

It really depends how you like your *Porgy*. If you simply like to enjoy the hit songs, there is a seemingly infinite choice of recordings of at least some of them by hundreds of popular singers. The best loved is probably that with Louis Armstrong and Ella Fitzgerald, though I'd hate to be without Miles Davis's free workings of the Gershwin melodies.

For the dramatic experience, though, go for the Simon Rattle-conducted version on EMI. Rattle gives the score the full operatic treatment but never neglects its jazz core. This was recorded in the studio using the cast of Trevor Nunn's phenomenally successful 1980s Glyndebourne production – and the entire cast has obviously benefited from close rehearsals with the great director. Willard White's Porgy, especially, is a complex, rounded portrayal (far better than his earlier recording for Lorin Mazel) – one can well understand how Nunn came to pick him as Shakespeare's Othello soon afterwards. There is not a flaw in the whole cast, though, in what remains one of the finest ensembles ever gathered in a studio.

Beware though: steer clear of the film of that Glyndebourne production. For some reason, the cast (minus Bruce Hubbard's mellifluous Jake, who had sadly died in the interim) was reunited for the cameras in 1993 – but required to dub their roles to the soundtrack they had made several years previously. Unsurprisingly, there is some very bad lip-synching and the drama feels, well, muted. There isn't yet any really satisfactory film, with the 1959 Sidney Poitier and Dorothy Dandridge starrer also disappointing.

The Producers

Music by Mel Brooks
Book and lyrics by Mel Brooks and Thomas Meehan
Premiere: 19 April 2001, at the St James Theatre, New York

Have a hit musical, and you'll find a multitude of people taking the credit or, more often, claiming that they had the idea earlier (when, invariably, the idea 'hadn't yet reached its time' – and given the time it takes for a show to reach the public, such claims are often true). *The Producers* was the smash of the 2001 Broadway season, and so far I have encountered at least three people who say they had approached Mel Brooks, or at least thought of doing so, with the notion of turning his 1968 movie into a stage musical years before (one of whom, interestingly, was the comedian Eric Idle for whom the eventual success of *The Producers* became the blueprint for his own film-to-stage musical, *Spamalot*). Not least the young Brooks himself – he went to the impresario Kermit Bloomgarten when he first thought of the plot, only to be told, 'There are too many scenes. Make it into a movie.'

Finally though, it was film maven David Geffen in the late 1990s who talked Brooks into it. There was initially scepticism even among fans of the madcap parodist, but the move should have seemed obvious – the song-and-dance routines in Brooks's movies, even the flops, were always wildly imaginative, with *The Producers'* high-kicking Nazi stormtroopers in *Springtime for Hitler* a natural focal point for the theatre. And, in that and other film songs, he had proved his mettle as a tunesmith – and was told as much by Jerry Herman, who reputedly turned down Brooks's offer to compose, saying he should do it himself.

So Brooks set to work alongside choreographer-turned-director Susan Stroman and a cast led by Nathan Lane and Matthew Broderick in the roles originally filmed by Zero Mostel and Gene Wilder. His only small fear, he mischievously told me in an interview, was that he'd be shot by a German sniper.

That there were more realistic problems for the show was hardly apparent at the opening. Lane and Broderick had formed a magical double-act (so much so that they capitalised on that success some years later, reuniting for a Broadway revival of Neil Simon's *The Odd Couple*), *The Producers* bagged a record twelve Tony Awards and obliterated New York box-office records. Its own producers were so confident that they set yet another record – pitching seat prices at an all-time high.

It was only after Lane and Broderick left that the show's in-built problem became apparent – the casting of the pivotal role of Max Bialystock. In true Yiddish-theatre tradition, Brooks had written a screamingly funny show that depended, not just on a star draw with split-second timing and an overflow of energy, but on a healthy injection of, well, Yiddishkeit. Schmaltz, chutzpah, a good dose of the oy-veys, they all have to be there in the show's spirit – and that depends on the casting of Max. So demanding is the role (he's rarely offstage and has a killer number near the end, 'Betrayed') that few performers could carry it off – and the songs, while hummable, were just not quite good enough to bring in audiences by themselves.

Lane had set an impossible standard, and the role became the show. As soon as he left, the problems started. Respected British actor Henry Goodman was recruited to replace Lane, then fired before his opening night ('I wasn't allowed to try one step that was different from Nathan,' he later grumbled). For the London roll-out, Richard Dreyfuss was so unnerved by the demands of the role that he went on television to warn people off attending before he felt ready (telling the studio audience of the popular *Frank Skinner* show, 'If I see one face from here at the show before Christmas, I swear I'll kill you'). Days later, he had withdrawn, citing a shoulder injury – to be replaced by Nathan Lane.

Although the show had respectable success almost everywhere it went, without Lane it never attained the blockbuster status of a seemingly endless run. The only Max whom the critics deemed as great a success as Lane was Jason Alexander, famous from TV's *Seinfeld*, in a limited run in Los Angeles. 'Casting Max', admitted producer Rocco Landesman, 'is a constant problem.' From the box-office viewpoint, lyricist Thomas Meehan was more specific: 'Since *Cats*, everyone expects a successful musical to replicate itself around the world, but most don't depend on the star like we do. Nobody cares who's playing the Phantom in New York, but they do care who's playing Max Bialystock.'

The Producers ran for seven years in New York, a great hit if not the generations-spanning run of some of its competitors. Its London stay lasted just over two years. Other international runs have often been relatively short – in Toronto it lasted just thirty-three weeks. Lane and Broderick repeated their performances for the so-so 2005 film of the musical. Brooks, bitten by the theatre bug, moved on to musicalise another of his own movies, *Young Frankenstein*, and dreams of creating an original show harking back to the classic age of the silver screen.

TRIVIA

At the first rehearsal of the London run of *The Producers*, original lead Richard Dreyfuss (he left the show before opening night, to be replaced by Nathan Lane) met co-star James Dreyfuss, and was informed by the younger actor that they were actually cousins.

Bialystock's big number, 'Betrayed', originally contained a homage to the Jule Styne show *Gypsy*. According to a working diary of the show, by company member Jeffrey Denman (*A Year with The Producers*), that passage had to be cut when *Gypsy* book-writer Arthur Laurents refused permission. When director Susan Stroman told the cast in rehearsal, they booed, but 'Betrayed' was duly trimmed.

THE PLOT

Down-on-his-luck theatre producer Max Bialystock is audited by mild-mannered accountant Leo Bloom, who reluctantly agrees to overlook some shady dealings in Bialystock's books, noting that nobody would be likely to check the accounts of a flop closely. In fact, he muses, a dishonest producer could use that idea to make more money from a flop than he could from a hit – simply by investing far more than the production would cost and keeping the difference. Bialystock is possessed by the idea, and begs Bloom to help him.

Eventually Bloom agrees, and they find a script, *Springtime for Hitler – A Gay Romp with Adolf and Eva at Berchtesgaden*, and visit its bird-obsessed, Nazi writer Franz Liebkind. After dancing the 'Guten Tag Hop Clop' with him, they secure his signature and turn their attention to finding the worst direct-~ ~ in the world. They find him in the person of the extremely ~ p Roger De Bris (who is invariably accompanied by his 'c nmon-law assistant' Carmen Ghia), whose vision of the ~ y is to 'keep it gay' with high-kicking girls dressed as rmtroopers – and the second act must be changed, since e Nazis losing the war is too depressing for Broadway. Bialystock and Bloom take on a gorgeous Swedish secretary, Ulla Inga Hansen Benson Yansen Tallen Hallen Svaden Swanson and Bialystock goes to woo his backers – literally, since his investors are dozens of little old ladies who are all sexually infatuated with him.

In the second act, Bloom and Ulla fall in love. The auditions for the main part of Hitler are a disaster, until Liebkind demonstrates how a song should go and (being suitably dreadful) is cast by Bialystock. All seems set for a glorious disaster. But in the theatre, nothing is guaranteed.

NUMBERS TO LISTEN OUT FOR

'I Want To Be a Producer'
'We Can Do It'
'Keep It Gay'
'That Face'
'Springtime for Hitler'
'Betrayed'
'Prisoners of Love'

RECOMMENDED RECORDINGS

There isn't a wide choice, but the film soundtrack isn't a patch on the Broadway cast recording, with Lane and Broderick joined by Cady Huffman's lovable Ulla. A shame they never caught the superior London line-up though, with Lane better partnered by Lee Evans (Broderick is a touch too vaudeville for my taste) and a just-the-right-side-of-believable Roger De Bris from Conleth Hill.

Rent

Book, music and lyrics by Jonathan Larson
Premiere: 29 April 1996, at the Nederlander Theatre, New York

No theatregoers who visited Broadway in the spring and summer of 1996 are likely to forget the winding queues stretching from the Nederlander. Yes, it is always heartening to see a line snaking from any theatre, but this was different. Because this show represented both triumph and tragedy in a back story that wouldn't have been out of place on the stage itself.

Writer and composer Jonathan Larson had given up much for this script, a rock opera treatment of Puccini's *La Bohème*, with the updated characters living under the shadow of Aids. Working and pushing for years to get it staged, he worked as a waiter to pay the bills. Eventually a New York Theatre Workshop production mutated into a full-blown Broadway show and word began to build. Hours after the dress rehearsal, aged thirty-five, Larson died of an aneurysm.

Whether the show's massive New York success has more to do with the musical itself or with the emotional pull of Larson's own story is open to question, but its popularity has stood the test of time so far. Although two London productions have failed, *Rent* has played in dozens of cities around the world and there has been a film version. Does this qualify it as a great musical? No, but it undoubtedly expressed some of the widespread concerns and attitudes of its time – to enormous popularity – and for that it deserves respect enough to be ranked in any top hundred list.

TRIVIA

After Larson's death, the cast cancelled the first preview and instead performed a run-through of the show for the writer's family and friends, in tribute to his achievement. There was silence at the end, until somebody in the audience called out, 'Thank you, Jonathan Larson!'

THE PLOT

Songwriter Roger and film-maker Mark are dismayed and angry when their ex-friend Benny, who had promised they could live in his apartment without paying, changes his mind and turns the power off until they agree to pay rent. Roger, who is HIV-positive and determined to write a song by which he will be remembered, meets the teenage heroin addict Mimi. Mark is besotted by a performer, Maureen, who is planning a big protest against Benny's plans for the building. All of them and their friends, however, live with the knowledge that Aids is rampant and among their number.

NUMBERS TO LISTEN OUT FOR

'Rent'
'One Song Glory'
'Light My Candle'
'Another Day'
'La Vie Bohème'
'Seasons of Love'
'Your Eyes'

RECOMMENDED RECORDING

Such has been *Rent*'s success that, should you wish to, you could buy soundtracks in Hungarian, Icelandic or Korean. The original Broadway cast recording will be fine for most, though – especially as it includes the terrific Adam Pascal and the pre-*Wicked* Idina Menzel.

The Rocky Horror Show

Book, music and lyrics by Richard O'Brien
Premiere: 19 June 1973, at the Royal Court Theatre Upstairs, London

London's esteemed Royal Court Theatre, parent to so many major new plays, from John Osborne's *Look Back in Anger* to Mark Ravenhill's seminal *Shopping and F***ing*, gave birth to perhaps its strangest-looking baby ever when it premiered Richard O'Brien's *The Rocky Horror Show* in 1973. It was, in every sense, a freakish one-off – at least, no other major musical has yet combined transvestism, free sex, alien life, drugs and ray guns. O'Brien himself has not yet spawned anything to begin to match *Rocky Horror* (indeed, he has written very little, in terms of musicals, since). It's not so surprising. The world couldn't take two shows like this.

Rocky Horror has transcended the normal bounds of musical theatre to become a worldwide cult. But it was not always thus. Richard O'Brien sat down to write the show while suddenly unemployed – he had been cast as Herod in the London premiere of Andrew Lloyd Webber's *Jesus Christ Superstar* but objected to his choreography and left the production. He had some help and advice from his friend and *Superstar*'s director Jim Sharman, who committed to directing the new work.

The two men realised that what O'Brien was writing was, to put it mildly, unconventional. They would need a producer willing to take a risk. The Royal Court came on board, but didn't have the funds to finance the whole thing themselves. It was they who suggested Michael White.

They'd found the right man. White, an inveterate party-goer (he always reportedly annoyed his friend Jack Nicholson by arriving at parties with better-looking girls than those accompanying the film star), would appreciate the piece's wildness. What's more, his tastes in theatre tended to the experimental – it was, after all, White who had produced the successful but controversial revue all about sex *Oh! Calcutta!*, as well as Joe Orton's scandalous comedy *Loot*. O'Brien played White some of the songs, told him the story and the producer was in. He loved the show, and would say, more than twenty years later, it was the only one of his productions that he could see any amount of times and still be thrilled by.

The team was fortuitous with its timing. It was still less than five years since the laws of censorship over British theatre had been removed. In its no-holds-barred celebration of sexual freedom, *Rocky Horror* might almost have been devised as a raspberry-blowing exercise at the Lord Chamberlain.

But the show was not an overnight success. The Royal Court's upstairs venue held only 63 seats, and though reviewers loved it and audiences came, it was not until White moved the production to an old cinema on the King's Road that a wider public could start to roll in. Still, success in the UK was not enough to guarantee an American triumph. And despite a transatlantic transfer for Tim Curry, whose turn as Frank'n'Furter had made him a star, and a cast that also included Meat Loaf, its debut Stateside – at the Roxy Theatre in Los Angeles, followed by a Broadway transfer – was a disaster. The reviews took no prisoners, and *Rocky Horror*'s American adventure lasted only 45 performances after opening night.

In a story that has nearly as many twists and turns as a Richard O'Brien plot (only none quite bizarre enough), it did not end there. White, a film as well as stage producer, thought the musical might have some sort of life as a movie. As befits this show's tortuous road to success, the shoot was freezing cold (Susan Sarandon, playing Betty, reportedly caught pneumonia after the pool scene), extremely uncomfortable and made under enormous time strictures (White continually found himself under pressure from the caretaker at the Berkshire castle where filming took place).

The film opened, and White seemed to have a flop on his hands. Jim Sharman (who also directed the film) and Meat Loaf (who appeared in it) went to see it in America and were the only people in the cinema. It was saved from obscurity only by the owner of the Waverly cinema in New York. Having been one of the few to see, and love, the film, he programmed it at his cinema more than six months after its US premiere, and played it night after night.

Gradually, word caught on that this was a new cult entertainment. Traditions sprang up – fans developed a large repertoire of audience-participation points (from hurling rice at the screen to squirting water pistols). Actors would come to introduce screenings. In fact, the popularity of the film was such that it is said there has not been one day since its release that it has not been showing somewhere around the world – making it unique in the history of film.

The film's success had an impact on the fortunes of the stage show (not least that later productions tended to incorporate changes made for the screen). Now *The Rocky Horror Show* was synonymous with a (relatively) wild night out, a diversion of choice for students and hen parties. More recent productions have made efforts to move back to the darkness of the original, but in any case O'Brien's crazy flight of fantasy – with its catchy songs and time-warped sense of humour (get it?) – had become one of the most popular entertainments the stage has known.

O'Brien wrote an unsuccessful sequel, *Shock Treatment*. But a more heartening final chapter in the story came in 2006 when the Royal Court, approaching its fiftieth anniversary, asked its audiences to vote for the one work they would like to see brought back. *Rocky Horror* won, and was given a special charity gala reading, with an all-star cast including O'Brien, Michael Ball, Anthony Head, Toyah Wilcox, Adrian Edmondson, Robin Cousins, Jamie Theakston, Christopher Biggins and original cast members Patricia Quinn, Little Nell and Rayner Bourton.

TRIVIA

The person believed to have initiated the tradition of audience participation during the film version is the kindergarten teacher Louis Farese. In 1976, on the Labour Day weekend, he yelled at the screen. His immortal lines were 'How strange was it?', shouted at Charles Gray's criminologist, and to a rain-soaked Janet, 'Buy an umbrella, you cheap bitch!' A fellow audience regular, Lori Davis, wrote a *Ten Commandments of Rocky Horror*, which set down some 'laws' in writing.

THE PLOT

The show is presented by a cinema usherette as the evening's science fiction feature. Once the action proper begins, Brad and Janet confess their mutual love and agree to marry. However, as a narrator explains, they must first make the journey to see their old science teacher. On the way, their car breaks down in bad weather, and the only abode near by is a spooky old castle.

They approach the castle, ask for help and are unsettled to note the strange characters who live there – not least the sinister butler Riff Raff, and a bisexual scientist who also happens to be insane. They are offered rooms for the night, and reluctantly accept. It is to be a night that neither of them will ever forget, assuming they live through it.

NUMBERS TO LISTEN OUT FOR

'Science Fiction/Double Feature'
'Dammit, Janet!'
'Over at the Frankenstein Place'
'Sweet Transvestite'
'The Time Warp'
'I Can Make You a Man'
'Touch-a-Touch-a-Touch-a-Touch Me'
'Once in a While'
'Rose Tint My World'
'Superheroes'

RECOMMENDED RECORDINGS

I have to confess that I have not heard every recording of *Rocky Horror*. There are more than two dozen, in a variety of languages. Want to hear the 'Time Warp' in Korean? Or Icelandic? Be my guest. I stuck to the Anglophone versions, and came to the conclusion that the best option is the film – not the soundtrack, the film itself. In audio only, I'd probably go for the dark, disturbing yet frenzied original 1973 London cast, but this is one of those shows where you really have to see as well as hear what's going on. The movie makes alterations to the musical but nothing that is too damaging, and it is thrillingly directed by Sharman. Tim Curry is a force of nature, while Richard O'Brien seems in on a private joke the rest of the characters haven't heard (which, as the writer, he may well have been). *The Sound of Music* this isn't, but there aren't many musicals more vivid or more alive.

Salad Days

Music by Julian Slade
Lyrics and book by Dorothy Reynolds and Julian Slade
Premiere: 5 August 1954, at the Vaudeville Theatre, London

A man who once played Lady Macbeth at university might seem an unlikely candidate to spearhead a British charge against New York's dominance of musical theatre (on second thoughts, that does sound like exactly the person to spearhead such a campaign) but, alongside his contemporary Sandy Wilson, Julian Slade got off to a flying start with this early effort, about two university students and the piano that makes everyone feel a bizarre compulsion to dance. It was a smash, running for 2,288 performances.

Unfortunately, Slade's promise was not ultimately fulfilled. He never wrote anything nearly this successful again, although he was never bitter about that fact, and London had to wait until the 1980s for its era in the sun. Still, *Salad Days* was a success although the odds were stacked against it – critics who were pessimistic about its chances of a long run, Slade's refusal to import star names when he imported the show to London from the Bristol Old Vic – and Slade had shown he could achieve a hit his way.

TRIVIA

It was the barmaid at the Bristol Old Vic who suggested the title. The theatre had just been showing Shakespeare's *Antony and Cleopatra*, and the Egyptian queen's mention of her 'salad days' had stayed with the girl.

Slade himself played the piano for much of the show's run.

THE PLOT

Two students meet a tramp, who promises to pay them in return for their looking after his piano. It is, however, a magic instrument and those who hear it cannot help but dance. Merriment and not a little chaos ensue, ranging from dancing policemen to a flying saucer.

NUMBERS TO LISTEN OUT FOR

'The Things That Are Done by a Don'
'It's Easy To Sing'
'We're Looking for a Piano'
'Oh, Look at Me, I'm Dancing!'
'Cleopatra'

RECOMMENDED RECORDING

There's a marvellous fortieth anniversary recording from 1994 on EMI. A fabulously starry cast including Janie Dee, Prunella Scales, Leslie Phillips, Willie Rushton, Roy Hudd and Timothy and Samuel West clearly have the time of their lives. Helpfully for a musical not that often revived these days, there is some dialogue.

She Loves Me

Music by Jerry Bock
Lyrics by Sheldon Harnick
Book by Joe Masteroff
Premiere: 23 April 1963, at the Eugene O'Neill Theatre, New York

Not as popular as *Fiddler on the Roof*, this is the one Bock and Harnick show that has been able to stand more or less alongside it – and is a favourite of musical-theatre aficionados. The original Broadway cast partnered a Broadway stalwart, Barbara Cook, with a British Shakespearean actor, Daniel Massey, to fine effect.

TRIVIA

An early writing job for Bock was contributing songs to *Your Show of Shows*, the Sid Caesar vehicle that was put together by a legendary writing team that included Woody Allen, Neil Simon, Carl Reiner and Mel Brooks.

THE PLOT

Georg Nowack and Amalia Balash, both clerks in Maraczek's Parfumerie in Budapest, cannot stand the sight of each other. They both find pen pals to whom they confess their troubles and become quite attached. Georg eventually realises that his correspondent is, in fact, Amalia. Bringing himself to tell her is another matter.

NUMBERS TO LISTEN OUT FOR

'Days Gone By'
'No More Candy'
'Tonight at Eight'
'I Don't Know His Name'
'Will He Like Me?'
'Dear Friend'
'Vanilla Ice Cream'
'She Loves Me'
'Grand Knowing You'
'Twelve Days to Christmas'

RECOMMENDED RECORDING

Cook and Massey make a marvellous couple in the original Broadway cast, so this remains first choice.

Show Boat

Music by Jerome Kern
Lyrics and book by Oscar Hammerstein II
Premiere: 27 December 1927, at the Ziegfeld Theatre, New York

For a Broadway audience completely unused to seeing black and white actors on stage together, the opening of *Show Boat* must have felt like a punch in the solar plexus. Overture, curtain, cue the opening chorus – 'Niggers all work on the Mississippi'. And even though the musical's political correctness has, inevitably, been challenged over the years, there is no denying the power of that first image, the undercurrent of bitterness that could not help but underline the word 'nigger' (so sensitive was its usage that future productions often had to substitute it for something less provocative) nor, most enduring of all, the sight of black worker Joe crying against the weight of historical oppression in the magnificent 'Ol' Man River'.

Placed in the context of a time when musicals were not expected to have a plot or a script of any real weight or consequence, this was revolutionary. (Hammerstein was to advance the revolution still further years later, when he added new dimensions of complexity to his characters in *Oklahoma!*) In an age where blacks and whites were still segregated across America, the show's stance was brave. Quibbles over what might now be seen as a patronising use of dialects have to be viewed in that light.

Just as a piece of drama – perhaps the first American musical of which that could be said – *Show Boat* still stands up. In fact, in some ways it has improved with age. What once was a slightly uneven mix of traditional numbers and the more dramatically aware now serves only to emphasise the way the work still resonates. A lovely period piece is, at various moments, shot through with an anger at racial injustice that still feels contemporary with the genocide in Darfur on daily news bulletins. If anything, it increases the work's power, knowing that a cry that rang out some nine decades ago still urgently needs to be heard. You come out of *Show Boat* humming the tunes, to be sure, but also feeling the blood pumping in your veins. Exactly what Kern and Hammerstein intended.

TRIVIA

Joe was written for Paul Robeson, but although he was to become identified with the role, he had to pull out of the first production when its scheduling changed.

THE PLOT

Cap'n Andy runs the show boat *Cotton Blossom*, performing up and down the Mississippi. When a gambler, Gaylord Ravenal, falls for Andy's daughter, the teenage Magnolia Hawks, boat-worker Joe warns her about spending too much time with gamblers like him. Joe then reflects on everything the river has seen, including racial prejudice ('Ol' Man River').

The show's stars, Julie and Steve, are warned that the sheriff is on his way to see them. Quickly, Steve cuts Julie's hand with a knife and sucks her blood, to everyone's amazement. He is able to resist the sheriff's accusation that the mixed-race Julie is living with a white man because, as he says, he now has black blood in him. The sheriff orders them both to leave town. Regretfully, Cap'n Andy bids farewell to the couple, and Gaylord and Magnolia are installed as the new leads in the show. Eventually, they are married. The show follows the twisting fates of the various characters over a period of nearly fifty years.

NUMBERS TO LISTEN OUT FOR

'Make Believe'
'Can't Help Lovin' Dat Man'
'You Are Love'
'Why Do I Love You?'

RECOMMENDED RECORDING

Given that *Show Boat* more than most musicals has one foot in operetta, it is no surprise that an EMI recording cast largely with opera singers – fine actors all – is the best in show here. Jerry Hadley is winning and properly just a touch seedy as Gaylord, Frederica von Stade is immensely winning as Magnolia, Teresa Stratas is a Julie of one's dreams and Bruce

Hubbard's Joe is a milestone in a career that was just taking off and was cruelly cut short. It is also a very extensive version, spread over three discs (though there is a highlights album). You want to sample the set at its best? Just listen to the expansive tempo taken for the beginning of 'Can't Help Lovin' Dat Man', before the rhythm snaps into life. Pure, theatrical magic.

Singin' in the Rain

Music by Nacio Herb Brown
Lyrics by Arthur Freed
Book by Betty Comden and Adolph Green
Premiere: 30 June 1983, at the London Palladium

A film musical about the making of a film musical, *Singin' in the Rain* works just as well on stage as it does on the big screen. Almost. What you miss is the kinetic camerawork in showy sequences such as the long ballet. What you gain, predictably, is an immediacy and increased sense of sheer delight in performing. I caught the 2001 stage version mounted by the UK's West Yorkshire Playhouse (presented at London's National Theatre) and still remember the ripples of pleasure that went through the audience when in the title song Paul Robinson began dragging his foot through the water, pulling it out to soak the front row.

The famous film, starring Gene Kelly, Debbie Reynolds and Donald O'Connor, premiered in 1952, became an instant classic. The stage first adopted it in 1983, when Tommy Steele brought it to the Palladium with great success. Steele himself co-directed, and the score, which needed filling out with extra songs, borrowed from the best – Cole Porter, Johnny Mercer, the Gershwins.

Two years later it enjoyed a respectable run on Broadway, where the esteemed Twyla Tharp provided the choreography. And the 2001 West Yorkshire Playhouse version, determinedly unstarry, was a triumph for the unfailingly inventive choreographer Stephen Mear, whose career subsequently took off (he is one of the best working on the scene today).

TRIVIA

That West Yorkshire Playhouse production featured Zoe Hart as Kathy – which became her first major London lead. Years earlier, as a child, she had created the role of little Cosette in the first London cast of *Les Misérables*.

THE PLOT

The silent-film star Don Lockwood is in trouble. He is perpetually at odds with his ridiculously demanding, squeaky-voiced leading lady Lina Lamont. He is in love with Kathy, a girl who says she cannot stand him and attracts the enmity of the powerful Lina. Worst of all, the silent-film era is coming to an end, and he, and especially Lina, are finding it impossible to translate their brand of romantic melodrama to the world of talkies. It is Kathy who comes up with a killer idea, to turn their new film *The Dueling Cavalier* into a musical comedy, called *The Dancing Cavalier*. When Kathy agrees to dub Lina's voice, her fortune seems made. Except for one thing – Lina Lamont.

NUMBERS TO LISTEN OUT FOR

'Fit as a Fiddle'
'Beautiful Girl'
'Make 'em Laugh'
'You Are My Lucky Star'
'Moses Supposes'
'Good Mornin''
'Singin' in the Rain'
'Would You'
'Broadway Rhythm'

RECOMMENDED RECORDINGS

Surprisingly, the Tommy Steele recording is not eclipsed by the film soundtrack. He brings his own very likeable style to

Don Lockwood's songs (such a shame that composer Nacio Herb Brown never did become the serial hit-deliverer that one feels he might have been) and Steele's enjoy-it-it's-a-classic approach is shared by the rest of the excellent cast. As mentioned, the song selection differs from the film – and sometimes for reasons of copyright – but it is extremely enjoyable and a must for Steele's legions of fans.

Still, there really is no substitute for Kelly, O'Connor and Reynolds. O'Connor especially delivers a masterclass in vocal (as well as, on screen, physical) clowning. Whichever version you opt for, you won't be disappointed. There's no way, surely, to listen to any decent rendition of this score without feeling a lightening of the mood and a tapping of the toes.

The Sound of Music

Music by Richard Rodgers
Lyrics by Oscar Hammerstein II
Premiere: 16 November 1959, at the Lunt-Fontanne Theatre, New York

People for whom the shows of Rodgers and Hammerstein are saccharine often cite *The Sound of Music* as their trump card. Singing nuns, Maria running atop grassy mountain peaks warbling that 'the hills are alive with the sound of music', an unbearably cute chorus of singing children – it's all too syrupy for words, say the cynics (and there are many of them – Andrew Lloyd Webber remembers his aunt being shocked that he loved this show). Of course, they are ignoring the political context, and they are usually talking about the fantastically successful 1965 film version which, with its resplendent Hollywood scoring and frankly unnaturally beautiful children, is an easy target.

But look, and listen, deeper. Note the way Captain von Trapp struggles to hold together his family, and his own temper, in the face of the growing pressures on him to fly the flag for the Third Reich, or the counterpoint of Liesl's and Rolf's youthful love – followed by his willingness to sacrifice even her for the Führer. This is not the stuff of an easy, leave-your-brains-at-home singalong (although it is true that the *Sing-Along-a-Sound-of-Music* cinema show has become a popular UK phenomenon in its own right).

The same burning social conscience that had pricked Hammerstein into writing about racism in *Show Boat* and later *South Pacific*, community exclusion in *Oklahoma!*, and a complex and sometimes brutal marriage in *Carousel* now turned him to questions of morality. And where is morality, loyalty to the highest morals and loyalties of mankind more tested than under a fearsome regime that seeks to control the thoughts of entire countries?

He poured all of this into Captain von Trapp's exquisite love song to his homeland – seemingly simple, yet filled with the purity of goodness and right – 'Edelweiss'. 'Bless my homeland for ever,' sings the Captain, even as he is preparing to flee it. The country has betrayed him and his family, and running away now is not an act of betrayal, as the Austria he loves no longer exists. This was the last song that Hammerstein ever wrote. He died less than a year after *The Sound of Music* opened.

It was not hailed as a masterpiece immediately. Some of the more negative reviews even went so far as to suggest that Rodgers and Hammerstein had set back the very art form they had done so much to progress. The public disagreed, and the show ran on Broadway for 1,433 performances. It did even better in London, where it opened in 1961 and notched up 2,385 performances.

A decade earlier, the ever popular Mary Martin had created the role of Nellie in Rodgers and Hammerstein's *South Pacific*. Now she returned for Maria, the unsettled nun who finds her home with the von Trapp family. For the second time, though, she lost out when the film version came to be made, this time to Julie Andrews (Mitzi Gaynor had been preferred for *South Pacific*). Martin herself was (eventually) sanguine about this, although the *South Pacific* rejection in particular had stung. She didn't enjoy making films, far preferring live contact with an audience (although her son, Larry Hagman, became a major television star thanks to two hit shows, *I Dream of Jeannie* and *Dallas*). Theodore Bikel was the Captain to Martin's Maria. Both were Tony Award-nominated, with Martin taking the prize.

In fact, Martin was attached to the show before Rodgers and Hammerstein came on board. Her friend, the stage director Vincent J. Donehue, had seen a German film about the real-life adventures of the musical von Trapp family (itself based on Maria von Trapp's autobiography) and he wanted to adapt it as a play with songs to showcase Martin's talents. The writers Howard Lindsay and Russel Crouse started work on the idea, and decided that it should use songs that the von Trapp family actually used to sing, plus a few more that would be specially composed.

They went to Rodgers and Hammerstein to supply those extra few songs. Unusually, since his health was fragile, Hammerstein agreed to restrict his input to the songs rather than the book – but both he and Rodgers felt that mixing musical styles of different composers would be messy. They undertook to write the entire score themselves, and one of the best known of all musicals began to take shape.

In the event, although the musical is not immensely accurate as a history, the broad facts are true enough. Maria did come to work for the family as a governess, but for only one of the children (who was suffering from rheumatic fever). She also married the captain in 1927 rather than 1938. But their escape from Salzburg was less dramatic than the show would have it. Rather than getting away under cover of a climactic singing competition, the von Trapps arranged for one of their regular mountain hiking expeditions. Maria, pregnant with her husband's tenth child, and the rest of the family smoothly boarded a train through the Alps to Italy and never returned. In fact, they didn't stop until they had cleared Switzerland and France, where they took a boat to England. From there they took to the seas once more, this time bound for America.

Once in the US they took to singing for their supper, literally. Weddings, bar mitzvahs and other events beckoned, and they were a success. In 1939 they had saved enough to buy their first farm, in Stowe, Vermont. Later, they built the Trapp Family Lodge which is still running today (managed by the youngest of the von Trapp siblings, Johannes). Maria and the Captain are buried next to each other in the Lodge grounds.

TRIVIA

Salzburg welcomes around 300,000 fans of *The Sound of Music* a year and, alongside Mozart, the musical is the city's major tourist attraction.

'Edelweiss' has often been thought of as an authentic Austrian folk song. In fact, it was written from scratch by Rodgers and Hammerstein.

The film was initially a flop in Austria, where locals had not heard of the stage show. Its first Austrian cinema run closed after only three days.

Maria von Trapp's great-grandchildren Melanie, Sofia, Amanda and Justin (all currently under twenty years old) still tour as a musical act.

At the UK's touring cinema show, the *Sing-Along-a-Sound-of-Music*, viewers are encouraged to attend dressed as characters from the film. There are always plenty of nuns, but more unusual costumes have included dresses made from brown paper packages tied up with string, and even grass for those hoping to pass themselves off as the hills that are alive.

THE PLOT

It is pre-World-War-II Austria, and the Nazis are on the rise. Against this background, the would-be nun Maria Rainer is sent by her Mother Abbess to act as governess for Captain von Trapp's seven children. As she teaches them about music and the Captain learns to open his heart, the political storm clouds are gathering.

'The Sound of Music'
'Maria'
'My Favourite Things'
'Do-Re-Mi'
'Sixteen Going on Seventeen'
'So Long, Farewell'
'Climb Every Mountain'
'Edelweiss'

RECOMMENDED RECORDINGS

Let's face it, Maria for the overwhelming majority of *Sound of Music* fans means Julie Andrews, and so it should. Her interpretation on the 1965 film soundtrack is fresh, beautifully sung and well characterised. Nobody else really comes close, but Mary Martin in the 1959 Broadway cast recording on Sony, more mature sounding (almost matronly at times) though she is, brings her own distinctive style to the part. And without those glitzy film orchestrations, the drama and the schmaltz are more finely balanced.

South Pacific

Music by Richard Rodgers
Lyrics by Oscar Hammerstein II
Book by Oscar Hammerstein II and Joshua Logan
Premiere: 7 April 1949, at the Majestic Theatre, New York

After *Allegro* put paid to Rodgers and Hammerstein's hopes of delivering three hit shows in a row, the timing for *South Pacific* could not have been better. In 1949 many Americans, and British for that matter, well remembered the loneliness of being stationed overseas with only your fellow soldiers as meaningful company. 'There Is Nothing Like a Dame' was not merely a comic song; although undoubtedly funny, it was an expression of exasperation and misery which struck more than musical chords.

Yet this was not about finding a subject to court popularity. As so often in their finest musicals together, Rodgers and Hammerstein tackled serious issues: *Oklahoma!* had brought the darker side of pioneer life to the stage; *Carousel* had analysed an unhappy and at times violent marriage; now *South Pacific* took a swipe at society's in-built racism.

The relationship between all-American GI Joe Cable and the Polynesian girl Liat shocked audiences in some parts of the US. The musical's hardest-hitting song, 'You've Got to Be Carefully Taught', in which Cable lashes out against the racist views that, he now knows, have infected even him, faced intense lobbying at the time from groups against its message that inter-racial marriage was OK. In standing up for this important subplot, Hammerstein was putting his hand into wounds he had helped to expose years previously with *Show Boat*. More than two decades on, those wounds still stung. The writers must have known that they could have been risking the entire show's future.

In fact, it was the southern American states where they ran into problems, with the idea of justifying inter-racial relationships branded a Communist plot. In Georgia, a bill was introduced to outlaw entertainment that contained 'an underlying philosophy inspired by Moscow'.

Despite this, the show was an enormous success (and its brave social stance might well have helped it win the 1950 Pulitzer Prize for Drama). Whether intended as a gimmick or not, the casting of an opera star, Ezio Pinza, in the central role of Emil de Becque, opposite Broadway darling Mary Martin was inspired. The bass's gravitas made a perfect contrast with Martin's patented brand of sunny hyperactivity.

There were other struggles to be had behind the scenes. Director Joshua Logan lobbied hard for Pinza to be replaced. His English, claimed Logan, was unintelligible. Rodgers and Hammerstein argued, always insisting that their opera star should just be given more time, more time. 'I knew that Pinza's ego', wrote Rodgers later, 'would not let him fail.' It didn't, and Pinza's portrayal became an instant classic.

Although it was Logan who initiated the idea of musicalising James A. Michener's short-story collection *Tales of the South Pacific* and brought Rodgers and Hammerstein on board, his relationship with the writers was far from easy. He wrote fair chunks of the book yet had to fight to be given proper credit, let alone royalties.

Nothing, though, could prevent *South Pacific*, in its flawless combination of action adventure, romance and sharp social observation, from being a success story. Nor, in my opinion, Rodgers and Hammerstein's very greatest musical.

TRIVIA

The original London production featured two aspiring actors in the chorus – Sean Connery and Mary Martin's son, Larry Hagman.

When she learned that Ezio Pinza was to be her leading man, Mary Martin considered turning down the role for fear of being shown up vocally by him. Richard Rodgers promised her that she would not have a single duet with Pinza. In fact, Nellie does sing with Emile, but only a little and they never sing at the same time.

It was only after casting Pinza and Martin that the show's creative team realised that they could not possibly meet the salaries of two such big stars. They told them the situation, and the two leads halved their fees, so keen were they to work together.

Hammerstein always disliked his lyrics to 'This Nearly Was Mine'. Use of the word 'paradise' irritated him, as he felt it was a cliché and too easy. Nevertheless, he never came up with anything better so 'paradise' remained in the song.

THE PLOT

American soldiers stationed on an island in the South Pacific during World War II are lonely and frustrated – the local intelligence has not been good enough for any operation to be launched against the Japanese. So they sit and await a breakthrough. That comes in the form of visiting marine

Lieutenant Joe Cable – he has discovered that a man who lives on the island, the plantation-owner Emile de Becque, has good enough knowledge of the surrounding area to make valuable spying viable. Emile, though, is reluctant. He is in love with the nurse Nellie Forbush, and unwilling to risk his life just as their romance is beginning to blossom.

Frustrated, Cable visits the mysterious island of Bali Ha'i, where he himself falls in love, with a Polynesian girl. Both Cable and Nellie, who has discovered that Emile has two children by his late Polynesian wife, must grapple with their prejudices. And in the meantime, the spying operation is on.

NUMBERS TO LISTEN OUT FOR

'Dites Moi'
'A Cockeyed Optimist'
'Some Enchanted Evening'
'Bloody Mary'
'There Is Nothing Like a Dame'
'Bali Ha'i'
'I'm Gonna Wash That Man Right Outta My Hair'
'Younger Than Springtime'
'Happy Talk'
'Honey Bun'
'You've Got to Be Carefully Taught'
'This Nearly Was Mine'

RECOMMENDED RECORDINGS

You have to be careful here, because there are some really awful recordings of *South Pacific*. It needs, among other things, a Nellie of immense charm (otherwise she sounds cloying) and an Emile of burnished tone and sensitivity (otherwise he sounds like an opera stiff shoehorned into a musical). A great example of how not to do it is the TER recording with a past-it Justino Diaz and Paige O'Hara – a Nellie so steely and relentless in her peaches'n'cream girlishness, she sounds as though her smile is fixed so wide as to be alarming.

The original cast recording has much going for it. Martin and Pinza make a lovely pair, but to modern ears she may sound a touch old-fashioned, even occasionally stately (though a very rare and rudimentary film of the original London production proves that, with the benefit of vision, stateliness was the last thing Martin's Nellie could be accused of). He, meanwhile, was just starting to go into vocal decline, with some greying around the edges of that deep and resonant voice.

The film soundtrack stands up well, although some may be allergic to those overblown Hollywoody orchestrations (I rather like them). Mitzi Gaynor is sweet and lovable as Nellie, Giorgio Tozzi the finest Emile on disc (those gorgeous, polished bronze tones have never sounded better than here). London's first Bloody Mary, Muriel Smith (strangely voicing the part in the film for the role's creator, here dubbed, Juanita Hall), is a suitably mysterious Bloody Mary and John Kerr's is a romantic and righteous Joe Cable.

What you think of the film itself will entirely depend on your reaction to director Logan's big stylistic gamble – the frequent use of colour tints. Many are allergic to this affectation, with Logan himself later questioning the idea. Rodgers hated it. If you don't like them, the bad news is that they were filmed in such a way that there is no way of removing them. I think it works, adding to the sense of mystique around these islands with the strange Bali Ha'i in their midst. The romance becomes tinged with a hint of Joseph Conradesque jungle fever (to which Cable temporarily succumbs), where love jostles with something occasionally approaching madness. The 2001 television film with Glenn Close and Harry Connick Jr is decent, though a mature Close is rather strangely cast against type as Nellie.

A couple of other recordings are worth considering. Following their huge-selling *West Side Story* recording, Dame Kiri Te Kanawa and José Carreras teamed up again for this musical. And the results aren't at all bad, if you can take a tenor, rather than a bass, as your Emile (at least there's no dramatic problem here with his accent, unlike in the Bernstein!). You also get a weird and wonderful Bloody Mary from Sarah Vaughn, and an over-vibrant Cable from Mandy Patinkin.

Then there's a very fine 1988 London cast recording. It would be a clear front-runner for anyone not minding a tenor Emile, except that the aptly named Emile Belcourt undertook the role far too late, with that beautiful silvery voice of his barely under control at times. Still, he is sensitive and likeable. Gemma Craven is a good-time girl (in the polite sense) as Nellie, determined to make the best of her surroundings. Andrew C. Wadsworth is a vocally smooth but dramatically biting Cable and Bertice Reading is a wonderfully oversized, cackling Mary. Overall, and unusually, I'd probably stick with the film soundtrack, with the 1988 London cast as back-up.

Starlight Express

Music by Andrew Lloyd Webber
Lyrics by Richard Stilgoe
Premiere: 27 March 1984, at the Apollo Victoria Theatre, London

A show so pacy it feels like it's on rails. It isn't, but *Starlight Express* hit upon a great gimmick when it put its cast into roller skates. It worked perfectly for a story about trains, enabling the cast to whiz around at high speed (some theatres in which it has played, such as London's Apollo Victoria, were rebuilt so that tracks would dissect the audience – meaning that the all-important races could be a 360-degree experience).

Yet it would be wrong to assume that *Starlight* is all fenders and no feeling. After all, composer Andrew Lloyd Webber wrote it for his children, Imogen and Nicholas, while his direct inspiration was that most gentle series of books by the Reverend W. Awdry that gave the world Thomas the Tank Engine. Lloyd Webber first wanted to create an animated musical, and even created the Really Useful Company (named after Thomas's ultimate accolade, as a 'really useful engine') in anticipation, but was turned down by Awdry.

Undeterred, he proceeded with his own railway yarn, one that proceeds at a far faster pace than any of the Awdry books. And for all its rock posturing, touches of metal in the music that are appropriate for a story about heavy-duty, high-speed locomotives, *Starlight* is not without charm. The *Starlight Express*, after all, or a variation on it, is every little boy's dream.

Having proved his musical touch with *Cats*, Trevor Nunn was once again brought in to direct. Arlene Phillips provided the choreography. Now firmly in his post-Tim Rice phase, Lloyd Webber turned to the clever and witty Richard Stilgoe to solve his lyricist problem (for *Cats*, Stilgoe had been one of the various writers invited to contribute the words to what would become the song 'Memory', with lyrics by director Nunn). Despite an efficient job on *Starlight*, Stilgoe lasted as long as most of the composer's writing partners, which is to say one show. A later reworking of the musical saw a new song written by then in-favour (and most enduring following Rice) lyricist Don Black.

Starlight Express has chuffed around the world. Its London run passed the eighteen-year mark, closing in January 2002 after 7,409 performances. It has played sports stadiums in Japan; it has run on ice in the US. An entire theatre was built for it in Germany's Bochum where, at the time of writing, it is still running, having been seen by something over 10 million people. In the region of 16 million people have seen the show worldwide, with a box-office gross totalling more than £352 million. The London production's closure was followed by a UK tour and Lloyd Webber insists that this is far from the end for his all-singing automatons. Animation and even 3D have been suggested as possible future directions for the trains that seem to stop everywhere.

TRIVIA

The production sent every new cast member to a special skate school for four weeks prior to attending rehearsals. Melanie Brown, aka Scary Spice of the Spice Girls, passed through *Starlight*'s skate school.

A theatre ghost was seen at some performances, sitting in Row Q of the Apollo Victoria.

According to the Really Useful Group, a postman named Alan Newman saw the musical 250 times, always sitting in seat L23 in the stalls. He has estimated that the combined cost of his tickets reached around £21,000.

THE PLOT

A bit hard to summarise, since the show has gone through various and sometimes major revisions for various productions and overhauls. But essentially, a little boy known as Control falls asleep while giving racing instructions to his toy trains. As he dreams, the trains come to life. Greaseball, the speedy diesel, challenges all comers. But the steam train Rusty stands up to their bullying and resolves to beat his boastful rival. His ambition is redoubled when he joins forces with Belle, the sleeping car.

NUMBERS TO LISTEN OUT FOR

'Rolling Stock'
'There's Me'
'Belle the Sleeping Car'
'Make Up My Heart'
'Starlight Express'
'I Am the Starlight'
'Only You'
'Next Time You Fall in Love'
'Light at the End of the Tunnel'

RECOMMENDED RECORDING

Received wisdom has it that the original is best but if, like me, you first encountered the musical on the 1992 'new' version, you might prefer to go for the juiced-up scoring. There are also several new songs, including the lovely number 'Make Up My Heart'.

Stop the World – I Want to Get Off

Music, lyrics and book by Anthony Newley and Leslie Bricusse
Premiere: 20 July 1961, at the Queen's Theatre, London

Although arguably Newley and Bricusse's most famous musical-theatre song comes from a less popular show ('Who Can I Turn to?' from *The Roar of the Greasepaint, The Smell of the Crowd*), *Stop the World* was their biggest stage success. And its number 'What Kind of Fool Am I?' still enjoyed huge success. Like fellow British composer Lionel Bart, Newley was a quintessential East End boy and absorbed his childhood influences – music-hall and variety – into his own work. *Stop the World*'s circus-tent setting, designed by Sean Kenny, caught that staginess. Newley himself led the popular first production in London and then in New York. Later actors in his role of Littlechap have included Joel Grey and Sammy Davis Jr but latterly the musical has not had the success it once did.

TRIVIA

Newley was such a film fan, he reportedly filmed his own first date with Joan Collins, whom he was later to marry.

THE PLOT

Littlechap is propelled through the various ages of man, throughout them all searching for the right woman (all played by the same actress) and his ideal of happiness.

NUMBERS TO LISTEN OUT FOR

'Lumbered'
'Gonna Build a Mountain'
'Once in a Lifetime'
'Someone Nice Like You'
'What Kind of Fool Am I?'

RECOMMENDED RECORDING

Since this show now seems so much a product of its time, it is best heard in the original London cast recording, with

Newley and Anna Quayle. Newley's vocal style has often been cited as an influence on David Bowie – judge for yourself!

Sunday in the Park with George

Music and lyrics by Stephen Sondheim
Book by James Lapine
Premiere: 2 May 1984, at the Booth Theatre, New York

Perhaps the thing his fans most admire about Stephen Sondheim is the way he constantly pushes himself, and his audiences, to break new ground. Every Sondheim show sets the composer a challenge, even though it may not always be one he is able to surmount, and none more so than *Sunday in the Park with George* (which, interestingly, missed out for the most part on the traditional Tony Awards but did bag a Pulitzer). 'George Seurat demanded that the world look at art in a shocking new way,' opined the *New York Times*'s Frank Rich in his first-night review. '[This show demands] that an audience radically change its whole way of looking at the Broadway musical.'

That's it in a nutshell. *Sunday* ditches much sense of plot in the conventional sense (at least until the second half); its characters are mostly ciphers with little or no back story; the leading man has few sympathetic features (apart from the fact that he happens to be a genius painter) and Act II suddenly shoots forward several generations and switches countries.

Neither does it all work. *Sunday* was born from a workshop production, for which the second act was only finished at the last minute, and the lack of out-of-town try-outs before the show was launched on Broadway was very clear in the original production (that second half felt far less confident than the first). Subsequent productions have improved on its flaws and the work as performed in its latest major London revival – at the Menier Chocolate Factory and then West End – felt much more even.

If this is no structural masterpiece though, it is a *tour de force* in other ways. Sondheim and Lapine attempted nothing less

than an examination of art and the mindset of the artist presented as a piece of drama. Painting as theatre.

The composer himself has long been fascinated by the
detail, the intricate work that goes into a painting – it is this
that draws him to a piece of visual art rather than any sense of
'life' in the image. What *Sunday* does, on a stroke of brilliance
that borders on genius, is to peer ever more closely at Georges
Seurat's pointillist masterpiece *Sunday Afternoon on the Island
of La Grande Jatte*. Just as a close look at the painting itself
reveals that it is made up of thousands of dots, so the musical
isolates the many characters in the frame – the soldiers destined to forever flirt with the nearby ladies, the salty sailor
with his dog and, ah, the girl with the parasol. She, aptly
named Dot, is here George's mistress – doomed to play a
distant second fiddle to his work, except when she herself
appears in it, given that parasol as protection from the eternal
sun in one of the artist's few gestures of consideration
towards her.

In George's and Dot's relationship Sondheim and Lapine
go beyond the paint to join together the dots of the artist's
mind. His songs, staccato and as pointillist as his work, obses-
sively return to the painting, to detail after detail – in his
world, his compulsion to 'finish the hat' is without question
more important than saving his relationship by taking Dot to
the Folies Bergère. Indeed, it's not a question. In his mind, he
has no option.

And yet, and yet. When all those dots are linked in a blaze
of harmony and orchestral colour – when the characters
assemble *en masse* at the end of Act I to re-create the painting
physically on stage – there is life in such intensity as only the
coming together of all that detail can provide. Bordering on
genius? Come on, this is the real thing.

If Act II never again reaches this level, it is in many ways a
reaction to that *coup de théâtre*, forming a fascinating arc. So
Sunday is uneven, but those moments where it does work burn
themselves into an audience's heart. Sondheim attempts what
nobody else has in this art form, and you have to love him for it.

TRIVIA

The original Broadway cast included in a small role Brent Spiner, later to find wider fame as the character Data on *Star Trek: The Next Generation*.

Act II of *Sunday* depicts George's great-grandson (also called George). In fact, Seurat's son died at the age of one, and he left no other descendants.

THE PLOT

Act I is set between 1884 and 1886, with the painter George (based on Georges-Pierre Seurat) furiously working on his most ambitious piece to date – *Sunday Afternoon on the Island of La Grande Jatte*, a canvas depicting the various bustling people moving through the Parisian park. Through all this, George faces hostility from the art establishment to his style, and the pleas of his mistress, Dot, for some attention.

Act II takes place a century later when Seurat's descendant, also named George, is mired in a creative rut – his once-lauded and innovative electric artworks now seen as stale. To make matters worse, he has to spend much of his time glad-handing potential sponsors. In an effort to seek new inspiration, he takes his grandmother (Dot's daughter) back to La Grande Jatte, where he comes to a startling realisation.

NUMBERS TO LISTEN OUT FOR

'Sunday in the Park with George'
'Colour and Light'
'Everybody Loves Louis'
'Finishing the Hat'
'We Do Not Belong Together'
'Sunday'
'It's Hot Up Here'
'Putting It Together'
'Children and Art'
'Move On'

RECOMMENDED RECORDINGS

The newest recording from the Menier Chocolate Factory production (or rather its West End transfer, which had an important cast change) is by far the most complete. Given that, and the fact that it includes Sondheim's later revisions, it is now a clear first choice for an audio-only recording. Daniel Evans is a quietly intense Act 1 George, more laid back and outwardly humble for his later incarnation.

Often finding Mandy Patinkin's vocal style overheated, I'd still go with Evans even if the original Broadway cast recording were as complete. That said, if any role fits Patinkin's particular brand of nervous energy, it's this one. And Bernadette Peters is absolutely charming as Dot, alternately funny and moving.

Strong as its score undoubtedly is, though, this is one of those shows that simply cries out to be seen – given its subject matter. Happily there is a DVD of the Broadway cast, with both Patinkin and Peters at the top of their game and Lapine's vibrant production shown off to magnificent effect.

Sunset Boulevard

Music by Andrew Lloyd Webber
Book and lyrics by Christopher Hampton and Don Black
Premiere: 12 July 1993, at the Adelphi Theatre, London

It's not that nobody had wanted to make a musical from Billy Wilder's hit film *Sunset Boulevard* before Andrew Lloyd Webber got to it. As early as the 1960s, dizzy with the success of *A Funny Thing Happened on the Way to the Forum*, Stephen Sondheim spoke to Wilder about the idea. The writer-director discouraged him, saying that the plot was so grand, 'about a dethroned queen', that it could musically be done justice only as an opera. The playwright Christopher Hampton also made his own enquiries, to be told by Paramount Studios that the stage rights had already been reserved. He did not know by whom, but would soon find out.

During the early planning stages of *Phantom of the Opera*, Lloyd Webber invited Hampton to lunch. He asked him to write the lyrics for *Phantom*, and Hampton laughingly replied that Gaston Leroux's Gothic novel was 'a terrible idea for a musical'. He suggested an alternative, *Sunset Boulevard*, only to learn that it was Lloyd Webber who had already purchased the rights. In fact the composer had already, years earlier, asked the lyricist Don Black to set two melodies intended for a possible *Sunset* musical (one of which, which Black entitled 'One Star', ended up as the song 'Memory' in Lloyd Webber's *Cats*).

So when, in 1989, having enjoyed his greatest triumph with *Phantom* followed by the respected but less successful *Aspects of Love*, Lloyd Webber finally turned to *Sunset*, he already had his enthusiastic collaborators chomping at the bit, eager to get started. In a strategic masterstroke, Lloyd Webber persuaded Black and Hampton to work together. They complemented each other perfectly. Black supplied the emotion and the poetry as well as his years of musical-theatre experience. ('You can't write a song with the word "anachronistic" in it and ex-pect it to be a big hit,' he patiently explained to Hampton.) The playwright brought to the show a literary shrewdness, satirical bite and the pace of a thriller.

Lloyd Webber, by this point in his career, could inhabit both worlds – and brought them together to awesome effect. For the mausoleum-like home of the faded film star Norma Desmond he all but suffocated her with lush orchestration; great, Gothic minor chords and motifs at once awe-inspiring and terrifying as the seductive, dead hand of nostalgia holds Norma – as well as her helpless prey, the screenwriter Joe Gillis – in its grip. Then, on the occasions Joe manages to break away to the world of 1940s Hollywood the score turns to the harsh, brash world of pop. Salvation lies nowhere in this tragic story – even Joe's love song with the angelic Betty sounds empty, hopeless.

Unlike the Phantom, another trapped monster, Norma has no final evasion. Her big exit is always going to be a flaming fall from grace – but in the harsh world of Hollywood she will take others with her. And that is about as operatic as musicals get.

Billy Wilder did come to see the show, and was delighted. He bounded up to the writers afterwards. 'You boys were very clever,' he told them. 'You didn't change a thing.'

TRIVIA

So central was the character of Norma that the show depended on a succession of star leading ladies. Patti LuPone created the role at the London world premiere, and she was followed by Glenn Close, Elaine Paige, Petula Clark, Betty Buckley and Rita Moreno. The Los Angeles Norma was to have been Faye Dunaway but, after she was withdrawn from the show by a worried creative team, she gave an angry press conference and demanded a financial settlement (widely reported as $1 million). History almost repeated itself when Patti LuPone was passed over for the Broadway opening in favour of Close, who had greatly impressed Lloyd Webber in the LA production. Another settlement was reported.

The show was in economic trouble before it even opened. At a time when Lloyd Webber had relatively little control over his Really Useful Company, it budgeted the production to break even when London's Adelphi Theatre was 85 per cent full. As Lloyd Webber later told me, 'This was crazy! You should budget for 85 per cent as being the maximum likely audience capacity you will get, not as your break-even point.' Although the show ran in the West End for around two years, both Lloyd Webber and Black are adamant that with better management it would have run far longer.

THE PLOT

An out-of-work and out-of-money screenwriter, Joe Gillis, flees his creditors. Bursting a tyre in the high-speed chase that ensues, he turns into the driveway of a large house on Sunset Boulevard to hide. A sinister butler, Max, ushers him inside. The lady of the house is mourning the death of her pet monkey, and Joe has been mistaken for the undertaker.

Recognising the lady as a once great film star of the silent era, Norma Desmond, Joe comments, 'You used to be big.' 'I am big,' she snaps. 'It's the pictures that got small.' Norma hires Joe to fine-tune a script she has written, based on the story of Salome, for a screen comeback – but Joe must live on the premises. He accepts.

Returning to the studio to settle some affairs, Joe meets Betty, the fiancée of his best friend Artie. Betty has read an old synopsis of Joe's and wants to work with him on it. The seeds of love are sown.

Norma, however, also falls in love with Joe, and proves a possessive employer. She throws a grand party for New Year's Eve – but the only guests are Joe and herself, with the ever faithful Max at the organ. Joe can take the claustrophobia no longer and storms out to meet Artie and Betty. While at their party he takes a phone call – Norma has attempted suicide.

Repeated phone calls from Paramount Studios convince Norma that the director Cecil B. De Mille wants to make *Salome*. She excitedly goes to Paramount and demands to see him. The return to her old domain is emotional, but it transpires that Paramount only wanted to borrow her vintage car for a movie. De Mille hides this fact from her.

Joe, however, reveals the truth one night when she has discovered his secret liaisons with Betty. He also tells a shocked and then alienated Betty the truth about his own sordid relationship with Norma. The screen legend is unable to accept the fact that her best days are over and, as Joe turns to walk out on her, she shoots him dead. When the police and press arrive, dazzled by the TV lights and maddened by the night's events, she descends the stairs for her last great close-up.

NUMBERS TO LISTEN OUT FOR

'With One Look'
'New Ways to Dream'
'The Perfect Year'
'As If We Never Said Goodbye'

The most atmospheric soundtrack hails from the 1994 Los Angeles cast, with a touching yet ever more unhinged Norma from Glenn Close. Alan Campbell is a properly vulnerable Joe despite the sarcasm, and George Hearn is a louring Max.

Sweeney Todd

Music and lyrics by Stephen Sondheim
Book by Hugh Wheeler
Premiere: 1 March 1979, at the Uris Theatre, New York

Stephen Sondheim is a great Anglophile, and his masterpiece *Sweeney Todd* is his love letter to England. A love letter of the twisted, stalker type, you understand – for *Todd* is one of the more bloodthirsty and haunting musicals. There are few that are blacker in tone (notwithstanding the same composer's own *Assassins*, whose titular characters' chief goal in life is to kill an American president), or that better chart the decay of a soul touched by evil, raked with rage.

It is also, in a brilliant subversion of musical-theatre traditions, killingly funny. When Sweeney archly promises one victim 'the closest shave you will ever know', suddenly the show doesn't seem so very far from the early days of vaudevillian musical comedy. Then another character has his throat slit, his body dumped down a chute and is baked into a pie and you're wandering, disorientated, in uncharted, shadowy territory.

If anywhere, you're actually closest to the contorted world of Alban Berg, the opera composer whose works include the brutal – and sometimes brutally amusing – *Lulu*, about an enigmatic victim of Jack the Ripper. Rarely have non-sung-through musicals come this close to opera, and it's no accident that this was one of the first musicals picked up as fair game by opera houses around the world.

Sondheim's most immediate influence was Christopher Bond's play, based on the Victorian penny dreadful *The String of Pearls*. Bond imagined Todd, not as the ogre of folklore, but as an unjustly exiled husband and father whose obsession with revenge leads him into sadistic madness.

The original production was not a huge success. Some blamed the production by Hal Prince which, large scale and monumental, somewhat neutralised the show's delicate balance of acidic wit and dark satire. Others were nonplussed by the graphic violence. And then there is always that complaint with Sondheim, that he 'doesn't write hummable tunes' (not true at all, but the charge stung the composer sufficiently that he scornfully wrote the same accusation into his next show, *Merrily We Roll Along*).

Starring Len Cariou and Angela Lansbury, it ran just over a year in New York, but the West End transfer did worse. With Denis Quilley and Sheila Hancock as Todd and Mrs Lovett, it only cleared 157 performances. Gradually, though, broadcasts, tours and recordings saw *Todd*'s stock rise. Today, it is considered one of the high points of musical theatre. Denis Quilley, meanwhile, was able to set the record straight with a critically acclaimed second 'stab' at the character at the National Theatre in 1994.

TRIVIA

During the first London production, Sheila Hancock was plagued by terrible stage fright.

THE PLOT

Sweeney Todd returns to London, his life having been saved at sea by the sailor Anthony Hope. Encountering the baker Mrs Lovett, he reveals his true identity – the exiled Benjamin Barker. He has returned to discover what happened to his wife and his daughter, and to the man who has lusted for them both, Judge Turpin. Anguished to hear that his wife has died and that his daughter Johanna is now Turpin's ward, he swears revenge.

Reunited with his old razors, Todd sets up shop as a barber above Mrs Lovett's pie shop. When his vengeance is frustratingly delayed, he begins a campaign of violence against society in general. Mrs Lovett suggests that they use his bloody war to boost business – and he agrees to give her the bodies of his victims to be baked into pies. Business booms, but Todd never forgets about Johanna nor about the judge, and when Anthony tells him that he has fallen in love (unwittingly) with Todd's daughter, the barber sees his opportunity.

NUMBERS TO LISTEN OUT FOR

'The Ballad of Sweeney Todd'
'The Barber and His Wife'
'My Friends'
'Johanna'
'Pretty Women'
'Epiphany'
'A Little Priest'
'Not While I'm Around'

RECOMMENDED RECORDINGS

There is a large and ever growing selection. And in this case, the first is not necessarily the best. True, Angela Lansbury's dotty and ever-so-slightly devilish Mrs Lovett has yet to be bettered on record (given that Julia McKenzie's for the National Theatre was only ever broadcast on radio), but the show doesn't quite feel 'sung in' yet. Len Cariou is a strong Sweeney but along those (wonderfully hammy) lines George Hearn is much better – vocally as well – on a DVD from the National tour. You also get Lansbury, in Hal Prince's unfairly derided original staging.

Apart from some brilliantly sinister, Hermannesque scoring, the movie soundtrack is a dead loss. Johnny Depp as Sweeney and Helena Bonham Carter as Mrs Lovett might have worked visually, but in sound only they're a disaster – he lurches from an underpowered pop singer's voice to a bat-out-of-hell heavy-metal fury with nothing in between while she, with little vibrato and no projection, sounds bizarrely like Lionel Bart's Oliver.

None of this actually matters in the 2007 Tim Burton-directed film. So claustrophobic and suffused with dread is the atmosphere, so brilliantly offbeat the comedy, that the soloists' strange vocal meanderings only add to the general feeling of unease. Alan Rickman's Judge is sublimely, well, judged, with real menace behind a quietly unpleasant demeanour. Major changes from the stage show include the cutting (bad pun) of the chorus, while Johanna and Anthony are played straight, without parody. Fabulous as it is, this vision of *Sweeney* won't be for all – what on stage was a Grand Guignol, vicious satire is here propelled headlong in its closing stages into slasher-horror territory (Burton doesn't spare the ketchup).

Overall, the best audio bet is a 2000 live concert performance with the New York Philharmonic Orchestra. The great Welsh bass-baritone Bryn Terfel was supposed to make his debut as the lead but pulled out, so George Hearn stepped in, clearly determined to show exactly what a real Sweeney is made of. His portrayal is even more richly rounded than before, the murderer's mental disintegration more detailed, the humour still blacker. Patti LuPone's Mrs Lovett unfortunately boasts an English accent indebted to Dick Van Dyke, but she sings with lustrous tone and just the right hint of infernal desire. A luxury cast includes the likes of Audra McDonald, Heidi Grant Murphy and the operatic bass Paul Plishka. And you can do worse for a pit band than the New York Phil.

Sweet Charity

Music by Cy Coleman
Lyrics by Dorothy Fields
Book by Neil Simon
Premiere: 29 January 1966, at the Palace Theatre, New York

The very young Cy Coleman found working with the famous Dorothy Fields daunting. 'I could never come up with my best ideas when she was in the room,' he told me years later. 'So I'd keep saying I had to go to the bathroom, and by the time I came out I'd know how we should continue.'

The result was a partnership that lasted some ten years until Fields died, but their first and greatest success together was *Sweet Charity*. The story of a dance-hall hostess (softened from the film – Fellini's *Nights of Cabiria* – from which the musical is adapted, where she is a prostitute) looking for love and never finding it is crammed full of memorable numbers, while with a kookily charismatic actress in the lead it rarely fails to catch fire on stage.

The original Charity, never bettered for offbeat charm, was Gwen Verdon, proving once and for all that she was so much more than one of Broadway's finest dancers (and the wife of the choreographer, Bob Fosse). But the very fine film version loses nothing in the casting of Shirley MacLaine.

The typically skewed world view of Fosse's dances is balanced by toe-tapping tunes from Coleman, ballsy lyrics by Fields and a book from the king of the crowd-pleasing one-liner, Neil Simon. 'I'm the only one in here I've never heard of,' says an awed Charity at a big-name party. It's hard not to love a character with lines like that.

TRIVIA

This is the only Dorothy Fields musical to date to have had a West End production.

THE PLOT

Dance-hall hostess Charity is pushed in a Central Park lake by her boyfriend. She returns to work where her friends tell her she allows herself to be pushed around too much by men. That evening she meets a famous movie star who, after she faints from hunger, takes her to his apartment. Things seem to be looking up, until the star's mistress returns and Charity is forced to hide in a cupboard.

Finally she meets a timid accountant, Oscar, with whom she falls in love. He is also in love with her, but then he doesn't yet know the secret of what she does for a living.

NUMBERS TO LISTEN OUT FOR

'Big Spender'
'Rich Man's Frug'
'If My Friends Could See Me Now'
'Too Many Tomorrows'
'There's Gotta Be Something Better Than This'
'The Rhythm of Life'
'Baby, Dream Your Dream'
'Sweet Charity'
'Where Am I Going?'
'I'm a Brass Band'
'I Love to Cry at Weddings'

RECOMMENDED RECORDINGS

The only thing to choose between the original Broadway and London cast recordings is Gwen Verdon as New York's Charity. Juliet Prowse is excellent in London, too – but Verdon is Verdon. Do watch the film version as well, though. MacLaine is adorable.

Tell Me on a Sunday

Music by Andrew Lloyd Webber
Lyrics by Don Black
Premiere: 26 March 1982, at the Palace Theatre, London
  (as *Song and Dance*)

Standing isolated on the stage of London's Royalty Theatre one day in January 1980, facing an invited audience and a battery of BBC Television cameras, Marti Webb was understandably nervous. She was, after all, about to perform Andrew Lloyd Webber's new one-woman show in front of millions as a live TV broadcast. Feeling terribly alone, she looked across at a friendly cameraman named Ron. He gave her an encouraging grin and promptly placed a sign atop his camera. It read, 'Good luck.' Forty-five minutes later, having taken her character – a girl who moves from London to America – through four broken relationships and put herself through a barrage of testing songs, she faced the ecstatic applause. She turned back to Ron. He had a new sign on his camera. It read, 'Well done!'

It was several months since Lloyd Webber had approached Don Black, a young lyricist whose musical *Barmitzvah Boy* had impressed him, with the idea that they do a song-cycle for a solo actress. Neither was entirely sure that it could work, but as Black worked closely with their chosen performer – Webb, a former London Evita – a structure emerged. Powerful numbers were interspersed with recited letters home and bitter arguments (of which the audience, of course, hears only one side). Webb's own willingness to tell Black the minutiae of her life found its way into the character, as did the lyricist's own disillusioning experiences of living in Hollywood (a town of broken promises is depicted in the satirical 'Capped Teeth and Caesar Salad'). And then there were the poetic, desperate torch songs; 'Tell Me on a Sunday' and 'Come Back with the Same Look in Your Eyes' were the show's meat and potatoes.

A test-the-waters performance at Lloyd Webber's Sydmonton Festival and then the TV broadcast were to have been the end of it. But producer Cameron Mackintosh, who had enjoyed such success with Lloyd Webber's *Cats*, had other ideas. He suggested a double-bill, reviving the original *Cats* idea (the feline singathon was originally offered to dance companies as one half of a dance programme). To pair with Webb's singing, Lloyd Webber created a showcase for the diminutive but explosive dancer Wayne Sleep, set to the composer's *Variations*. Borrowing a phrase from *Tell Me*, the evening was called *Song and Dance*. It played London for two years, with Webb's successors in the *Song* half including Gemma Craven and Sarah Brightman.

In New York the show was lengthened and starred US star Bernadette Peters. An American lyricist, Richard Maltby, was brought in to work with Black on Americanising the show. It did well, though Black felt the changes were 'hokey' and that Peters didn't really inhabit the role (although she won a Tony Award). Yet he himself worked with Lloyd Webber on fleshing out the show to 80 minutes for a 2003 West End revival, with the tabloid-friendly Denise Van Outen. The character was made bolder, more in control of her destiny (and hence with the times) – she even tried out speed-dating.

TRIVIA

As he did with Webb, Black incorporated elements of Van Outen's life into his updated show – one of the character's break-ups is modelled on the actress's split with the Jamiroquai pop star Jay Kay.

THE PLOT

(Slightly differs according to performing versions.)

As an English girl moves to New York she breaks up with her boyfriend and meets the Hollywood producer Sheldon Bloom. He takes her to LA, where she hardly sees him. Realising that he doesn't really care about her, she moves out and soon meets a man several years younger than she is. She is devastated when she finds out through a friend that he has been unfaithful. The third man she meets is married and this time it is she who realises that she is not really in love with him. She moves on with her life.

In *Song And Dance*, the evening's end sees one of the men (the dancer of the second half) reunited with the singer.

NUMBERS TO LISTEN OUT FOR

'Sheldon Bloom'
'Capped Teeth and Caesar Salad'
'The Last Man in My Life'
'Unexpected Song'
'Come Back with the Same Look in Your Eyes'
'Take That Look off Your Face'
'Tell Me on a Sunday'
'Nothing Like You've Ever Known'

RECOMMENDED RECORDINGS

Gutsy as Marti Webb is, and London to the core, the Van Outen recording is the one to have. Her voice is less impressive than her predecessor's (in fact, Webb was also her successor, as she replaced her in the 2003 revival) but even that works in her favour, as she seems to throw everything she has into the role – that the vocal lines don't all lie easily for her only increases the intensity.

The Threepenny Opera

Music by Kurt Weill
Lyrics and book by Bertolt Brecht
Premiere: 31 August 1928, at the Schiffbauerdamm Theatre, Berlin
  (as *Die Dreigroschenoper*)

Nobody ever seems quite to know how to classify Weill's early, European works – musical, cabaret even, opera? – and if *The Threepenny Opera* (a working of John Gay's *The Beggar's Opera*) is a musical, it is a very unusual one. But then, that is only to be expected from a collaboration with Bertolt Brecht, never one for sticking to the rules of theatrical niceties. Even in the somewhat more genteel translation by Marc Blitzstein which became popular in America, the show still invariably comes across as an acerbic, savage in its way, social satire. Its most famous song, 'Mack the Knife', might have been cosied up by the likes of Louis Armstrong (who took to reciting the names of favourite singers as part of his revamped lyrics) but there is nothing remotely cosy about the complete work.

TRIVIA

The song 'Mack the Knife' was inserted into the show only to pacify a difficult-to-please leading actor.

THE PLOT

The notorious criminal Macheath is planning to marry Polly Peachum. She is the daughter of London's beggar king, who controls a vast network of the city's down-and-outs. He is furious that Polly has fallen for Macheath and resolves to get his would-be son-in-law hanged. Macheath has protection from an old friend, who is now the chief of police. But Peachum is more powerful than either of them can easily handle, and it is far from certain that Macheath can escape the gallows.

NUMBERS TO LISTEN OUT FOR

'Mack the Knife'
'Pirate Jenny'
'Love Song'
'Barbara Song'
'Ballad of the Easy Life'
'Useless Song'
'Solomon Song'

RECOMMENDED RECORDINGS

The Threepenny Opera does not want, either for audio or filmed versions. First choice will be whether you want it in English or in the original German. If in German there is a marvellous early selection of music recorded with the show's original orchestra, Theo Mackeben and the Ruth Lewis Band – here using a reduced orchestration – and Weill's wife Lotte Lenya a matchless Jenny. Fascinatingly, these records were made by the German label Telefunken who, even after Weill's music was banned by the Nazis, continued exporting them to the US. Lenya is again the Jenny in the best English-language recording, of the 1954 Off-Broadway cast, where she is joined by Scott Merrill's charismatic Macheath.

West Side Story

Music by Leonard Bernstein
Lyrics by Stephen Sondheim
Book by Arthur Laurents
Premiere: 26 September 1951, at the Winter Garden Theatre,
New York

At the top of page one of Leonard Bernstein's copy of Shakespeare's *Romeo and Juliet*, the composer scrawled, 'An out-and-out plea for racial tolerance.' The handwriting seems rushed, difficult to make out, and underlined in a broad, emphatic sweep. Clearly Bernstein had been inspired.

Perhaps surprisingly, for a show that is now part of Broadway history, exactly how that inspiration would manifest itself was a matter of much discussion over several years. Bernstein and writer Arthur Laurents liked choreographer-director Jerome Robbins's idea to musicalise *Romeo and Juliet*. They just didn't quite know how. An early suggestion was for a show called *East Side Story*, about conflicts between Catholics and Jews on the streets of New York. Still, it didn't quite work.

In fact, so troubled was the show's genesis that Robbins had difficulty getting its co-creators actually to commit to spending time on it with him. 'I'd try to get the guys together and couldn't,' he told the author Lawrence Thelen for his book *The Show Makers*. 'They didn't want to do it!' Bernstein and Laurents even tried to divert Robbins with another idea for a musical, but he held firm. Eventually the writers stumbled upon a newspaper article in Los Angeles about street clashes between Puerto Rican immigrants and native-born Americans. Six whole years after Robbins first brought them together ('Jerry hasn't given up,' noted an amazed Bernstein in his journal), they had their setting.

Stephen Sondheim wanted to be a composer as well as lyricist, but his mentor Oscar Hammerstein insisted that he learn the lyricist's craft thoroughly first. So he sought work on *West Side Story*, as the project was by now called. Bernstein was deeply impressed, writing in his diary, 'A young lyricist named Stephen Sondheim came and sang us some of his songs today. What a talent!' Originally, Sondheim was to share the lyricist credit with the composer, who did actually work on the lyrics, but then Bernstein generously ceded full credit (and the percentage points, which he would later take to pointing out, turned out to be a lot of money given the huge success of the show) to his young colleague.

Robbins wanted, and got, an unusually long rehearsal period. Four or five weeks was the norm for a new musical. Robbins had eight. But then, what he wanted to achieve was daringly, thrillingly new for musical theatre. For this was a mainstream show in which dance would play a major part. Sequences such as the opening street brawl, or the bestial, on-heat movements for the dance at the gym would help to establish vividly the enormous pent-up energy of these characters – quick to violent anger, just as intense in love. Shows since *Oklahoma!* had incorporated elements of ballet before, but *West Side Story* would move it centre stage, weave it through the tapestry. 'I was really so far ahead of myself,' mused a satisfied Robbins, years later.

Meanwhile, Bernstein was welding together his classical training, his feel for a ritualised, Latin and African-influenced jazz and his ear for a great, populist melody. Not since Gershwin died had a score come along that at once challenged, served the theatrical moment, and at the same time immediately sealed its place in the American songbook. If Bernstein was never to deliver the great American opera he seemed to promise, this was yet a great American musical experience.

The show was a smash, and its success seemed only to grow with time. A first Broadway run of 732 performances was topped by its London transfer, while revivals came thick and fast – and still do to this day. The 1961 film starring Natalie Wood bagged 10 Oscars, while seemingly every popular singer of the day was eager to record his or her version of the marvellous Bernstein songs, classics as soon as they appeared.

The writers were delighted ('I laughed and cried,' wrote Bernstein after the first out-of-town try-out). Only Sondheim had a regret. His lyrics for Maria's excited number 'I Feel Pretty' were, he felt, wrong. The lines were too complex, too sophisticated for a young girl dizzy with love. And yet the song became one of the score's best known, most recorded, and has cropped up in various Hollywood films. Talk about rubbing it in.

TRIVIA

The first Maria, Carol Lawrence, might have been passed over for the role in the film in favour of the more famous Natalie Wood, but she had a solid career on screen as well as on stage. She also published a cookbook, entitled *I Remember Pasta*. *I Remember Mama* is the name of a Rodgers and Hammerstein musical, generally considered so bad that it is commonly referred to by musical-theatre fans as *I Dismember Mama*.

THE PLOT

Taking their differences to the streets of New York, gangs of Puerto Rican immigrants (the 'Sharks') and native-born Americans (the 'Jets') fight each other at almost every opportunity. Both sides are furious when Tony, an ex-Jet, and Maria, the sister of one of the Sharks, fall in love. Tony and Maria hope that their love can transcend the violence all around them, but the two sides have other ideas.

NUMBERS TO LISTEN OUT FOR

'Jet Song'
'Something's Coming'
'Maria'
'Tonight'
'America'
'Cool'
'One Hand, One Heart'
'I Feel Pretty'
'Somewhere'
'Gee, Officer Krupke'
'I Have a Love'

RECOMMENDED RECORDINGS

There are very few bad recordings of *West Side Story*. Ironically, one which comes in for more criticism than most is the one conducted by the composer himself. Given that, as one of the world's most revered conductors, he would have had his pick of almost any singers on the planet, it is amazing that he made a fundamental mistake in casting. Nothing wrong with the great tenor José Carreras, nor the equally admired soprano Kiri Te Kanawa. But as Tony and Maria, especially when the plot hinges on he being American and she being Hispanic? Gorgeous as much of their singing is, the tenor's Spanglish and, to a lesser extent, similar accent problems from the Anglophone Te Kanawa doom the album (they were far better matched in a follow-up *South Pacific*).

Incidentally, the story I heard about this album was that Bernstein, in his cups one night, stated that he wanted 'that tenor beginning with J' as his Tony. When asked if he meant José Carreras, he nodded. It was only when it was too late that he realised the mistake – he had meant the all-American tenor Jerry Hadley (Bernstein's merciless treatment towards Carreras in the sessions, seen in a 'making of' documentary, would seem to lend credence to this story). It's all a shame, as Bernstein's conducting predictably takes no prisoners.

If it's vocal quality you're after, then you could do worse than seek out a Warner recording with the generous-voiced Michael Ball and Barbara Bonney. But for all the youth and fire that galvanises this show, the original Broadway cast album on Sony, starring Carol Lawrence and Larry Kert, is a must-hear. Energy, passion, even desperation – it's all there.

Wicked

Music and lyrics by Stephen Schwartz
Book by Winnie Holzman
Premiere: 30 October 2003, at the Gershwin Theatre, New York

Despite the hype, an ingenious idea and undoubted success around the globe (in London alone, the show took its first £100,000 in little more than an hour of the box office opening), *Wicked* is not such a shoe-in for a musicals top 100 as you might expect. The brilliant notion, taken from the Gregory Maguire book upon which this is based – an alternative take on *The Wizard of Oz*, told from the viewpoint of the Wicked Witch of the West – takes it far, but it comes perilously close to catastrophe long before Dorothy shows up to drop a house on the Wicked Witch of the East.

It is hardly fair to accuse the early scenes, where Wicked-Witch-to-be Elphaba and her 'Good' counterpart Glinda meet at a Hogwarts-like school for magic lessons and more, of any kind of Harry Potter rip-off. This is a story about magic, after all, and in this world, any school worth its salt is likely to teach the ways of the wand. But for all its slickness, Schwartz and Holzman seem bored here – as if writing by numbers. So you get makeovers and practical jokes, bullying and pulling together. It's just not very funny or charming.

Once the girls travel to the Emerald City to ask the Wizard for help, though, we might be in a different show altogether. Suddenly they must negotiate a world of ethical ambiguities where good and bad no longer seem nearly so certain. The characters might be far from Kansas, but the problems they face are not so distant from those of present-day America. For all its talking animals and yearning love songs, this is a moralistic musical for the age of global terrorism.

And this, as if they have been waiting for this moment, is where the writing suddenly catches fire, with electric dialogue (one superb scene pits Elphaba's confused rebel against the Wizard's disturbingly persuasive argument of totalitarianism) and songs that soar as high as the Wicked Witch herself. Elphaba's climactic 'No Good Deed' is propelled by the frustrated fury of someone trying to use her powers for good, yet never knowing quite what 'good' is.

If, in the end, this was a show that beat the critics – reviews in London and New York were lukewarm – it was a triumph of marketing. *The Wizard of Oz* meets a Hogwarts-style magic school for a girlie buddy tale? They built it, and teenage girls were bound to come (which they did, in their thousands). In so doing, the producers might have discovered that there is more power in selling instantly recognisable brands than in a thousand magic wands. But on balance, this show deserves its success. Especially if its armies of fans then march on to see *Hairspray*.

TRIVIA

A special version of *Wicked*, lasting only half an hour, was created specially for the Universal Studios theme park in Japan.

Celebrities spotted among audiences at the London production of *Wicked* include Jennifer Aniston, Shirley Bassey, Tim Burton, Matt Damon, Mick Jagger, Ricki Lake, Lucy Liu, Emma Thompson and Vince Vaughn.

Part of *Wicked* is musically modelled on part of Mussorgsky's opera *Boris Godunov*, of which Stephen Schwartz is a great admirer.

THE PLOT

Glinda the Good Witch tells the Munchkins about how she came to meet Elphaba, the notorious Wicked Witch of the West. Elphaba, despised and ill-treated because she was born with green skin, had been sent to Shiz University with her sister. She and Glinda dislike each other at first sight but eventually learn to see each other's good qualities and become best friends.

Elphaba reveals outstanding talents for magic, and she is soon summoned to meet the mighty Wizard of Oz himself. It is when she discovers that not only is the Wizard a fake but his ideas of exactly how her powers should be used are very different from her own that she goes on the run – leaving Glinda to decide where her loyalties lie. Meanwhile, someone drops a house on Elphaba's sister . . .

NUMBERS TO LISTEN OUT FOR

'Popular'
'Defying Gravity'
'Wonderful'
'No Good Deed'
'For Good'

RECOMMENDED RECORDING

Decca Broadway's original cast album is a spirited and vivid affair. Idina Menzel, so praised as Elphaba, brings an appropriately individual, off-centre energy to the role – only the
character's vulnerability seems less than convincing. The stars
for me are Kristin Chenoweth, adorable and funny as Glinda,
and Joel Grey's hokum-peddler of a Wizard. It's worth pointing out that the sound quality is superb, lending an extra sheen
of magic to the proceedings. It'd be nice to have a London
cast album though (not planned at the time of writing), if only
to capture Kerry Ellis's genuinely moving Elphaba.

The Witches of Eastwick

Music by Dana P. Rowe
Book and lyrics by John Dempsey
Premiere: 18 July 2000, at the Theatre Royal, Drury Lane, London

An unexpected choice for a top-100 musicals list, perhaps.
Producer Cameron Mackintosh had been disappointed by
initial reactions to his last big new show, *Martin Guerre* (by
Les Misérables writers Boublil and Schönberg), and he turned
to another duo whose work he has championed, Dempsey and
Rowe, to deliver a hit. Their track record wasn't great – the
satire *The Fix* at the Donmar Warehouse had been damned
by negative reviews. But Mackintosh had faith, and having
spent years developing serious new shows such as *Guerre* and
Miss Saigon, he felt the time had come for a return to good
old-fashioned musical comedy. The day after those scathing

reviews for *The Fix* came out, he took Dempsey and Rowe to lunch and asked them what they intended to write next.

He showed them a list of movie titles from Paramount Studios whose rights were available for stage adaptation. Without much hesitation, both Dempsey and Rowe seized on the John Updike story turned starry 1987 movie.

The musical lies somewhere between the crowd-pleasing film and the much more vicious book (Updike's satire of small-town America doesn't flinch from the odd repellent murder and neither do Dempsey and Rowe). Yet for musical-theatre purposes, the story had two absolute gifts – a trio of women whose voices could, and in Rowe's hands do, soar and intertwine almost like characters from a Richard Strauss opera, and a charismatic male lead who could be marked out by pounding rock'n'roll.

The blending of the three female voices, the witches of the title, Rowe and Dempsey got absolutely right from the start. Numbers such as the wishful 'Make Him Mine' contain surprising little harmonies while 'I Wish I May' weaves the voices together in determined unison. The 'pop' songs for the Satanic Darryl van Horne took a bit of polishing, so that when the show opened at Drury Lane (to mixed reviews) he had one belter of a number, 'Dance with the Devil', and one dud – 'Who's the Man'. Mackintosh moved the show to the smaller but still grand Prince of Wales with a largely new and better cast (even the fine Ian McShane was outshone by his successor, the leering Clarke Peters – the casting of whom the London *Evening Standard* likened to 'a shot in the erogenous zones'), and the show was tightened, with 'Who's the Man' replaced by the far better 'The Glory of Me'.

Witches lasted little more than a year. How long it might have run without the 2001 terrorist attacks in New York (which both hit tourism in London and scuppered plans for a US transfer) can never be known. It has had foreign productions since, in Australia, the Czech Republic and, eventually, America (in 2007). But whatever its commercial potential, it's a terrific show.

TRIVIA

Although it wasn't for a Cameron Mackintosh production, *Witches* lyricist John Dempsey partnered with fellow writers from the Mackintosh stable, Claude-Michel Schönberg and Alain Boublil, on their 2006 show *The Pirate Queen* (which was not a success). Composer Dana P. Rowe has not been involved with anything so high profile again after *Witches*, but composed *The Ballad of Bonnie and Clyde* for the 2005 New York Musical Theater Festival.

Ian McShane, formerly a British television star, arguably had his career revived by *Witches*. A few years afterwards he landed a lead role in the major HBO series *Deadwood*, making him a star in the US.

Lucie Arnaz, who created the role of Alex, is the daughter of TV legends Lucille Ball and Desi Arnaz.

THE PLOT

Three lonely women in the small American town of Eastwick idly wonder aloud to each other what sort of man they would wish for if they had the ability to order one on demand. Unbeknownst to them at this point, they possess magical powers and, sure enough, a man who fulfils all of their desires arrives in town – in the magnetic person of Darryl van Horne.

Van Horne begins a three-way affair with the friends. But despite their every desire, not least physical, being fulfilled, they begin to suspect that Darryl might be a strangely malevolent influence on the town, and on themselves. When his flashes of temper turn lethal, and he threatens to ruin the life of a young girl they care about, they resolve to put an end to his tenancy in Eastwick.

NUMBERS TO LISTEN OUT FOR

'Eastwick Knows'
'Make Him Mine'
'Waiting for the Music'
'Something'

   'I Wish I May'
   'Dance with the Devil'
   'Evil'
   'The Glory of Me'

RECOMMENDED RECORDING

There is only one, of the original London cast. Maria Friedman, Lucie Arnaz and especially Joanna Riding make an enjoyable coven of witches, sweet of voice in the trios. Ian McShane is broodingly infernal. A pity that the rejigged, superior, London version was never recorded, but this will do very well for now.

Wonderful Town

Music by Leonard Bernstein
Book and lyrics by Betty Comden and Adolph Green
Premiere: 25 February 1953, at the Winter Garden, New York

On the Town had three sailors arrive in New York looking for love and thrills. Bernstein's next musical, *Wonderful Town*, had two sisters arriving in New York looking to make their fortunes. If it wasn't exactly covering radically different ground, the similarities did not stop there. Comden and Green, flush from their success with their first Bernstein collaboration, joined him again here – and both shows parody musical styles (only here it is dance music rather than *On the Town*'s plays on opera).

   Destined to be all but eclipsed by its predecessor and by both of its successors – *West Side Story* and *Candide* (the latter if only because it is always seemingly being still worked on) – there is lots of good material in *Wonderful Town*. Some of the numbers have become cabaret favourites, particularly perhaps the witty and sardonic 'One Hundred Easy Ways to Lose a Man'. Yet where Comden and Green delivered typically clever lyrics, their book is much less even, which makes the show more loved as a recording than on stage. Its cause has also probably not been helped by the fact that the movie version jettisoned its title in favour of the name of the play on which it is based, *My Sister Eileen*. Not only that; it rejected the Bernstein songs and had new ones written by Jule Styne!

TRIVIA

Bernstein, just back from honeymoon, was approached in a hurry to write the score and given only four weeks to finish. He agreed straight away. Comden and Green wrote later, 'He always liked deadlines.'

George Gaynes, who co-starred in the original, later found widespread fame as the soft-centred commandant in the *Police Academy* films.

THE PLOT

Sisters Ruth and Eileen have left Ohio to make their way in New York. Their apartment is not all that they had hoped, troubled as it is with explosions from the subway being constructed beneath them and visits from clients of the last tenant, who was a prostitute.

Cracking the job market is also fraught with difficulty but at least, as a despondent Ruth notes, Eileen's charms have an effect on the men they meet. Ruth does soon meet a man to love, if only they could first get along.

NUMBERS TO LISTEN OUT FOR

'Christopher Street'
'Ohio'
'One Hundred Easy Ways to Lose a Man'
'What a Waste'
'A Little Bit in Love'
'Conversation Piece'
'A Quiet Girl'
'Conga'
'Swing!'
'It's Love'
'Wrong Note Rag'

RECOMMENDED RECORDINGS

The original 1953 Broadway cast recording is Rosalind Russell's great moment on disc as an unforgettable Ruth. But the whole cast shines. There's also a great, classically inclined, concert performance on DVD, with the Berlin Philharmonic conducted by Simon Rattle – with Kim Criswell, Audra McDonald and the operatic baritone Thomas Hampson – which has an enormous sense of fun.

Musicals That Changed the World

There are some people, people who don't like musicals, who tend to think of the art form as trivial. 'It's so trivial,' they'll say, 'so transient.' Not so. Well, OK, if you're talking about *Thoroughly Modern Millie*, no argument from me there. But some shows actually count for something quite apart from the virtues of a terrific piece of theatre in itself. Some shows have actually changed the world. A few have managed to do this, perhaps the most impressive feat of all, without actually being very good.

Changed the world? Is that not Jule Styne-like hyperbole? Well, maybe. But some landmark musicals have had an effect, on economies, on politics, on the wider culture. Sometimes they have amplified what was already occurring. Sometimes they have created movements themselves.

Oklahoma! is always, along with *Show Boat*, top of anyone's list of the shows that invented the modern musical and that's discussed elsewhere in this book. But when Curly first wandered on stage with his dreamy smile, singing 'Oh, What a Beautiful Morning', he wasn't just dragging musicals into a new era of vital, coherent plot lines. In times of crisis the arts can do much to restore the feelgood factor to society. The grit of the *Oklahoma!* residents, their determination to win out and enjoy themselves despite hard conditions, gave Americans a point of empathy and a confirmation of hope in the midst of the Second World War. Members of the armed forces flocked to the show, often shortly before leaving to fight overseas. As Curly stands up to the boorish Jud and the good times return to this Oklahoma community, Americans were inspired. They might have wept as the coffins came home, but *Oklahoma!* helped remind them what they were fighting for – a way of life, a sense of right in the world – and what the Allies stood to lose.

It wasn't all peaches and cream around this era. Some twelve years earlier, George Gershwin and the great satirist George

S. Kaufman, in shows such as *Of Thee I Sing* (and indeed its darker, though less successful, sequel *Let 'Em Eat Cake*), served up contemporary commentary with a shot of bourbon. The partnership yielded among the first examples of that era of popular entertainment taking on the politics of the day – *Of Thee* centres on a presidential candidate elected on a family-values ticket, only to become mired in a sex scandal. In England, mind you, political satire had been essayed by musicals before they were even musicals. Gilbert and Sullivan's *Iolanthe* saw fairies take over the House of Commons (for that matter *HMS Pinafore* was fairly withering about the recruitment policy for the military's officer classes – Sir Joseph Porter KCB merrily confesses that 'a junior partnership . . . was the only ship I ever had seen' prior to running Her Majesty's Navy).

It's also worth noting that the politics–musicals relationship goes both ways. Candidates have been quick to jump on successful bandwagons. In the US, for instance, Bill Clinton used the song 'One Day More' from *Les Misérables* as a focal point for his 1992 presidential campaign. Satire is one thing, but apparently politicians think that musicals can also be used to convince the masses of their undoubted sincerity.

It will be no great shock to anyone who has seen it that 1968's *Hair* keyed into one of the great cultural movements of the time – the pacifist anti-Vietnam protests, most flamboyantly expressed by the hippies. What isn't so remembered now though is the fact that that show did not become a success thanks to the usual theatregoing public. It wasn't until about three years into the New York run that the musicals-loving crowds started to turn up *en masse*. Instead, the houses were filled by people in love and in tune with the show's depiction of a culture that *Hair* helped to move from underground to overground and on to Broadway. It gave the hippies a high-profile place to converge, the pacifists a rallying point.

Not for nothing did revivals of *Hair* begin to pop up during the second Iraq War – when Daniel Kramer, director of an important production on the London Fringe, staged it complete with images powerfully reminiscent of alleged prisoner abuses by the Allied troops and spoke openly about how he hoped it would once again find an audience among the new pacifists.

And yet *Hair* helped to change society in another way, alongside Andrew Lloyd Webber's *Jesus Christ Superstar*. They made rock music, if not polite, then at least acceptable to polite society. These shows used rock music – actual (chart-topping) pop songs which, in the case of *Superstar*, were released on a (highly successful) record album before the show was ever staged. And yet the Lloyd Webber show in particular integrated these songs into a powerful dramatic context. Suddenly the psychedelic vocal harmonies of *Hair*'s 'The Age of Aquarius' and the frenetic electric guitar riff of *Superstar*'s 'Heaven on Their Minds' were opening hit shows in the middle of the Great White Way. This was Middle America's home turf. The music that had swept the country's youth and was condemned in some areas as inspired by Satan was doing its thing at Saturday matinees before the nice dinner at Sardi's. At once these shows brought new audiences, rock audiences, to the theatre and helped to make rock music acceptable to polite society.

Across the Atlantic, Kenneth Tynan and the West End were doing the same for sex. Or, more generally, for freedom of expression at a time when the era of censorship, embodied in the Lord Chamberlain, was all but over. The Lord Chamberlain's powers to restrict what theatres offered to the public were abolished in 1968. *Oh! Calcutta!*, Tynan's self-styled 'nude review', opened in London in 1970 (after an initial production in New York the previous year) and took full advantage. This risqué show with its full-frontals and in-your-face explicitness ran for a full four years in New York (spawning in the process multiple regional productions across the US) – a staggering show of rejoicing in a theatre that suddenly felt free and a culture that seemed to have undergone a revolution. Just as *Hair* and *Superstar* gave rock music a social makeover, so the success of *Oh! Calcutta!* took sex out of the bedroom and paraded it nude down the high street. The fact that it eventually became something rather seedy, in its last days frequented by tired businessmen in search of a cheap thrill, doesn't diminish that initial impact. As with every relationship, if you don't keep it fresh the sex becomes routine in the end. But it's fun while it lasts.

When the glorious 1980s came and with them the era of the mega-musical – those shows that trouped, tapped and trotted dutifully around the globe – musical theatre suddenly had real economic clout to wield. Entire areas were affected. *Les Misérables* almost single-handedly transformed Chicago from a routine touring venue to arguably the most important out-of-town date before New York. Later, shows from *The Producers* to *Spamalot* would have their big try-outs there, with all the attendant publicity and scrambling for tickets. It certainly didn't hurt the city's now burgeoning reputation as the true cultural powerhouse of America.

Meanwhile the tourism industry of Vietnam was given an enormous boost by *Les Misérables*'s success there. And the Cameron Mackintosh stable produced hit after hit – *Cats*, *Phantom*, *Les Mis*, *Miss Saigon* – to help bolster, perhaps even save, a Broadway that was flagging, with the threat of the redevelopers hanging over some of its greatest theatres. For the future, it remains to be seen what effect plans to seed a local musical-theatre culture in China will have on the tourist industry in the big cities there. Some years ago, *Phantom* haunted Beijing – and audiences were saturated in marketing by-products (a personal favourite, not that I ever sniffed it, was Christine's perfume range). It's not just the rears on seats any more. And that kind of spending can really begin to have an effect.

Then – its own kind of mini-revolution – came *Mamma Mia!* Which definitely falls into the 'not that good' category (yes, yes, pleasant enough, but after about half an hour I find your eyes glaze over and you fall into a kind of pleasant but brain-dead stupor – it's the musical-theatre equivalent of reality TV). Nevertheless, it has been an enormous box-office success and provided a blueprint for risk-shy producers (who can blame them, given the immense costs of producing a musical these days?). After *Mamma Mia!* came an endless slew of song-catalogue shows. If the Abba *oeuvre* had worked for them, impresarios reasoned, why not mine the backlist of Queen? And Madness. And Rod Stewart. And Take That. *Ad*, seemingly, *infinitum*. This, added to the *Lion King* effect, where Disney proved that famous screen titles could effectively be made anew for the stage, had the unfortunate but far-reaching consequence of instilling a play-safe culture in the West End and Broadway. Want to musicalise *Lord of the Rings*? Tell me where to sign. A risky new show about singing felines? Er, pass. This particular revolution constitutes the biggest threat to musicals themselves that the genre has ever faced.

But over the years there's no doubt that financially, socially, culturally, politically even, musicals have made their mark. They can, near as dammit, change the world – and not just for the night.

Musicals Go to the Opera

In 2002, the ultra-trendy film and theatre director Baz Luhrmann – at the height of his fame following the movie *Moulin Rouge* – attempted to kick-start an operatic invasion of Broadway with *La Bohème*. Announcing that he would open the window on what he saw as the stuffy world of opera, he cast virile young leads, tweaked the surtitles (a particularly self-conscious instance from Act 1 read, 'He was making out with a hot chick') and updated the setting to the 1950s. In fact, it was remarkably similar to a previous *Bohème* of his for Australian Opera. This time, though, it moved from San Francisco to Broadway and in so doing made a statement. Grand opera is part of the musical-theatre family. It can communicate in the same way. And, Luhrmann's backers hoped, could do similarly well at the box office. The New York opening was glitzy and well received. The reviews were good, and A-list celebrities (Hugh Grant, Sandra Bullock, Harvey Keitel among them) emerged gushing for the news cameras. The show bombed, losing a reported £3.5 million and closing after only seven months.

Opera and musicals may be part of the same family, but they don't eat together. Nearly every time a similar experiment to Luhrmann's has been tried in a musical-theatre stronghold, it has failed. Yet the two art forms do share the same genes. Musicals, for all their vaudeville influences, really emerged from opera – or, to be more precise, operetta. The men who forged the musical were mostly European immigrants, raised on the speak-then-sing formulas of Offenbach, Lehár and Gilbert and Sullivan, which they imported to the New World. It is surely no accident that the one outstanding example of an opera succeeding on Broadway is Sullivan's *The Pirates of Penzance* (albeit in a ludicrously overdone staging by Joe Papp that crushed all the humour out of it).

So why should audiences for musicals be reluctant to embrace opera? Some musical composers straddled both worlds: Weill,

Gershwin and Bernstein provided bridges between them. While they also absorbed jazz and folk influences, Rodgers, Porter, Berlin and the like composed ballads as dreamily romantic as any by Lehár. Bernstein created deft operatic parodies (in *On the Town*) and structures (in *West Side Story*) that his audiences would have recognised and appreciated. Gershwin pointed the way forward with his through-sung 'folk opera' *Porgy and Bess*, which is not only an opera using jazz themes; it cries out for big, operatic voices. The folk operas became rock operas during the age of Lloyd Webber and Rice, and Boublil and Schönberg – until, tellingly, the British pair tired of the precursor 'rock' and called *Evita*, simply, an opera. At this point, the genteel spirit of Offenbach was ditched in favour of the red-blooded melodrama of Puccini. It has been said that, as opera itself moved away from easily hummable scores, the musicals were the natural continuation of the melodic traditions of the nineteenth century.

Arguably the most operatic composer of them all is Stephen Sondheim, whose use of leitmotifs (recurring themes throughout the show with their own messages) and melodies that wind in unexpected directions actually places him closer to modern opera composers than to either the old grand opera or operetta. At times, especially when he is at his most offbeat – in, say, the alienating territory of *Assassins* or the comic horror of *Sweeney Todd* – you might be forgiven for thinking that you're hearing one of Alban Berg's psychological opera-dramas. Interestingly, the composer has turned down all offers to compose for an opera house as he feels a new work needs a long, uninterrupted run in which to bed down, which the opera world traditionally does not offer.

None of which, clearly, washes with the public. They are very welcoming, though, when an opera singer moonlights in the musicals world. This has yielded some unforgettable performances. Ezio Pinza's turn in *South Pacific*, followed by Giorgio Tozzi on the film soundtrack is the stuff of legend. That role was written for a true bass. And not surprisingly opera stars have tended to gravitate towards the more operatic roles – two more great basses, Willard White and Simon Estes, have both been superb Porgys, the superstar bass-baritone Bryn Terfel a fabulous Sweeney Todd. But neither have they shied away from lighter fare – particularly on record. The English sopranos Josephine Barstow and Valerie Masterson have both graced the TER label's roster (Barstow a trenchant yet vulnerable Nancy in *Oliver!*, Masterson a lovely Anna in *The King and I*). American baritone Thomas Hampson sings Gershwin, Porter and the gang as to the manor born (of course, when it doesn't work – Frederica von Stade in *Anything Goes* for EMI, Thomas Allen in *Kiss Me Kate* – the results can be excruciating). 'Supertenor' José Carreras and the creamy-voiced Kiri Te Kanawa produced some sumptuous vocalising in Leonard Bernstein's own recording of *West Side Story* (almost, but not quite, overcoming the ridiculousness of casting that saw a Latin singer play an all-American boy and an Anglophone soprano as the Puerto Rican Maria; the characters' nationalities being the point of the show). The big surprise is that more opera singers have not delved into the 1980s British shows, although I did hear that Placido Domingo was once keen to give a concert performance of *Les Misérables*.

So why the big divide? Producer Cameron Mackintosh once told me that opera singers did steadfast determination very well, but other things less well. Listening to Hampson's lightness of touch (it helps that he's American and steeped in Broadway traditions) or the vocal grace of a Masterson or a Dawn Upshaw, it is hard to believe. Besides which, some admired West End and Broadway stars, Barbara Cook and Philip Quast among them, actually have classical voices.

It is, I suppose, a question of expectations and perception. Musicals are first and foremost about direct communication with an audience – sung in the local language, heavily miked to make it all as easy for the spectator as possible, involvement in the drama before anything else. Operas are still seen as events one has to put effort into. The language can be one remove; a concentration on the sound above what is actually being seen on the stage can be another (this is changing but still fairly widespread). And the fact that being born with an unusual throat shape that gives you a remarkable singing voice does not mean you are also a born actor can be yet another.

And there is one more nagging thought. Musicals were born as escapist entertainments. Since the decline of the through-sung shows, there has been a return to a rather old-fashioned style of musical comedy – *The Producers*, *Hairspray*, even *Avenue Q*. Good as these are, the shows that are moving the form on are not the big commercial hits. And these comedies are where musicals get furthest from opera. So perhaps, after all, people really want their musicals to make them feel good; almost all the most famous operas are tragedies.

Musicals may not feel that they need opera, but the opera world certainly feels that it needs musicals. Opera houses now almost routinely programme *On the Town*, *Sweeney Todd*, and even less obviously classically inclined shows such as *The Sound of Music*, in an effort to bolster box office and broaden their companies' appeal. The theory is: get 'em in for *On the Town*, and they'll come back for *The Magic Flute*. In terms of box office, it seems to work. So in a way the back-and-forth between opera and the musicals is as busy as ever – even if today it is almost totally one-sided.

Movies and Musicals

According to news reports, some film fans who bought tickets to see Tim Burton's 2008 film of *Sweeney Todd*, starring Johnny Depp, were surprised when a sailor rowed into view in the first scene, opened his mouth and started singing, 'There's no place like London.' The trailer had not shown anybody actually singing and they had not realised that *Todd* was a musical, still less the screen version of Stephen Sondheim's stage masterpiece. Come to think of it, Joel Schumacher's 2004 film of *Phantom of the Opera* also featured a trailer with nobody singing (though, so popular has the stage show been that it is difficult to imagine that many people hearing those crashing signature chords would have been confused). Clearly, though, Hollywood has an identity crisis when it comes to musicals – there are plenty now in production, but it seems that some studios don't want to admit to the habit publicly.

A habit it is, one as old as talking pictures themselves, although its nature has changed over the decades. The very first major talkie, *The Jazz Singer*, featured Al Jolson singing. Even though most cinemas weren't equipped to play the soundtrack, still it sent shock waves through the industry, not least because it heralded the beginning of the end for many of its biggest stars.

Musicals on film quickly became a gravy train for cinema. Millions flocked to see spectacular fare such as 1933's *42nd Street* (a film that caught all the grit and glamour of Broadway itself, with its famous line, 'You're going out there a youngster but you've got to come back a star!') and the jaw-dropping choreography of the Busby Berkeley shows. Stage hits found wider audiences through the camera lens. Some of the more high-profile efforts have dated horribly (for an anti-racism musical, 1936's *Show Boat* ironically features the most grotesque fake-Negro dance numbers) or, inevitably, were misconceived – *South Pacific*'s lens-colouring techniques have infuriated many

(I love them, but I'm greatly in the minority). But they spread the word far and wide.

The studio with the most hits, MGM, also took the business of making musicals more seriously than its rivals. Producer Arthur Freed set up his own ad hoc production unit, specifically to work with the studio's talent on musicals – his training was rigorous, and consequently the Freed Unit turned out stars of the order of Judy Garland and Gene Kelly. Among its success stories were – and here come all the films you grew up on – *The Wizard of Oz, Meet Me in St Louis, Easter Parade, On the Town, Annie Get Your Gun, Show Boat, An American in Paris, The Band Wagon* and *Gigi*.

Often, as in so many areas, the fare was star-led. Musicals became vehicles for generations of all-singing, all-dancing entertainers. Crosby, Garland, Fred Astaire and Ginger Rogers, later Sinatra, Streisand, Liza Minnelli; it almost seemed as though they burned brightest who sang the loudest. There were even movie musicals about movie musicals, as with perhaps the most famous of all, 1952's *Singin' in the Rain* (another Arthur Freed triumph). Until the bottom fell out of the musicals racket.

The moment is usually pinpointed at 1969, and specifically the release of *Hello, Dolly!* The costs of making a musical had been steadily shooting up, but this proved just too much. Budgets seemed to go out of the window during its filming. Its star, Barbra Streisand, wore a gown in one scene that reportedly cost $8000. A single sequence took three months to get right. The movie won Oscars, but almost sunk its studio – Twentieth Century-Fox was able to put out only one film for the whole of the following year. It didn't help that *Hello, Dolly!* was the third in a three-flop sequence of Fox musicals (the others being *Doctor Dolittle* and *Star!*).

Oh, there were isolated attempts after that to revive the form. But the musicals themselves were changing. As the old song-and-dance comedies faded, to be replaced by 1970s offbeat experimental shows such as *Hair* and *A Chorus Line*, then by the 1980s operatic sung-through dramas, Hollywood didn't know quite how to react. Both *Hair* and *A Chorus Line* were filmed, with mixed results (ranging from so-so in the case of the anti-Vietnam show to dire for *A Chorus Line*). Employing big-name directors didn't seem to help: *Hair* had Milos Forman; *A Chorus Line*, Richard Attenborough. And various plans to film the new wave of *Les Misérables* and *Phantom of the Opera* fell through. Only *Jesus Christ Superstar* of the Lloyd Webber *oeuvre* was tackled, in 1973, and done very well by Norman Jewison (the composer wasn't convinced), and much later *Evita* in 1996 (with a wellnigh unwatchable second half courtesy of Alan Parker and Madonna).

There were of course the glorious one-offs, such as 1978's *Grease* or to a lesser extent 1975's *Tommy*, but these were the exceptions to the rule. During the dark decades for the film musical, toes were kept tapping by a variety of animals and make-believe creatures from the Walt Disney stable, and of course the ever-ready-to-warble Muppets.

So what changed to bring the movie musical roaring back to life? A new generation of directors and producers, who prided themselves on their involvement with stage shows, in-herited the baton. The Australian director Baz Luhrmann had opera productions on his résumé, and was musically as well as visually in tune enough to turn his jukebox jamboree *Moulin Rouge!* (2001) into something resembling a real musi-cal (in fact, the story is a play on Puccini's *La Bohème*). Nicole Kidman and Ewan McGregor won enormous critical kudos – and, perhaps to their surprise, street cred among the young – for their leading roles. And, suddenly, musicals were in fash-ion again.

But still not making money. *Moulin Rouge* was esteemed a critical success but nothing to set the cash tills singing. Then came 2002's *Chicago*. Its director, Rob Marshall, was a former stage choreographer and had assistant-directed Sam Mendes on their hit revival of *Cabaret*. He got the *Chicago* job almost by default. Producer Martin Richards had held the film rights to the show for years. Originally he had planned to make it with the show's first choreographer, Bob Fosse, except that neither of them could figure out how to manage the transition from stage to screen. Finally, one afternoon, Richards received a call from Fosse: 'I know how to do it, I know how to film *Chicago*!' said the excited director, promising to tell Richards when he was back in New York. That was the last time they spoke; Fosse died soon afterwards.

Various other directors had been slated to take on the project over the years, including Nicholas Hytner (offers were also reportedly made to the likes of Luhrmann and Milos Forman). None of them had an answer. How could what was essentially a series of cabaret turns, albeit strung together by a plot, work on screen? It was Marshall who came up trumps, lobbying for the film and devising a conceit whereby any singing is seen through Roxie's imagination.

With A-listers Renée Zellweger, Catherine Zeta Jones and Richard Gere on board – and co-produced by Miramax – the film grossed $170,684,505 (according to trade magazine *Variety*) and bagged six Oscars. After that, the floodgates opened. Musical projects were green-lit and fast-tracked. Big stars told their agents to get them a musical. And so the production line rolled – off it came a miscast but flashy *Phantom of the Opera*, the excellent *Dreamgirls*, the even better *Hairspray*. And, er, a really rather bad *Rent*. Mel Brooks turned his movie-turned-stage-musical *The Producers* back into a movie, this time with the songs (but without the directorial flair). And Sondheim's *Sweeney Todd* took a turn for the gorier in the hands of Tim Burton.

Still on the stocks at the time of writing are *Damn Yankees*, *Guys and Dolls*, *Pippin*, *Sunset Boulevard*, *Urinetown* and possibly *Bombay Dreams*. The roots of today's film industry lie deep in stage musicals, and the relationship goes both ways. The Weinstein brothers, who co-produced *Chicago*, are big funders of Broadway shows. While Disney and now animation rival Dreamworks have concentrated on reinventing their film catalogues for the stage, Universal has cannily invested in new work such as *Wicked*. After all, it is potentially a relatively cheap (cheaper, at least, than starting a movie from scratch) way of seeding new material before committing it to celluloid.

Meanwhile, musicals continue to draw from the movie well. Stifling the yawns (actually, some of these are rather good), a parade of movies-turned-musicals has hit Broadway and elsewhere: *Dirty Dancing*, *Dirty Rotten Scoundrels*, *The Full Monty*, *Spamalot*, *The Producers*, *Hairspray*, *Lord of the Rings*, *Legally Blonde* and so on.

The hit rate for musical films is pretty low. Which is why no doubt some studios are wary of admitting up front what audiences are going to see. But with the rise of reality TV shows helping to make musicals truly trendy again, it isn't likely that film producers will kick the habit just yet.

My Ten Favourite Musicals

Guilty as charged. There's little academic value in having a 'top 10 musicals' list, as by the time you get to such a small number you're necessarily giving the hook (as in 'give me the hook or the ovation', from *La Cage aux Folles*'s most celebrated of gay anthems, 'I Am What I Am') to so many great shows that are 'their own special creation' (*La Cage* again, same number). But lists are always fun – I generally have a 'top five musicals' permanently dancing round in my head; four tend to be fixed, with the fifth chopping and changing (clearly, I am my own special creation in some ways). All are examples of an art form that can at once be populist, daring and emotionally complex at its finest. Of course, the responsible way to do this would be to rate the most important shows in terms of influence – *Hair* would make that list, as would *Gypsy*, *Oklahoma!* certainly. But since when were musicals meant to be responsible? So, in their spirit of excitement, and glamour, here are the ten shows that have had the greatest never-to-be-forgotten impact on – me. Forget the order, or change it around. Up to you.

Show Boat

I'm somewhat surprised to see this roll off the keyboard as the first entry to spring to mind. It falls under that capital-letters category of Important Musical, of course, but it's very much a period piece, of its time, with at least one foot still in operetta (think of pretty but very obviously 'placed' songs such as 'Make Believe' and 'You Are Love'). And yet, it portrays the progression of an era in American history with the unstoppable momentum of the rolling Mississippi river. As the motific 'Ol' Man River' charts the decades, changing social attitudes and the ebb and flow of its characters' fortunes, *Show Boat* will not be denied. Brave and, yes, important. But you leave the theatre moved and, in an unexpected way, humbled. Time may not, as *Mack and Mabel* famously has it, heal everything. But it has a habit of putting us in our place. And just as Gaylord discovers the true meaning of love, so – with the first black US President in the White House – the show's prescient suggestion that other, wider wrongs must one day be righted, now also seems to reinforce that healing spirit.

West Side Story

You knew it had to be here. It's fashionable now to count the once derided *Mass* as Leonard Bernstein's masterpiece but, while that work is fascinating, *West Side Story* is all but perfect. Perfect in structure, perfect in characterisation (despite what Stephen Sondheim says about Maria's too sophisticated lyrics – yes, he wrote them, he should know, but to me they seem right for the period). Not that there's very much pretty about perfection, at least not here. Everywhere there's urgency (think of the edgy propulsion of Tony's 'Something', or even the staccato nervousness of 'I Feel Pretty') – the love music isn't decorative, it's deadly earnest, with the risk-all seriousness of purpose or devotional piety. Eventually it spills over into the savagery of a rumble (as the lovers' rhapsodising merges with the angry build-up to the climactic fight). I remember the producer Bill Kenwright telling me about *West Side Story* being his first theatrical experience – the cinema being full. He sat in his seat, unmoving, even through the interval, mesmerised by what he was seeing. The aggression, the energy, the feeling that the stakes were as high as they could be. No, Bernstein never bettered this. You really can't improve on perfection.

South Pacific

It all came together here for Rodgers and Hammerstein. Politics and romance intertwined, and if, as Andrew Lloyd Webber says, 'All great musicals have to be a little bit of their time', there was plenty here to which audiences then – but also now – could relate. Many of the theatregoers of the 1940s would well remember the sense of impatience with a war that dragged on and on, the loneliness of the soldiers, their feeling of impotence. This emotional backdrop at once throws all the more importance on the consuming love of two couples and prevents it seeming overly sentimental. Meanwhile, the looming hills of the mystical island Bali Ha'i throw a haze of unreality over everything. As Bloody Mary sings of being 'lost in the middle of a foggy sea', the whole show is about inaction – waiting to fight, deciding whether or not to fall in love, fretting about what they might think back home, watching to see what the enemy might be capable of. When the action arrives, every plotline jerks forward at pace: what is unclear becomes clear; indecision becomes decision; questions considered at leisure become urgent matters of life and death. It is a brilliantly worked show, filled with songs that etch themselves on your heart.

Guys and Dolls

The theatre critic Kenneth Tynan once, famously, called Frank Loesser's visit to Runyonland the second-best American play ever written. Well, it's hard to compare it to the likes of *Death of a Salesman* and *Long Day's Journey into Night*, but if it's true that a comedy is harder to pull off than a tragedy then Loesser accomplished something approaching true genius. Amidst all the unforgettable Broadway caricatures – Harry the Horse, Nicely-Nicely Johnson, Big Julie – this show, with the deftest of touches, goes beyond Runyon's short stories to brush, never so lightly, poignancy, and above all the not-to-be denied heart-rush of true love. The songs are gems, flawless.

Sweeney Todd

From the restless opening organ, suddenly pierced by the scream of a factory whistle, Stephen Sondheim's love letter to Grand Guignol, written in blood, continually wrongfoots. Romantic heroines become hysterical figures of warped fun, the darkest peerings into psychological horror give way to knockabout verbal comedy (the demon barber's 'Epiphany', a howling embrace of his most murderous instincts, for instance, is succeeded within a matter of moments by his duet with Mrs Lovett, 'A Little Priest', a devilishly delicate exchange of wordplay – Noël Coward as dance of death). The audience is constantly kept on the edge, never sure whether to laugh or scream. And every so often comes an ensemble number such as 'The Ballad of Sweeney Todd' or 'City on Fire' to remind us that, yes, this is a deeply disturbing story. And, yes, we're laughing along, which is the most disturbing thing of all.

Jesus Christ Superstar

It is a shame that the main things people tend to remember about this musical, apart from the fact that it's the show that made the names of Andrew Lloyd Webber and Tim Rice, are the fact that the concept album came before the stage show (a revolutionary notion at the time), the protests from outraged Christian groups and the lines 'Jesus Christ, superstar, do you think you're who they say you are?' sung by a funky Judas with a backing group of rocking angels. To think of these is to mis-understand a show that is structurally perfect and dramatically speaking a searing experience. This is very far from a rock album strung together and thrown on the stage, using the pretext of the Christ story as an excuse for some flamboyant numbers. In fact, at a time when rock music wasn't really 'allowed' in musicals, Lloyd Webber and Rice use it to free up the drama – the outsider's life of the pop star providing a loose but apt metaphor both for Jesus as cult figure and Judas as uncomprehending rebel. The rage of a subjugated people, the seeming craziness of new ideas, the bewilderment of Pilate; they're all caught in the curving guitar lines, falsetto shrieks and hammering rhythms. But the structure itself is as taut and unsparing as, well, verses from the Bible. And at two points in the drama – the flogging of Jesus and the disorientated clos-ing coda – the writers let the words go altogether and let the music say what cannot be said. Yes, this is a serious work, to be taken seriously. And it packs a dramatic punch that almost no other musical has matched.

My Fair Lady

This show was never all about Julie Andrews. Her expulsion from the role for the film showed that (when the English actress's star-making stage turn was rejected in favour of Audrey Hepburn, a glamorous Eliza whose singing voice had to be dubbed by Marni Nixon). Neither is it all about Rex Harrison's Professor Higgins. Harrison, speaking the lines as he bent the part to suit his own gifts, was undoubtedly definitive. But then others have redefined it – notably Jonathan Pryce and Alex Jennings. No, this is all about the ideal marriage of Bernard Shaw's wit and the emotional charge provided to the Irish author's *Pygmalion* by Lerner and Loewe. The Americans' music and lyrics provide the emotional elaboration; Shaw is never heartless, but Broadway's treatment put that heart on his sleeve, or at times up it.

Fiddler on the Roof

I might have lost all respect among serious musicalphiles for choosing Bock and Harnick's klezmer musical, otherwise known as 'bar-mitzvah band's default songlist' (cue the groan). Hear me out. It's the small moments that do it. Not the chest-shaking theatrics of 'If I Were a Rich Man', or even the tear-jerking nostalgia of the watching relatives at a wedding in 'Sunrise, Sunset'. No, it's the line that forms the quiet centre to 'If I Were a Rich Man' (yes, there is the odd calm moment): 'Then I'd have the time that I need to sit in the synagogue and pray, and that would be the sweetest gift of all.' It's the short but wordless *nigun* chant at the end of 'Sabbath Prayer' before the word 'Amen'. Come to think of it, it's the absence of any song whatsoever for the non-Jewish husband of Chava. Through all of these comes a deep, sincere and age-old spirit, the soul of an ancient religion, a culture that has persevered in crushing adversity. There is the well of, yes, tradition that sits at the centre of this show and prevents it, for all that the hits are still played at every happy Jewish event around the world *ad nauseam*, from lurching into caricature or hokum. The image of a people trying to stay true to itself despite everything is universal. The idea of a man struggling to stick to what he believes to be right and to adapt those beliefs to a fast-changing world, even while he shudders at some of its new ways, remains sympathetic. The depiction of a society that celebrates what life can offer even while it bemoans and fears what it frequently delivers is eternally topical. And the tunes are great. Though I never want to hear one at a bar mitzvah again.

Les Misérables

Again, this could just be me. *Les Mis* fell somewhat out of favour (with me, I mean) for a while. The synthesiser-led score sounded *so* 1980s, while musical inspiration in the second half seemed seriously thin on the ground compared with what had preceded it. There is truth in both charges (not that the first is a killer: all musicals sound of their time; the great ones make a virtue of it). Seeing it again fairly recently, none of this seemed to matter. The sweep of the story, a country in revolution, fighting for new freedoms, all seen through the prism of Jean Valjean's struggle to be a good man in an unforgiving society – it is, simply, riveting. There are few moments in musicals, in theatre, that carry such a stirring sense of destiny approaching as the great Act I ensemble 'One Day More' (you have to go back to opera, to Verdi's *Macbeth* or Mozart's *Don Giovanni*, for an equivalent). Valjean is a man determined to change his fate – a fate embodied by his nemesis, the uncompromising policeman Javert. It is that sense of trying to seize control of life that shoots through *Les Mis* – whether it be the impetuous love of Marius and Cosette, the mutinous students or even the conning, thieving Thenadiers. Not all manage to write their own page in history (and neither is the chapter ending always what was intended – we now know the moral fall-out of the French Revolution), but Boublil and Schönberg (and Victor Hugo, of course) salute those who try and try for the general good. Atmospheric, powerful, *Les Mis* is not to be resisted.

Sunday in the Park with George

I have been arguing with myself over my final Top 10 spot for some time. My wife Kareen decided for me. 'What are the options?' she demanded. '*Oliver!*, *Kiss Me Kate*, *Cabaret*, I suppose *Sunday in the Park with George* . . .' I started to recite. 'Has to be *Sunday in the Park with George*. It's the one show you always want everyone to see. It had an effect on you.' And yes, she's right. So there are more consistent musicals than this. There are others with better books. As for plots, well, *Sunday* hasn't exactly got one in the traditional sense. What started life as an experiment turned into an adventure – a journey to see just how far the musical could go. Somewhere before the horizon, but not much before, it meets the world of pointillist art and, eventually, the visual and the theatrical forms become one. The end of the first half of this show, where the most famous painting of Georges Seurat is physically re-created on stage, is an apex of the (musical) genre. It is a reaching for the ideal, for some kind of higher level of existence – as Georges might put it – through art. For that feeling of being most alive in the work; a theme of the show. *Sunday in the Park with George* doesn't always attain that level, doesn't perhaps finally reach the horizon. Strange as it may seem, I have come to believe that it's all the more moving for it. Sondheim has charted unknown waters, and in so doing has excitingly shown just how much more there is to be explored. But he has reached further, strained harder than most. You've got to love this show, and him, for that.

Ten Terrible Musicals

It's hard to come up with a list for 'the ten worst musicals of all time' – which is what everyone really wants to read – in a genre that can so easily turn ridiculous. After all, singing at each other can seem ludicrous enough in itself (while Judi Dench once said that in musicals, 'characters sing when words are no longer enough', it is a sad truth that in many shows people burst into song for far less exalted reasons). Meanwhile, post-*Phantom*, shows routinely seem to feel they must reach a certain level of, often empty, spectacle. And after the success of, sigh, *Mamma Mia!* (the Abba tribute show masquerading as a musical that has about as much dramatic involvement as an episode of TV's *Big Brother*, and is about as popular) some producers don't feel they even have to do more than join the dots. Big, moving sets? Check. Hit songs ready-made circa *Top of the Pops* nineteen eighty-something? Check. Ben Elton to string it all together? Check. The result? The Rod Stewart mash-up *Tonight's the Night*. Which definitely makes it to the list of ten below. Because while most bad musicals are simply that, bad, as in boring and tedious, some are so dreadful that they become collectors' items. Terrible in the watching, wonderful though for dinner-table anecdotalising. And all the more rare because they don't usually stick around for long enough for many people to see them. Never mind the opening night of *Les Misérables*, were you there for the single dismal performance of Mike Reid's *Oscar Wilde*?

The Fields of Ambrosia

Music by Martin Silvestri
Book and lyrics by Joel Higgins
Premiere: 12 March 1993, at the George Street Playhouse,
    New Brunswick

Ah, the fields of Ambrosia, 'where everyone knows ya'. Favourite moments from this couldn't-make-it-up show are legion. The ambiguous title refers to a paradisiacal idea of heaven, as dreamed of by the victims of a travelling executioner, who fries his victims in his electric chair. Quite a way to make a living, and apparently meat for a musical. If nothing else, it gave rise to the immortal opening song line, as a character emerges from being gang-raped in a forest and gingerly buttons up his flies: 'If it isn't one thing it's another.'

Voyeurz

Music, book and lyrics by Michael Lewis and Peter Rafelson
Premiere: 22 July 1996, at the Whitehall Theatre, London

British producer Michael White has a reputation for courting the risqué. He was, after all, the man behind Kenneth Tynan's nude review *Oh! Calcutta!*, as well as *The Rocky Horror Show* and the UK premiere of *A Chorus Line* (yes, I know that's about as far from risqué as you can get, but in its way it was bold and experimental, then). So when he put his money behind a musical from the lipstick-lesbian rock group Femme 2 Femme, it didn't seem like a bad bet. Quite the opposite in some ways. At the very least, a sex-themed show that promised girl-on-girl titillation and pumping pop should have attracted the same sort of people who limped along to *Oh! Calcutta!* in its last years (the sad days when its reputation as a trailblazer had given way to the stale promise of bare flesh). It didn't happen. Not only that, there were reports in British newspapers of even relatives of cast members leaving before the end. 'We should have done it in a club,' remarked White ruefully some years later, suggesting that it wasn't really for the traditional musicals crowd. Hmm. As a stag night event, it might have worked. With some better music, and a better script. Maybe.

As it is, *Voyeurz* gyrated for under two months. Reviewing for the *Financial Times*, and referring to White's earlier success against the odds, Ian Shuttleworth opined, 'Twenty-odd years

ago, the first production of *The Rocky Horror Show* drew less
than enthusiastic reviews, but it has since become a classic . . .
if, in decades to come, the appalling *Voyeurz* undergoes a similar
rehabilitation, then we might all just as well give up now.'

Carrie

Music by Michael Gore
Lyrics by Dean Pitchford
Book by Lawrence D. Cohen
Premiere: 13 February 1988, at the Royal Shakespeare Theatre,
    Stratford upon Avon

Somehow, on paper, this must have seemed like a good idea.
After all, the Royal Shakespeare Company was involved. They
even managed to hook that doyen of Broadway stars Barbara
Cook (and later on Broadway itself Betty Buckley; Cook
having left after the show's three weeks in Stratford). It was
helmed by the RSC's illustrious artistic director Terry Hands.
And yet, on stage, its destructive force was scarcely less cata-
strophic than that of the titular telekinetic teenager with a
serious grudge. This show, just to give an idea of the depth of
its reputation, has even inspired a book, Ken Mandelbaum's
chronicle of bad musicals – *Not Since Carrie*.

Cook, who played Carrie's ill-fated (in so many ways)
mother, once described the project's attraction, and its problems, to me:

> The supernatural tale, the horror, it was all supposed to be
> a metaphor for a girl's difficulties fitting in and her prob-
> lems relating to her mother. It sounded intriguing and
> original. But the people in charge didn't know how to do a
> musical from scratch. Terry Hands wasn't sure enough of
> himself to be ruthless, to cut bad songs and to demand
> replacements. They had no idea about what a character
> should sing where. For instance, at one point, my character
> decides to kill her daughter. Can you imagine what that

would be like? I said to them, 'There should be a song in which the mother talks about the pain of the decision and ideally makes the decision in the song.' Not an easy assignment, I understand. But they delivered this pretty song about how quiet the house would be without my daughter around!

There was nothing pretty about the murderous reviews. And yet, the stars emerged more or less unscathed. Cook's reputation was already beyond reproach; Betty Buckley even earned some kudos for throwing everything she had into a no-win role. And young Linzi Hately, in the main part, has gone on to have a very decent musical-theatre career. The greatest irony, indeed, may be that despite her share of West End productions, she has never done anything to have earned her anything like such personal fame, or notoriety, again.

Tonight's the Night

Music and lyrics by Rod Stewart
Book by Ben Elton
Premiere: 7 November 2003, at the Victoria Palace, London

This should more properly have been called *Enough's Enough*. Enough creaky pop-star catalogue shows. And enough lyrics from sell-out British comedian Ben Elton. OK, confession time. I had loved the sincerity of Elton's work on Andrew Lloyd Webber's *The Beautiful Game* (a heartfelt attempt to grapple with the complexities of violent regional conflict), and his still unerring instinct for a one-liner and a ludicrous situation had seen him through the unapologetically cash-in Queen homage *We Will Rock You*. But this? Taping Rod Stewart hits together with the flimsiest of storylines – something about a guy who does a deal with the devil to shake it like Rod Stewart, or whatever – and nil characterisation? It was the laziest of efforts, and played like a commercial contract rather than entertainment. Its saving grace was the fact that it played for less than a year (particularly since this show, together with the same producer's *We Will Rock You*, set a new highest-ever London ticket price at £55). Even cynicism, it turns out, required some effort.

Which Witch?

Music by Benedicte Adrian and Ingrid Bjornov
Lyrics by Kit Hesketh Harvey
Book by Piers Haggard
Premiere: 22 October 1992, at the Victoria Palace, London

'A powerful tragedy of romantic passion set in Rome and Heidelberg in the early sixteenth century,' boasts the official website for this iconic (one way or another) Norwegian musical. Such is the national pride invested in this show that when *Daily Mail* theatre critic Jack Tinker visited Norway and asked for a tour of one of the major theatres, he was refused, and told – this after Tinker and his colleagues had slated the show's London opening – 'Your name is sheet in Norway.'

As flops go, this is a curious one, both a great success in its home country and one of the most dismal failures ever seen in the West End. In Norway it sold in excess of 110,000 cast albums. And yet its London production lasted a paltry 76 performances. Part of the problem, perhaps, was that what had started life as a concert in the Bergen International Festival couldn't survive as a fully staged work. Partly it was the over-the-top infernal orgy scenes. The fact that one of its writers had once been awarded 'nul points' in the Eurovision Song Contest couldn't have helped. Either way, the reviews were savage. 'Flops', decreed the *Daily Telegraph*, 'don't come much floppier.'

Twang!!

Music and lyrics by Lionel Bart
Book by Lionel Bart and Harvey Orkin
Premiere: 20 December 1965, at the Shaftesbury Theatre, London

The exclamation marks might have struck twice for Lionel Bart, but they didn't work their charms in the way they had for both *Blitz!* and *Oliver!* Robin Hood has never really worked as a musical for anyone, despite various attempts, and Bart – by this time at the height of his success and displaying dictatorial tendencies (the original director Joan Littlewood, so the story goes, walked out because Bart wanted to control every aspect of this production) – was felled by his own arrow after a paltry 43 performances. With his own money sunk in the show, this did for Bart's finances and his morale. He never really recovered, so one of Britain's most brilliant tunesmiths spent the next three decades talking about the shows he might create, but never did.

Dance of the Vampires

Music by Jim Steinman
Lyrics and book by Jim Steinman and Michael Kunze
Premiere: 20 December 2002, at the Minskoff Theatre, New York

After Michael Crawford's success of Andrew Lloyd Webber's *Phantom of the Opera*, his fans could be forgiven for thinking that his more than fifteen years of absence from the musical-theatre scene was due to a nervousness about how to follow the biggest hit in musicals history. Crawford, one of the most talented actors of his generation and one of its few genuinely bankable musical stars, holed up in Las Vegas earning gazillions in a special-effects cabaret. He emerged, finally, in 2002 for this version of the 1967 bloodsucking Roman Polanski farce. But it wasn't the audience who got it in the neck.

'Michael Crawford will live to rue the day he chose this ludicrous musical as the vehicle for his Broadway return,' predicted *Variety* magazine. In truth, there have been far worse musicals (and the original Austrian production had already done well in German), but the level of expectation surrounding this made its brief run a flop that fell with all the impact of a crashing chandelier. To date, Crawford has not really recovered – his next bow was in Lloyd Webber's less than rapturously received *The Woman in White* (though he personally attracted positive reviews).

Grace – The Musical

Music by Cy Coleman
Lyrics and book by Seth Gaaikema
Premiere: 25 October 2001, at the Grace Theatre, Amsterdam

Honestly, I don't know if this really is one of the worst musicals of all time but it was certainly one of the most ostentatious. The fact that it was a structural mess was all the more glaring considering that an entire, lavish theatre was built in the Dutch capital especially for it, complete with restaurant and vintage cars placed strategically outside to evoke the period. It was the dream of the amiable businessman turned theatre producer Bert Maas, who brought in Broadway legend Cy Coleman to deliver a hit centred on Maas's heroine, Grace Kelly. Sadly, the show couldn't decide whether to be an old-fashioned musical comedy, a family tragedy or what. I vividly remember a prancing priest, but much of the rest I seem to have blotted out. A defence mechanism, I expect.

Oscar Wilde

Music, lyrics and book by Mike Reid
Premiere: 19 October 2004, at the Shaw Theatre, London

Brit radio DJ Mike Read followed one dubious show, *Cliff – The Musical* (the life of Cliff Richard given the *Buddy* treatment), with a more literary foray. It certainly created a stir, when *Oscar Wilde: The Musical* closed the morning after the night before. 'Reviews were poor,' said the press spokesman in a crashing understatement on a day when, for instance, the *Guardian* commented, 'Read has Wilde warble, "Think of me when the sun goes down." It will be hard not to when the nightmares kick in later.' Only five seats had been sold for the second night, meaning at least that refunds wouldn't be a problem. *Wilde* officially became the West End's shortest-running musical ever, a record that its leading man Peter Blake was breaking for the second time – his turn in the previous year's *Money to Burn* at Leicester Square's The Venue had lasted precisely one press night and a matinee.

Breakfast at Tiffany's

Music by Bob Merrill
Lyrics and book by Edward Albee
Premiere: 12 December 1966, at the Majestic Theatre, New York

After a deeply troubled out-of-town run, during which audiences heckled, critics poured scorn and the leading lady Mary Tyler Moore had to cope with constant speculation that she was to be replaced, drastic measures were called for. Producer David Merrick replaced his book-writer Abe Burrows with Edward Albee (who came up with an unexpectedly experimental script about a writer creating his characters) and changed the title *Holly Golightly* to the better-known movie name *Breakfast at Tiffany's*. But the great glory of this by-all-accounts dreadful show was its closing (remember that line from *Macbeth*, 'Nothing in his life became him like the leaving of it'?). After the fourth New York preview Merrick issued a statement to say that, 'Rather than subject the drama critics and the theatregoing public to an excruciatingly boring evening, I have decided to close.' In a matchless closing flourish, Merrick added that Cartier's jewellers had begged him to keep the show going so as to damage the reputation of their arch rival, Tiffany's. Merrick knew how to meet a flop with style.

Further Reading

Any self-respecting collection of books about musicals should include the following (and yes, that is the same James Inverne – but I promise I was not influenced by the fact that I stand to earn book royalties if you go out and purchase those, so feel free to buy those first):

Jeffry Denman, *A Year with The Producers*
Moss Hart, *Act One*
James Inverne, *Wrestling with Elephants: The Authorised Biography of Don Black*
James Inverne, *The Impresarios*
Howard Kissel, *David Merrick: The Abominable Showman*
Colin Larkin (ed.), *The Guinness Who's Who of Stage Musicals*
Ken Mandelbaum, *Not Since Carrie: 40 Years of Musical Flops*
Sheridan Morley, *Spread a Little Happiness: The First Hundred Years of the British Musical*
Frederick Nolan, *The Sound of Their Music: The Story of Rodgers and Hammerstein*
Richard Rodgers, *Musical Stages: An Autobiography*
Meryle Secrest, *Leonard Bernstein: A Life*
Meryle Secrest, *Stephen Sondheim: A Life*
Mark Steyn, *Broadway Babies Say Goodnight*

Index of People, Shows, Sources and Theatres

Main entries for musicals are indicated in **bold**.
Composition and writing credits are indicated in *italics*.